Writing Groups for Doctoral Education and Beyond

Writing is the principal means by which doctoral candidature is monitored and measured; this, combined with the growing tendency to use publications as proxy measures of individual and institutional productivity, underlines the centrality of writing in academia. One of the central questions for scholars in higher education, therefore, is 'How do we make writing happen?', and it is this question that the book seeks to answer.

The book provides detailed illustrations of collaborative writing pedagogies that are powerfully enabling, and through theoretical and conceptual interrogation of these practices the authors point the way for individuals as well as institutions to establish writing groups that are lively, responsive and context-specific.

Key topics include:

- new pedagogical responses for increased writing productivity and the 'push to publish';
- innovations for supporting academic writing quality, confidence and output;
- scaffolding the thesis writing process;
- new theoretical explorations of collaborative writing approaches;
- writing group formulations and pedagogical approaches;
- writing groups for non-native speakers of English;
- writing as women in higher education.

A particular strength of this book is that it showcases the potential of writing groups for advanced academic writing by pulling together a unique mix of authors and scholarly approaches, representing a wide range of new theoretical and pedagogical frames from diverse countries.

Writing Groups for Doctoral Education and Beyond will be attractive to academics seeking new ways to advance their writing productivity, as well as doctoral students, their supervisors and those who are tasked with the job of supporting them through the completion and dissemination of their research.

Claire Aitchison is Senior Lecturer in Postgraduate Literacies at the University of Western Sydney, Australia. She is an emerging scholar with a growing reputation in the use of writing groups in doctoral education and for the support of academic publishing.

Cally Guerin is Lecturer in Researcher Education and Development at the School of Education, University of Adelaide, Australia. Her research and publications focus on doctoral education, with a particular interest in writing skills development for both international and local doctoral students.

Writing Groups for Doctoral Education and Beyond

Innovations in practice and theory

Edited by
Claire Aitchison and Cally Guerin

Routledge
Taylor & Francis Group
LONDON AND NEW YORK

First published 2014
by Routledge
2 Park Square, Milton Park, Abingdon, Oxon OX14 4RN

and by Routledge
711 Third Avenue, New York, NY 10017

Routledge is an imprint of the Taylor & Francis Group, an informa business

© 2014 Claire Aitchison and Cally Guerin

The right of the editors to be identified as the authors of the editorial material, and of the authors for their individual chapters, has been asserted in accordance with sections 77 and 78 of the Copyright, Designs and Patents Act 1988.

All rights reserved. No part of this book may be reprinted or reproduced or utilised in any form or by any electronic, mechanical, or other means, now known or hereafter invented, including photocopying and recording, or in any information storage or retrieval system, without permission in writing from the publishers.

Trademark notice: Product or corporate names may be trademarks or registered trademarks, and are used only for identification and explanation without intent to infringe.

British Library Cataloguing in Publication Data
A catalogue record for this book is available from the British Library

Library of Congress Cataloging in Publication Data
Writing groups for doctoral education and beyond: innovations in practice and theory / edited by Claire Aitchison, Cally Guerin.
pages cm
Includes bibliographical references and index.
1. Academic writing—Study and teaching (Graduate)
2. Dissertations, Academic. 3. Authorship—Collaboration.
4. Group work in education. I. Aitchison, Claire. II. Guerin, Cally.
PE1404.W723 2014
808'.0420711—dc23
2013040763

ISBN: 978-0-415-83473-5 (hbk)
ISBN: 978-0-415-83474-2 (pbk)
ISBN: 978-0-203-49881-1 (ebk)

Typeset in Galliard
by Book Now Ltd, London

Printed and bound in the United States of America by Publishers Graphics, LLC on sustainably sourced paper.

Contents

List of illustrations   vii
Notes on contributors   ix
Acknowledgements   xv

PART I
Setting the scene   1

1 Writing groups, pedagogy, theory and practice: an introduction   3
CLAIRE AITCHISON AND CALLY GUERIN

2 Writing together for many reasons: theoretical and historical perspectives   18
ANTHONY PARÉ

3 Pick-n-Mix: a typology of writers' groups in use   30
SARAH HAAS

PART II
Theory and reflection   49

4 Learning from multiple voices: feedback and authority in doctoral writing groups   51
CLAIRE AITCHISON

5 Writing groups as critical spaces for engaging normalized institutional cultures of writing in doctoral education   65
DOREEN STARKE-MEYERRING

6 Transparent transactions: when doctoral students
and their supervisors write together 82
MICHELLE MAHER

7 Doctoral students create new spaces to write 94
ROWENA MURRAY

8 Walking the labyrinth: the holding embrace of
academic writing retreats 110
SALLY S. KNOWLES AND BARBARA GRANT

9 The gift of writing groups: critique, community
and confidence 128
CALLY GUERIN

PART III
Pedagogy in practice 143

10 Scaffolding the thesis writing process: an ongoing
writing group for international research students 145
LINDA LI

11 'If they're not laughing, watch out!': emotion and
risk in postgraduate writers' circles 162
LUCIA THESEN

12 A weekly dose of applause!: connectedness and
playfulness in the 'Thesis Marathon' 177
JUDITH WOLFSBERGER

13 The Studio Model: developing community
writing in creative, practice-led PhD design theses 190
WELBY INGS

14 An intimate circle: reflections on writing as
women in higher education 204
AGNES BOSANQUET, JAYDE CAHIR, ELAINE HUBER,
CHRISTA JACENYIK-TRAWÖGER AND MARGOT MCNEILL

15 Shut up & Write!: some surprising uses of cafés
and crowds in doctoral writing 218
INGER MEWBURN, LINDY OSBORNE AND GLENDA CALDWELL

Index 233

Illustrations

Tables

3.1	Typology of writers' groups	32
3.2	What happens in a writers' group	37
3.3	Writer's log sample	41
5.1	Support sought and received by doctoral students for different writing projects	70
7.1	Micro-group respondents' characteristics	97

Figures

3.1	'Pick-n-Mix' typology	42
5.1	Writing support sought by doctoral students for different writing projects	69
5.2	Writing support received by doctoral students for different writing projects	70
8.1	Walking the labyrinth at Jarrahdale, Western Australia	110
8.2	The Classical labyrinth	112
13.1	Working through each writer's focus question	193
13.2	Talita Tolutau's information graphic	200
13.3	Volume two from Moana Nepia's PhD thesis	201
14.1	Word cloud of writing retreat reflections	214

Contributors

Claire Aitchison is a Senior Lecturer (Postgraduate Literacies) in the Learning Skills Unit at the University of Western Sydney (UWS), Australia, where she supports writing development for higher degree research students, early career researchers and academics. She has been running and writing about writing groups since 2002. Claire's research interests are pedagogies for doctoral education particularly the use of writing group and retreat pedagogies to support thesis writing and writing for publication. Relevant recent publications include *Publishing Pedagogies for the Doctorate and Beyond* (Routledge, 2010) with Barbara Kamler and Alison Lee; 'Writing groups for doctoral education' in *Studies in Higher Education* (2009); Aitchison and Lee (2010) 'Writing in, writing out: doctoral writing as peer work', in Walker and Thomson's *The Routledge Doctoral Supervisor's Companion*; and 'Tough love and tears: learning doctoral writing in the sciences' (2012) in *Higher Education Research & Development (HERD) Journal* with Catterall, Ross and Burgin. Her work in support of doctoral writing using writing group pedagogies was awarded a Citation for Outstanding Contribution to Student Learning by the Australian Learning and Teaching Council (2008) and she is a co-recipient of the UWS Vice Chancellor's Award for Leadership in HDR Teaching Excellence (2011).

Agnes Bosanquet is an early career Researcher and Lecturer in Macquarie University's Learning and Teaching Centre in Australia. Her PhD in Cultural Studies performed an autoethnographic response to Luce Irigaray's philosophy of sexual difference, transcendence and the mother/daughter relation. From her research in Cultural Studies, Agnes values critical theory, creative methodologies and questions about power relations, discourses and practices of inclusion and exclusion, locations of knowledge and constructions of subjectivity. As an academic developer, Agnes applies this critical legacy to her research, which explores changing academic roles and identities, theories and models of curriculum and graduate attributes.

Jayde Cahir is an early career Researcher in Macquarie University's Learning and Teaching Centre in Australia. She has researched the everyday use of mobile phones and text messaging for the past six years and more recently explored how these technologies can be used in learning contexts. Jayde is currently the lead researcher on an evaluation study of Open Source Learning Management Systems, and has also worked across several research projects including Spectrum Approach to Mentoring and Undergraduate Research Australia. Jayde's research interests include, but are not limited to, communication technologies, learning technologies, the scholarship of learning and teaching and academic writing.

Glenda Caldwell is a Lecturer in design at the Creative Industries Faculty at Queensland University of Technology in Australia. Glenda teaches digital fabrication and visualization of social networks and is currently studying for her PhD.

Barbara Grant is Associate Professor in the Faculty of Education at The University of Auckland, New Zealand, where she teaches, supervises and researches in the field of higher education. For the past 15 years, she has run twice-yearly week-long writing retreats for academic women, including doctoral students, in Aotearoa, New Zealand, as well as many similar retreats in other countries. Barbara has published widely in the areas of supervision, writing retreats and academic development, and is the author of *Academic Writing Retreats: A Facilitator's Guide*, published in 2008 by HERDSA (Australia). Along with being guest editor for two special issues of international journals (IJAD and IETI), Barbara is the Executive Editor for *Higher Education Research & Development*.

Cally Guerin has worked and published in doctoral education since 2008, coordinating a comprehensive suite of research skills training and academic development programs for research students and their supervisors in her role as a Lecturer in Researcher Education & Development, School of Education, University of Adelaide, Australia. Her research interests include doctoral pedagogies, academic mobility, academic integrity, researcher identities and writing skills development for both international and local doctoral students. Her recent publications on writing groups have appeared in the *Studies in Continuing Education* (2012) and *International Journal of Doctoral Studies* (2013).

Sarah Haas, currently a Teaching Fellow at the University of Ghent in Belgium, has been teaching writing for two decades. She has run courses, retreats and groups for research writers in the UK, Denmark, Japan, Belgium, and the US. She earned her PhD in applied linguistics in 2011, and her research interests lie in the area of writer support. She is interested in finding ways to facilitate the development of self-directed writers, in writers' understanding and control of their own writing processes and in the various workings of writers' groups and writers' retreats.

Elaine Huber is currently studying for her PhD in Education at Macquarie University, Australia. She is coming to the end of the first year of her study in which she is investigating the praxis of evaluation of locally funded learning and teaching projects in Higher Education. Elaine also works at the central Learning and Teaching Centre as the Head of Educational Design and

Support, a role in which she indulges her other main passion, educational technologies. She has been researching, working in and studying the field for over 12 years and hopes to make a valuable contribution with her research.

Welby Ings is a Professor in Design at AUT University, New Zealand. He holds a PhD in applied narratology and is an elected Fellow of the British Royal Society of Arts. He has published and spoken widely on issues of language, writing and practice-led scholarship. He has been a consultant to many international organizations on issues of creativity and learning. Welby is also a multi-award winning designer, filmmaker and playwright. In 2002 (in recognition of his innovative approaches to creativity and learning), he received the New Zealand Prime Minister's inaugural award for Tertiary Teaching Excellence.

Christa Jacenyik-Trawöger is a Program Research and Development Officer at Macquarie University's Learning and Teaching Centre in Australia. She has managed research projects exploring leadership in the context of peer review and cross-cultural supervision. She is currently a co-investigator on learning and teaching evaluation projects. Her research interests focus on collaborative peer review of learning and teaching, academic writing and cross-cultural communication within the higher education sector.

Sally S. Knowles is a Research Development Advisor in the Office of Research and Innovation at Edith Cowan University (ECU) in Australia, where she supports staff with their writing for research and publication. To help writers sustain and enhance the quality of their writing experiences, Sally seeks to create a vibrant research writing culture that is socially robust and collegial. Since 2003, following Barbara's retreat model, she has facilitated over 50 academic writing retreats for several Australian Universities and research institutes. She has organized and participated in a cross-institutional community of women scholars called *Women Writing Away (WA)* who have been meeting seasonally in a restorative bush setting for the last nine years. Sally co-ordinates an ECU on-campus writing group called *Writing Infusions*. She has a strong interest in how practice-led research from the creative and performing arts can infuse the research and writing practices of so-called 'traditional' researchers.

Linda Li is an Assistant Professor in the Academic Skills Centre at the University of Canberra, Australia. She conducts thesis writing workshops and provides individual consultations to support writing development for research students. She has been facilitating a writing group for international research students since 2005 and has published on this work in *Innovations in Education and Teaching International* (2011). Her other articles on doctoral education and academic writing development have been published in *Active Learning in Higher Education* (2011), *Journal of Academic Language and Learning* (2009, 2011), *International Journal of Pedagogy and Learning* (2008) and *Journal of University Teaching and Learning Practice* (2007). She won a Citation

Award for Outstanding Contribution to Student Learning by the Australian Learning and Teaching Council (2011) and a teaching award at the University of Canberra (2011) for her work in support of the thesis writing of higher degree research students.

Michelle Maher is a research Associate Professor at the Center for the Advanced Study of Learning in Higher Education (CASTL-HE) at the University of Virginia, USA, and Associate Professor in the department of Educational Leadership & Policies in the College of Education at the University of South Carolina, USA. Dr. Maher studies the development of knowledge, skills, and professional identity in graduate students, particularly in regard to disciplinary writing. She also studies the influence of disciplinary cultures on student learning outcomes in graduate education. Her work has been published in *The Journal of Higher Education, Science, Studies in Higher Education* and *The Review of Higher Education*.

Margot McNeill is a Senior Lecturer in Macquarie University's Learning and Teaching Centre in Australia. She currently manages the Change Management stream of the institutional implementation of a new Learning Management System and teaches on the Centre's postgraduate programme. Her research interests and much of her project work explore technologies for learning and teaching, particularly to support assessment of higher order learning outcomes.

Inger Mewburn is Director of research training at the Australian National University and editor of the blog *The Thesis Whisperer*. She teaches communications to higher degree by research students and conducts research on doctoral education.

Rowena Murray graduated with MA (Hons) from Glasgow University, UK, and PhD from Pennsylvania State University, USA, and is a Fellow of the Higher Education Academy, UK. She worked in Academic Practice at the University of Strathclyde, UK, and is now Professor in the School of Education at the University of the West of Scotland, UK, and Adjunct Professor at Swinburne University, Melbourne, Australia. Her teaching and research focus on academic writing, the subject of her journal articles and books, including *How to Write a Thesis, Writing for Academic Journals* and *The Handbook of Academic Writing* (co-authored with Sarah Moore). Her research has been funded by Nuffield Foundation and British Academy.

Lindy Osborne is a Lecturer in Architecture at the Creative Industries Faculty at QUT, Australia. Lindy has won a number of awards for her buildings and for her teaching practice. She is currently studying for her PhD which explores the role of architecture in learning.

Anthony Paré is a Professor in the Department of Integrated Studies in Education, McGill University in Montréal, Canada. He was a founding member of the University Writing Centre and its long-time director. He has taught and studied writing for 30 years. His research examines academic and workplace writing, situated learning, school-to-work transitions, the development of professional literacies and doctoral writing. He teaches courses in literacy, discourse theory, response to literature and writing (practice and theory). His publications include books, chapters and articles on topics related to the study and practice of academic and professional communication.

Doreen Starke-Meyerring is an Associate Professor in the Department of Integrated Studies in Education at McGill University in Montréal, Canada, where she teaches graduate and undergraduate courses in discourse, writing and internet studies. Her research examines the implications of digital technologies, globalization and an increased focus on knowledge production for the study and teaching of writing in higher education, specifically in doctoral education. Currently, she is completing a multi-year cross-institutional research project examining current practices, policies and processes of doctoral student writing at Canadian research-intensive universities. Her recent publications include *Research Communication in the Social and Human Sciences: From Dissemination to Public Engagement* (2008), *Designing Global Learning Environments: Visionary Partnerships, Policies, and Pedagogies* (2008) and *Writing in Knowledge Societies* (2011).

Lucia Thesen is a Senior Lecturer in the Centre for Higher Education Development at the University of Cape Town in South Africa. Since the 1980s she has been working at the intersection of the politics of academic communicative practices and access for students on the margins of the university. From her current position as coordinator of Postgraduate Literacies, she is committed to supporting postgraduates in their writing of research and to debating the current forms in which research is communicated in writing in the English language. She is co-editor (with Ermien van Pletzen) of *Academic Literacy and the Languages of Change* (2006) and (with Linda Cooper) *Risk in Academic Writing: Postgraduate Students, Their Teachers and the Making of Knowledge* (in press).

Judith Wolfsberger (formerly Huber) founded the independent business Writers' Studio in Vienna, Austria, in 2002. The Writers' Studio offers workshops, writing groups, individual coaching and the 'thesis' marathon for masters and doctoral students, and supports non-academics in the field of professional and creative writing. She is author of the highly successful guide book for students *Frei geschrieben: Mut, Freiheit und Strategie für wissenschaftliche Abschlussarbeiten* (2012). Judith Wolfsberger holds a Mag (MA) in History and Philosophy of Science from the University of Vienna, Austria, and was an exchange student at the University of California at Berkeley, USA.

Acknowledgements

In 2012, our colleague Alison Lee, a mentor and great supporter of academic writing groups, passed away. Her absence has been keenly felt throughout the production of this edition. This book is dedicated to her memory.

We would like to acknowledge all those scholars who have participated in writing groups at our institutions and in the process built our collective expertise over the years.

As editors we would also like to thank and acknowledge our contributors who have engaged so generously in this project, thereby enriching our own enjoyment and learning. They have collaborated with us and with each other, replicating something of a mini writing group through the process of peer review and in the development of the chapters. Along the way we have also shared many of life's big events including new babies and new jobs.

Thanks also to Roger, Louis, Philip, Lily and Victoria.

Part I

Setting the scene

Chapter 1

Writing groups, pedagogy, theory and practice

An introduction

Claire Aitchison and Cally Guerin

Writing, doctoral research and scholarly life

Scholarly writing is a central component of academic life. And yet we continue to hear that it is a disputed site: a source of anxiety for many students and academics, a contentious space for both learners and teachers of academic writing; an area of disputed responsibility in research education, and higher education teaching and learning more generally. Many doctoral candidates and credentialized academics report ongoing challenges regarding scholarly writing, not the least of which is a desire for supportive environments within which writing will happen. This book is positioned by two key pressure points for writing in the academy, namely writing associated with the requirements of doctoral study, and scholarly publication more broadly. Here we showcase examples of how writing groups can respond in innovative ways to these imperatives.

For the university labour force—doctoral scholars, tenured academics, funded researchers and institutional administrators—writing for publication is a value-adding activity that reaps high returns. Publications are used as proxy measures of individual, institutional and national productivity and quality; reputation, and the funding that flows from it, is directly tied to global competitive ranking systems that are based largely on research outputs, impact and citation rankings (Sinclair *et al.* 2013). Because writing and publishing have implications for university funding and reputation, this in turn creates extra pressure on doctoral students for timely completion of their theses and the production of related publications (Murphy 1998; Lillis & Curry 2010). For both doctoral students and academics, a strong publication record is indispensable for securing certification, establishing an academic career, promotion, grants, awards and privileges. Despite rhetoric to the contrary, higher education institutions continue to reward academics who publish over those whose contribution may be in teaching, administration or service to the community. So, at all stages, the ability to write well and develop and maintain a strong publication output is a fundamental literacy for academic success (Bourdieu 1983, 1991).

For the overwhelming majority of doctoral students, written documentation of research, in whatever form, remains the means by which one is admitted into the academy. During candidature, written work is the principal measure by which researcher progress is monitored and measured, and is even more central in those systems in which there is no oral viva or defence. For doctoral students, writing a thesis or dissertation (be that the production of a traditional 'big book', a practical work plus exegesis, or portfolio of publications) is a hurdle that can stall, even derail, candidature (Aitchison & Paré 2012). Increasingly, too, doctoral students will not only produce the text(s) required for graduation, but also aim to develop a healthy publication record during the period of their candidature (Aitchison *et al.* 2010; Kamler & Thomson 2006; Lee & Aitchison 2011).

On one hand then, getting writing done is an essential component of scholarly life, and yet much research shows that it continues to be marginalized and squeezed out of the everyday practices of researchers and academics (Hemmings & Kay 2010; Murray, Steckley & MacLeod 2011). There is a direct relationship between writing output and academic status and occupation. Unsurprisingly, senior tenured academics are responsible for a significant proportion of institutional publications, particularly when these writers are located in research centres, carry reduced teaching loads, and have well-resourced opportunities and time to write (Hemmings & Kay 2010). Doctoral scholars also account for a significant proportion of institutional output. However, in our experience at least, they, along with untenured academics and early career researchers, form a kind of underclass of 'writing labourers', often producing publications on top of normal workloads and outside of paid working hours. This unequal situation contributes to the growing levels of frustration and stress reported by academics worldwide.

Further complicating the situation, many academics report lacking the confidence and skills to support the writing development of their research students (Catterall *et al.* 2011; Paré 2011). And when those students are also struggling to write in a foreign language, or across traditional methodological or disciplinary boundaries, the challenges are even greater (Guerin *et al.* 2013). In many cases, supervisory practices for doctoral students continue to undervalue, even neglect, writing development (Aitchison & Paré 2012). We note here Bill Green's observations about the general absence of *education* in so much talk of doctoral studies (Green & Lee 1995; Green 2010). It is our intention that the present publication, with its explicit focus on pedagogy, contributes to redressing this omission.

By contrast, however, the market has not been slow to recognize the urgent need for help with writing, and there has been an extraordinary growth in non-institutional writing support for scholars. Doctoral students, their supervisors and academics seeking guidance and support for their writing are increasingly taking up the services offered by private consultants, web-based communities and the plethora self-help books (Thomson & Kamler 2013; Aitchison & Mowbray 2014).

It is in this context of rising pressure on doctoral students and academics for greater writing productivity that this book is located.

New approaches for changing contexts

We operate in an increasingly global system of higher education within which doctoral education holds a special place—being both buffeted by global and national policy changes, and at the same time resisting and reinterpreting its place within this complex context. There have now been a number of important accounts of change and innovation in doctoral education (see, for example, Golde & Walker 2006; Lovitts 2007; Parry 2007; Bitusikova 2009; Boud & Lee 2009; Walker & Thomson 2010; Devos & Manathunga 2012; Lee & Danby 2012; Group of Eight 2013). Much has also been written about the pressures on doctoral students and academics for greater writing productivity as measured in publication outputs (McGrail *et al.* 2006; Rocco & Hatcher 2011; Lee & Danby 2012; Murray 2012; Thomson & Kamler 2013).

Changed pedagogical practices in research education have altered for a number of reasons. Increased workloads of supervisors, the growth of interdisciplinary, multi-method research and cross-institutional studies mean that the previously tight fit between student and supervisor is increasingly less likely. The sheer volume of students entering higher research degree programs mitigates against the capacity of institutions to provide the older style, intimate supervisor–student formulations characteristic of former eras. In addition, there is greater cultural and linguistic diversity within the research student and supervisor population, which brings greater variation of experience and expectation about the form and function of research education, and the place of writing within it.

The doctorate itself and its functions have changed considerably in the last two decades. The desire for greater transparency, transferability and standardization that fuelled the Bologna Process has influenced systems beyond Europe (Group of Eight 2013). The expansion in professional and practice-based doctorates has been particularly marked in Australia and the UK, reflecting the growing requirement for doctoral programs to respond to the needs of industry and governments as they compete in the global knowledge economy (Danby & Lee 2012).

These factors, along with the pressure for fast throughput and timely completions, a more competitive job market for doctoral graduates and the recent impact of the global financial crisis on higher education more generally, have created a dynamic, even volatile, context for doctoral research education globally. In turn, these changes are forcing new pedagogical responses in doctoral education—and specifically for research writing. As the primacy of the supervisor–student dyad is disrupted, suites of other opportunities are being made available to doctoral students, including workshops, seminars, disciplinary and institutional conferences, masterclasses, coursework programs and so on. But still, much innovation remains due to individual initiative, often small-scale and local (Aitchison *et al.* 2010). Similarly, there is a keenness amongst early career researchers and academics to find ways to support their writing (Lee & Boud 2003; Murray 2005; Grant 2008; Murray *et al.* 2011; Thomson & Kamler 2013). Indicative of an unmet need is the growing number of writing related websites and blogs, mostly again the initiative of individuals as indicated in this diverse sample:

http://explorationsofstyle.com/
http://researchvoodoo.wordpress.com/
http://doctoralwriting.wordpress.com/
www.thedutchphdcoach.com
http://thesiswhisperer.com/
http://www.phd2published.com
www.patthomson.wordpress.com

New approaches to doctoral education are burgeoning and, as a consequence, we are required to think more carefully about how we might understand, take up and evaluate these emerging pedagogies. Within this rapidly expanding field, we focus on one increasingly popular practice: writing groups for postgraduates and faculty. As signalled by Bill Green (2009), it is imperative that we stop to investigate, interrogate and share practices, as this volume does.

What do we already know about writing groups?

While writing groups have become ubiquitous for creative writers, and collaborative writing arrangements in school and undergraduate classrooms are common, in doctoral education writing groups are still relatively novel and under-researched. The first book-length discussion of the history of writing groups and their application in undergraduate studies and composition programs in the North American tradition was published by Anne Ruggles Gere (1987).

A number of recent texts on scholarly writing and publishing (see for example, Murray 2005; Murray & Moore 2006; Rocco & Hatcher 2011) refer repeatedly to the value of writing groups. Similarly, publications for supervisors and doctoral students frequently recommend writing groups (see, for example, Kamler & Thomson 2006; Murray 2007; Thomson & Kamler 2013; Thomson & Walker 2010) for building writing acumen and scholarly know-how.

Elsewhere, literature on writing groups for research students and academic staff reports on: specific programs (see, for example, Aitchison 2009; Bastalich 2011; Cuthbert & Spark 2008; Delyser 2003; Ferguson 2009; Guerin *et al.* 2013; Haas 2011; Mullen 2003; Larcombe *et al.* 2007; Li & Vandermensbrugghe 2011; Maher *et al.* 2008; Parker 2009); the value of peer learning/mentoring and community building (Boud & Lee 2005; Caffarella & Barnett 2000; Guerin *et al.* 2013; McAlpine & Asghar 2010; Stracke 2010); and discussions of scholarly identity formation (Guerin 2013; Lee & Boud 2003; Kamler & Thomson 2008). In addition, a smaller number of articles attend to pedagogical specifics of writing forms and practices (Aitchison 2009, 2010; Cuthbert *et al.* 2009; Lee & Boud 2003).

In many ways the benefits of writing groups for doctoral students seems self evident, but, as this emerging literature makes clear, our understanding of when, how and why writing groups operate in academic scholarship is still fragmented and under-theorised. As we conceived of this volume, we had many discussions about likely authors and topics. Above all, we were seeking to create a text that was more than simply another 'feel good' book on writing groups. We wanted this edition to stretch our understanding of the practices and the diversity of writing groups; in particular, we sought to find and expose new ways of interpreting what was going on in such groups. In seeking out potential contributors we prioritized our desire for new perspectives, theoretical frames and innovative practices. In addition, we wished to invite both newer and more established scholars into this space. Our aim was to create a dialogue where different voices, perspectives and practices could come together across countries, systems and disciplines in discussions around writing groups for doctoral researchers.

And so the chapters here present close-up encounters with practices of scholarly writing in collaborative settings, identifying the pedagogical and theoretical elements and thus contributing to a more nuanced understanding of the everyday practices that make writing groups work for research scholars.

As advocates of writing groups, we are careful also to acknowledge the limitations of this approach. In particular, we wish to caution against uncritical or romanticized views of these emerging practices. We know a lot more about the successes than the failures of this pedagogy. As authors in this volume warn, writing groups are not for everyone, and without support and know-how many experience frustrations in their attempts to establish and maintain groups. Making writing groups work can be challenging. As Thesen, in this volume, says, the group 'sometimes feels very fragile. The flattened hierarchy ... does not solve all problems'. Writing groups can complement but not substitute for sound supervision and programmatic support. We don't believe writing groups are the ultimate 'fix'; however, we do see that the kind of social practice pedagogies enacted as writing groups have specific characteristics that match the requirements of advanced research scholarship and writing. Writing groups put mechanisms of academic writing and knowledge-making at the centre of scholarship.

Definitions, dimensions and declarations

Writing groups, writers' groups, writers' circles, writing retreats and writers' retreats. The contributors in this volume use all these descriptors; for some authors there are subtle differences in their use of these terms, and for others terms are used interchangeably.

We use 'writing groups' as an umbrella generic term to refer to situations where more than two people come together to work on their writing in a sustained way, over repeated gatherings, for doing, discussing or sharing their writing for agreed purposes. We understand writing groups as having 'a strong reliance on the pedagogical principles of identification and peer review, community, and writing as normal business' (Aitchison & Lee 2006: 265). We use this term to capture a variety of formulations and practices of groups of writers, whether they are situated within an institution, course or curriculum, or whether they operate in other voluntary or associated domains of academia, in synchronous or asynchronous time and space, in physically co-located or online environments. For us, the defining characteristic is the sociality of an endeavour that is focused on writing.

The writing groups showcased in this book include some that are quite specifically for, and by, doctoral writers, but many are more fluid in composition and purpose, reflecting the nature of research study, wherein traditional hierarchical boundaries of teacher and student, expert and novice, curriculum and assessment are broken down, horizontalized (Boud & Lee 2005) and reformulated.

Another dimension of diversity in this volume concerns what Lillis and Curry (2010) call 'textual ideologies', that is, 'clusters of views held about the nature of language, the writer, his/her location, the status s/he is granted as a user of English' (23). In this collection, reflecting not only the authors' country of origin but also their philosophical or disciplinary orientations, a variety of descriptors are used for those for whom English is not a first language. We note the extraordinary number of such labels—for example, terms such as non-native speaker (NNS), Non-English speaking background (NESB), English as an additional language (EAL), culturally and linguistically diverse (CALD), English as a second language (ESL)—and we recognize, too, how labels permeate this field, positioning both the user and the person being labelled. Where possible, and following Canagarajah (2002) and Lillis and Curry (2010), we have given preference to the term 'multilingual writer' because it avoids negative deficit positioning, and elsewhere we favour ESL in recognition of its global currency.

The majority of the authors in this volume are native speakers of English. Most work in contexts where cultural and linguistic diversity abound, and with scholars seeking to write theses and publications in English. We recognize that native speakers of English hold a privileged place because of the dominance of the English language and Anglophone traditions for scientific and academic publishing—and thereby for systems of knowledge production (Canagarajah 2002; Lillis & Curry 2010; Thesen & Cooper 2014 in print).

We also acknowledge the direct implications of this hegemonic positioning of English as the *lingua franca* of scholarly research for writing group practices. Inevitably, peer-to-peer relations are influenced by linguistic diversity in groups. On the one hand, multilingual scholars are positioned in specific ways in relation to their native-English-speaking peers in writing groups; on the other hand, those for whom English is a first language are required (at some level, at least) to negotiate expectations of their 'expert status' in regard to writing in English. Linguistically diverse groups must necessarily grapple with these factors in group facilitation, modes of interaction, group relations and knowledge-making (see, for example, Guerin, Li, Ings and Aitchison in this volume).

Writing, pedagogy and practice

Clearly, there can be no one simple approach to developing and supporting scholarly writing. The act of producing text and of writing is a complex, situated, social and political act that makes and reflects identity, position and power. A variety of theoretical frames are put to work by the authors of these chapters as they critically interpret the practices they describe; within this diversity, however, there are some unifying perspectives about writing, pedagogy and practice.

It can be risky for editors to try to situate the work of their contributors by claiming, on their behalf, theoretical influences; nevertheless, in one way or another, we see all of the authors in this book as taking a social practice approach. By this we mean that we see the chapters as sharing a common notion of academic writing as 'being rooted in specific cultural traditions and ways of constructing knowledge ... as embedded in power relations ... as involving issues of differential access to material or "non-discursive" resources ... as well as questions of linguistic and ethnic identity ...' (Lillis & Curry 2010: 21). Thus, writing and knowledge-making are intertwined. Perhaps not all our contributors would use the label, but we see this 'academic literacies' orientation, with its practice–theory interface, as situating both the broader complexities of the changing academic and doctoral landscape along with the deeply individual/subjective processes of embodiment and identity formation that accompany research scholarship.

The approach to writing and text in this volume is profoundly social—and, at the same time, deeply embedded in practice. Placing writing at the nexus of the social and practice enables a reconsideration of scholarly writing and writers as socio-material phenomena shaped by the mutually constitutive influences of embodied relational practices among human and nonhuman actors. Thus, for us, practice theory (e.g., Schatzki 2001; Kemmis 2005) has useful application to scholarly writing. The everyday practices around writing by doctoral students and scholars 'talk back' to the forces that demand certain kinds of writers and writing—but these practices are also, in turn, powerfully shaped by such influences. Writing groups instance this duality of the social and the practice, coming together in whatever formulations work for the particular group, in its particular context, for the purposes of advancing the shared objective of writing.

It is this very plasticity that is the essence of the writing group approach. As Sarah Haas (Chapter 3) so clearly demonstrates in her 'Pick-n-Mix' metaphor for writing groups, the permutations and configurations, the everyday routines, materialities and practices of groups of writers, are countless and open-ended. And within this diversity, as we show in this volume, is a plethora of embedded, constituent pedagogical practices, some overt and 'teacherly', others tacit and organic. In demonstrably pedagogic style, for example, in Chapter 10, Linda Li uses strategies from process writing and rhetorical genre theory in her facilitation of writing groups for multilingual students. She shares her practice of collaborative text work 'playing around' with participant texts that are projected onto a screen for group discussion and review. There are few opportunities in the academy for such close up textual work on language, and yet, for novice writers seeking to master advanced academic English, such facilitated opportunities are invaluable for building skills, confidence and community.

More conventional perspectives on pedagogy focus on student–teacher relations; however, in doctoral education this simple equation needs to be reconsidered and broadened out to reconceptualize teaching/learning relationships (Boud & Lee 2005). In Michelle Maher's chapter, for example, we see how, when supervisors and research students come together as fellow academic writers, they learn from each other in quite different ways from institutionally sanctioned pedagogies. Importantly, more junior scholars learn by observing the modelling of disciplinary writing practices. In his chapter, 'The Studio Model: Developing community writing in creative, practice-led PhD design theses', Welby Ings illustrates how he incorporates creative industry practices of collaboration and critique into a writing group approach to supervision, which is in turn supplemented by the students' own online writing community, a mode particularly favoured by multilingual and culturally diverse research students. By way of contrast, in Chapter 5, Doreen Starke-Meyerring draws from a major study to present the observations of students themselves about how institutions can work to stifle (or enable) attempts for productive collective writing.

Where accounts of pedagogy in doctoral education literature don't focus on student–supervisor practices, then the gaze turns to programmatic arrangements (Danby & Lee 2012), of which there are several examples in this book. However, even where writing groups are sanctioned by institutions, they seem to take on a life of their own. Sarah Haas (Chapter 3), Claire Aitchison (Chapter 4), Cally Guerin (Chapter 9) and Lucia Thesen (Chapter 11) operate from centrally located units to provide programmed writing group opportunities for doctoral scholars. Their examples attest to the ways in which some structural elements are useful enablers, and also demonstrate how groups doggedly re-form themselves by establishing their own norms, routines and behaviours. For example, in her role as an academic developer, Guerin helps students to establish groups and facilitates their initial meetings, with the express purpose of creating opportunities in which students themselves can then go on to develop their own arrangements and practices.

Three of the authors here reflect on two quite different retreat practices. Using the metaphor of the labyrinth, Sally Knowles and Barbara Grant depict a contemplative, organic retreat style that accommodates the rhythms of individual writers—and yet is firmly based on a set of four interrelated practice principles which are beautifully and usefully detailed. A key aspect of Rowena Murray's retreats is the more overt regulation and timing of writer productivity—and it is this aspect, the habituating of writing, that participants sought subsequently to reproduce in 'micro-groups', demonstrating what she calls behavioural, cognitive and social coherence.

But pedagogies for learning doctoral writing stretch across multiple and cascading networks of relations. Writers embody not only desires for the production of certain kinds of texts, but also carry with them the weight of expectations of other structural and human networks. Evidence of the reach of such social networks can be found in Chapter 15, where Inger Mewburn, Lindy Osborne and Glenda

Caldwell describe a self-organizing, global, online writing initiative. Here, layers of actors (students, academics, supervisors and the unidentified) collaborate to write together, marshalling their efforts across time and space. In Chapter 4, Claire Aitchison explores the impact and uptake of review and feedback that originates from within and beyond a writing circle, a situation that requires writers to negotiate multiple influences on their texts. In this edition there are numerous examples of such sanctioned and unsanctioned practices that mobilize complex networks of relations for the co-construction of knowledge.

The 'practice turn' (Hagar *et al.* 2012) would have us attend to not only the human actors, but also the contextual materiality of writing group activities. In many cases, the formation of writing groups arose in direct response to the pressures felt by individuals to increase writing productivity. In 'talking back' to these pressures, some used time as a mechanism for productivity. The 'Shut up & Write!' (Chapter 15) and 'Thesis marathon' (Chapter 12) models transform the pressures for writing performativity into bite-sized, socially mediated allocations of time and space for doing writing. For Lucia Thesen's groups in South Africa (Chapter 11) and for Judith Wolfsberger's participants in Vienna (Chapter 12), the positive emotions of laughter, applause and the sense of belonging activate learning and commitment in opposition to the more negative pressures of doctoral candidature.

Reports of doctoral writing pedagogy often tend to be narrowly conceived and ignore the extraordinary range of activities that operate, often unrecorded, even unnoticed, outside formal, sanctioned institutional arrangements. For example, a more fluid, less formal arrangement seemed appropriate for a group of women writers that included casual and permanent, academic and professional staff, doctoral researchers and early career researchers, all of whom were struggling to find time to write along with competing work and domestic demands. In this group, Bosanquet and colleagues (Chapter 14) experience learning and doing scholarly writing as an overtly gendered practice, where intimacy and connection operate as the central mechanism for enabling writing.

In exploring the actual material practices of these groups and events in this volume, we have stretched—perhaps to its limits—the concept of pedagogy. By viewing pedagogy as 'the process through which knowledge is produced' (Danby & Lee 2012: 4), we have confirmed a view of writing pedagogy as socially, situated and practice-oriented. This perspective values diverse 'learning enablers', such as human actions, cognitions and affect, as well as non-human structural, spatial and material factors.

Unifying themes and concepts

The chapters in this collection present a complex matrix of intersecting and overlapping thematic and theoretical insights; themes both expected and surprising resonate between these discussions in a rich array of contemporary understandings of the kinds of development that are possible within writing groups.

A key theme to emerge from these chapters relates to the spaces in which writing groups are conducted. While many institutions are openly supportive of writing groups as a strategic pedagogy for doctoral education (Li; Thesen; Aitchison; Guerin), others relegate writing groups to the margins. Some writing groups operate off-campus, as retreats undertaken in peaceful surroundings (Knowles & Grant; Murray), in the public space of coffee-shop encounters (Mewburn, Osborne & Caldwell), and in the private spaces of domestic households (Maher; Bosanquet et al.). Some spaces are created by supervisors for their own group of research students (Ings; Maher), while others are initiated by doctoral students and scholars themselves (Murray; Bosanquet). For some, the writing group provides an almost subversive space in which to enjoy the activity of writing that, despite pressures to increase publication outputs, is (curiously) somehow frowned upon by the institution (Starke-Meyerring); Wolfsberger proffers yet another form of writing group that occurs in the space of private enterprise outside the dictates of the institution. The location itself can be a physical or a virtual space (Ings), and communication technologies are increasingly used to facilitate these meetings (Mewburn, Osborne & Caldwell). Each of these variations on the spaces in which writing groups meet has at its core the recognition that there is value in creating separate, safe and collegial possibilities where researchers can focus explicitly on writing as a central activity of academic life.

These chapters demonstrate conclusively that writing groups do a lot more than simply develop writing skills: writing groups also provide an important emotional space for doctoral students and early career researchers. For many, the companionship of the group imparts a sense of connectedness and belonging to an academic community for those in the process of developing researcher identities. Sometimes this is because of a shared practice, as in the Shut up & Write!/typing pool style of writing group (Mewburn, Osborne & Caldwell; Murray), or because of a shared location, such as attending a residential writing retreat (Knowles & Grant). But this sense of connectedness and belonging seems to be produced by most forms of writing groups, as Guerin seeks to interpret through the lens of gift exchange theory, arguing that reciprocal giving of feedback sets up a dynamic that binds individuals into these communities.

The writing groups described in these chapters are testament to the positive emotions inspired by sharing the challenges of academic writing. In a post-apartheid South Africa, Thesen takes up Bakhtin's ideas of laughter to explore how it troubles and disrupts more pedestrian notions of risk. Wolfsberger is influenced by Bolker to structure a pedagogy that foregrounds applause and connectedness. While there is acknowledgement of the powerful effect of negative emotions in relation to writing (Starke-Meyerring), we also see here the potential of deeply nurturing environments formed by participants in writing groups (Bosanquet et al.; Knowles & Grant). There are risks in offering one's writing for critique, of course, as Paré, Thesen and Guerin explore. On the whole, though, one of the resounding impressions left by these chapters is that writing groups are, quite simply, a lot of fun.

Gender is another common theme. In keeping with the literature on writing groups, the vast majority of the contributions here are written by women, and most writing group participants described in these chapters are also women. While there is more work to be done on the gendered nature of writing groups, Bosanquet and colleagues reflect on the significance of their (accidentally) all-women writing group, finding resonance between their experiences and the perspectives of feminist theories of writing. Wolfsberger also considers the implications of working mostly with women in her writing groups. Perhaps there is evidence here of the ways in which at least some women seek to create different kinds of relationships in opposition to more competitive institutional hierarchies. Of course, there are dangers in drawing broad conclusions based on gender, but it is encouraging to think that gendered writing groups can contribute to collaborative models of collegiality within universities in a time of increasing pressures and challenges.

Another concept that unifies the chapters is food, which can function on many levels in writing groups. Knowles and Grant point out that good food plays a pivotal role in creating a focused, energetic atmosphere in writing retreats. It can evoke the nurturing intimacy of the home (Maher); it can act as a symbol of celebration (Wolfsberger); it can fuel conversation and reflection (Bosanquet *et al.*); it can facilitate social preliminaries to silent writing (Mewburn, Osborne & Caldwell); and it can create social bonds through gift exchange (Guerin). Eating and drinking together draws these individuals into a group that looks after its members; these social elements complement the work accomplished inside the group and speaks to the holistic identity of the researcher.

And finally, a number of these chapters are linked by their use of wonderfully evocative metaphors to explain their activities. Knowles and Grant explore the ancient poetry of the labyrinth as a metaphor for the focused thinking that is possible in the uninterrupted pathway provided by the structure of the labyrinth. Unlike the labyrinth, the metaphors of the writing sprint (Mewburn, Osborne & Caldwell) and the marathon (Wolfsberger) evoke vibrant images of movement which stand in contrast to images of the quietly labouring writer. Mewburn, Osborne and Caldwell use the 'pomodoro technique', employing the tomato-shaped timer to regulate spurts of writer productivity. On the other hand, Wolfsberger's marathon metaphor takes up the idea of the long-distance exertion required of dissertation writing by using props: a runner's track to mark progress, goals, a cheering audience, with awards and celebrations of success.

Overview of chapters

This book is loosely arranged into three sections. In the first section, this introductory chapter maps out the central concerns in contemporary scholarship on writing groups by presenting the overarching pedagogies, theories and practices that frame the volume. In Chapter 2, Paré provides a detailed historical and theoretical background for contemporary uptake of writing groups in research education. Next, Haas presents a typology of writing groups that identifies the key characteristics of groups and the many variations she has observed within those categories.

The 'Theory and Reflection' section opens with Aitchison's exploration of the complexities occasioned by the multiple sources of feedback that doctoral students must negotiate in the context of writing groups. Starke-Meyerring then considers the inhibiting and silencing of writing by institutions, and the potential of writing groups to circumvent these barriers. Traditional hierarchies are often dissolved in writing groups, and Maher explores this when doctoral students and their supervisors write together. Chapters 7 and 8 reflect on writing groups as retreats. Here, Murray explores the ways in which participants subsequently take the retreat experience into their everyday world. Then, using their contemplative model of retreats, Knowles and Grant focus on the emotional and environmental conditions that can aid the writing process. Finally, this section concludes with Guerin, who uses the lens of gift exchange theory to interpret the exchange relations of writing groups.

The third section of this volume, 'Pedagogy in Practice', showcases specific realizations of writing groups. We start with Li's explanation of the pedagogies she employs with multilingual scholars in a facilitated writing group. Thesen interrogates theoretical and practice dimensions of laughter and risk in the postcolonial context of writing groups in a South African university. In Chapter 12, Wolfsberger explicates the pedagogical motivations of playfulness and applause in writing programs located outside the university system. Two novel approaches to writing groups for doctoral students in creative, practice-led PhDs are outlined by Ings: one facilitated by a supervisor in a face-to-face setting; the other led solely by peers online. The nuances of writing together as women are explored in Chapter 14 by Bosanquet, Cahir, Huber, Jacenyik-Trawöger and McNeill. In the final chapter of this collection, Mewburn, Osborne and Caldwell describe their experiences of the global Web 2.0 movement 'Shut up & Write!', which harnesses mobile and social media technologies.

References

Aitchison, C. (2009) 'Writing groups for doctoral education', *Studies in Higher Education*, 34(8), 905–16.

—— (2010) 'Learning together to publish: writing group pedagogies for doctoral publishing', in C. Aitchison, B. Kamler and A. Lee (eds) *Publishing Pedagogies for the Doctorate and Beyond*, London: Routledge.

Aitchison, C. and Lee, A. (2006) 'Research writing: problems and pedagogies', *Teaching in Higher Education*, 11(3): 265–78.

Aitchison, C. and Paré, A. (2012) 'Writing as craft and practice in the doctoral curriculum', in A. Lee and S. Danby (eds) *Reshaping Doctoral Education: International Approaches and Pedagogies*, London: Routledge.

Aitchison, C. and Mowbray, S. (2014) 'Shadow writers in doctoral education? The good, the bad and the unknown', paper presented at Quality in Postgraduate Research conference, Adelaide, April.

Aitchison, C., Kamler, B. and Lee, A. (eds) (2010) *Publishing Pedagogies for the Doctorate and Beyond*, London, Routledge.

Bastalich, W. (2011) 'Beyond the local/general divide: English for academic purposes and process approaches to cross disciplinary, doctoral writing support', *Higher Education Research and Development*, 30(4): 449–62.

Bitusikova, A. (2009) 'Reforming doctoral education in Europe', *Academe Online*, 95(1).

Boud, D. and Lee, A. (2005) '"Peer learning" as pedagogic discourse for research education', *Studies in Higher Education*, 30(5): 501–16.

—— (2009) *Changing Practices of Doctoral Education*, London: Routledge.

Bourdieu, P. (1983) 'The field of cultural production or the economic world reversed', *Poetics*, 12: 311–56.

—— (1991) *Language and Symbolic Power*, Cambridge: Polity Press.

Caffarella, R. S. and Barnett, B. G. (2000) 'Teaching doctoral students to become scholarly writers: the importance of giving and receiving critiques', *Studies in Higher Education*, 25(1): 39–52.

Canagarajah, A. S. (2002) *The Geopolitics of Academic Writing*, Pittsburgh, PA: University of Pittsburgh Press.

Catterall, J., Ross, P., Aitchison, C. and Burgin, S. (2011) 'Pedagogical approaches that facilitate writing in postgraduate research candidature in science and technology', *Journal of University Teaching and Learning Practice*, 8(2).

Cuthbert, D. and Spark, C. (2008) 'Getting a GRiP: examining the outcomes of a pilot program to support graduate research students in writing for publication', *Studies in Higher Education*, 33(1): 77–88.

Cuthbert, D., Spark, C. and Burke, E. (2009) 'Disciplining writing: the case for multi-disciplinary writing groups to support writing for publication by higher degree by research candidates in the humanities, arts and social sciences', *Higher Education Research and Development*, 28(2): 137–49.

Danby, S. and Lee, A. (2012) 'Framing doctoral pedagogy as design and action', in A. Lee and S. Danby (eds) *Reshaping Doctoral Education: International Approaches and Pedagogies*, London: Routledge.

Delyser, D. (2003) 'Teaching graduate students to write: a seminar for thesis and dissertation writers', *Journal of Geography in Higher Education*, 27(2): 169–81.

Devos, A. and Manathunga, C. (eds) (2012) 'Special issue: contemporary issues in doctoral education', *Australian Universities' Review*, 54(1).

Ferguson, T. (2009) 'The "write" skills and more: a thesis writing group for doctoral students', *Journal of Geography in Higher Education*, 33(2): 285–97.

Gere, A. R. (1987) *Writing Groups: History, Theory, and Implications*, Carbondale, IL: Southern Illinois University Press.

Golde, C. M. and Walker, G. E. (eds) (2006) *Envisioning the Future of Doctoral Education*, San Francisco, CA: Jossey Bass.

Grant, B. (2008) *Academic Writing Retreats: A Facilitator's Guide*, Sydney: Higher Education Research and Development Society of Australia (HERDSA).

Green, B. (2009) 'Changing perspectives, changing practices: doctoral education in transition', in D. Boud & A. Lee (eds) *Changing Practices of Doctoral Education*, London: Routledge.

—— (2010) 'Challenging perspectives, changing practices', in D. Boud & A. Lee (eds) *Changing Practices of Doctoral Education*, London: Routledge.

Green, B. and Lee, A. (1995) 'Theorising postgraduate pedagogy', *Australian Universities' Review*, 38(2): 40–5.

Group of Eight (2013) *The Changing PhD: Discussion Paper.* Available online: http://www.go8.edu.au/university-staff/go8-policy-and-analysis/2013/the-changing-phd (accessed 4 September 2013).

Guerin, C. (2013) 'Rhizomatic research cultures, writing groups and academic researcher identities', *International Journal of Doctoral Studies*, 8, 137–50.

Guerin, C., Xafis, V., Doda, D. V., Gillam, M., Larg, A., Luckner, H., Jahan, N., Widayati, A. and Xu, C. (2013) 'Diversity in collaborative research communities: a multicultural, multidisciplinary thesis writing group in Public Health', *Studies in Continuing Education*, 35(1): 65–81.

Haas, S. (2011) 'A writer development group for Master's students: procedures and benefits', *Journal of Academic Writing*, 1(1): 88–99.

Hager, P., Lee, A. and Reich, A. (eds) (2012) *Practice, Learning and Change: Practice-Theory Perspectives on Professional Learning*, Dordrecht: Springer.

Hemmings, B. and Kay, R. (2010) 'University lecturer publication output: qualifications, time and confidence count', *Journal of Higher Education Policy and Management*, 32(2): 185–97.

Kamler, B. and Thomson, P. (2006) *Helping Doctoral Students Write: Pedagogies for Supervision*, London: Routledge.

—— (2008) 'The failure of dissertation advice books: toward alternative pedagogies for doctoral writing', *Educational Researcher*, 37(8): 507–14.

Kemmis, S. (2005) 'Knowing practice: searching for saliences', *Pedagogy, Culture and Society*, 13(2): 391–426.

Larcombe, W., McCosker, A. and O'Loughlin, K. (2007) 'Supporting education PhD and DEd students to become confident academic writers: an evaluation of thesis writers' circles', *Journal of University Teaching and Learning Practice*, 4(1): 55–63.

Lee, A. and Boud, D. (2003) 'Writing groups, change and academic identity: research development as local practice', *Studies in Higher Education*, 28(2): 187–200.

Lee, A. and Aitchison, C. (2011) 'Working with tensions: writing for publication during your doctorate', in T. S. Rocco and T. Hatcher (eds) *The Handbook of Scholarly Writing and Publishing*, San Francisco, CA: Jossey-Bass.

Lee, A. and Danby, S. (eds) (2012) *Reshaping Doctoral Education: International Approaches and Pedagogies*, London, Routledge.

Li, L. Y. and Vandermensbrugghe, J. (2011) 'Supporting the thesis writing process of international research students through an ongoing writing group', *Innovations in Education and Teaching International*, 48(2): 195–205.

Lillis, T. M. and Curry, M. J. (2010) *Academic Writing in a Global Context: The Politics and Practices of Publishing in English*, London: Routledge.

Lovitts, B. E. (2007) *Making the Implicit Explicit: Creating Performance Expectations for the Dissertation*, Stirling, VA: Stylus.

McAlpine, L. and Asghar, A. (2010) 'Enhancing academic climate: doctoral students as their own developers', *International Journal for Academic Development*, 15(2): 167–78.

McGrail, M., Rickard, C. and Jones, R. (2006) 'Publish or perish: a systematic review of interventions to increase academic publication rates', *Higher Education Research and Development*, 25(1): 19–35.

Maher, D., Seaton, L., McMullen, C., Fitzgerald, T., Otsuji, E. and Lee, A. (2008) 'Becoming and being writers: the experiences of doctoral students in writing groups', *Studies in Continuing Education*, 30(3): 263–75.

Mullen, C. A. (2003) 'The WIT cohort: a case study of informal doctoral mentoring', *Journal of Further and Higher Education*, 27(4): 411–26.

Murphy, P. (1998) 'Journal quality assessment for performance based funding', *Assessment and Evaluation in Higher Education*, 23: 25–31.

Murray, R. (2005) *Writing for Academic Journals*, Maidenhead: Open University Press.

—— (2007) *How to Write a Thesis* (2nd edn), Maidenhead: Open University Press.

—— (2012) 'It's not a hobby: reconceptualizing the place of writing in academic work', *Higher Education*, 66(1): 79–91.

Murray, R. and Moore, S. (2006) *The Handbook of Academic Writing: A Fresh Approach*, Maidenhead: Open University Press.

Murray, R., Steckley, L. and MacLeod, I. (2011) 'Research leadership in writing for publication: a theoretical framework', *British Educational Research Journal*, 38(5): 765–81.

Paré, A. (2011) 'Speaking of writing: supervisory feedback and the dissertation', in L. McAlpine and C. Amundsen (eds) *Doctoral Education: Research-based Strategies for Doctoral Students, Supervisors and Administrators*, New York: Springer.

Parker, R. (2009) 'A learning community approach to doctoral education in the social sciences', *Teaching in Higher Education*, 14(1): 43–54.

Parry, S. (2007) *Disciplines and Doctorates*, Dordrecht: Springer.

Rocco, T. S. and Hatcher, T. G. (eds) (2011) *The Handbook of Scholarly Writing and Publishing*, San Francisco, CA: Jossey-Bass.

Schatzki, T. R. (2001) 'Practice theory', in T. R. Schatzki, K. Knorr-Cetina and E. van Savigny (eds) *The Practice Turn in Contemporary Theory*, New York: Routledge.

Sinclair, J., Barnacle, R. and Cuthbert, D. (2013) 'How the doctorate contributes to the formation of active researchers: what the research tells us', *Studies in Higher Education*, (iFirst, August 2012): 1–15. DOI: 10.1080/03075079.2013.806460.

Stracke, E. (2010) 'Undertaking the journey together: peer learning for a successful and enjoyable PhD experience', *Journal of University Teaching and Learning Practice*, 7(1): 1–12.

Thesen, L. and Cooper, L. (2014 in print) *Risk in Academic Writing: Postgraduate Writers, Their Teachers and the Making of Knowledge*, Bristol: Multilingual Matters.

Thomson, P. and Walker, M. (eds) (2010) *The Routledge Doctoral Student's Companion: Getting to Grips with Research in Education and the Social Sciences*, London: Routledge.

Thomson, P. and Kamler, B. (2013) *Writing for Peer Reviewed Journals: Strategies for Getting Published*, London: Routledge.

Walker, M. and Thomson, P. (2010) *The Routledge Doctoral Supervisor's Companion*, London: Routledge.

Chapter 2

Writing together for many reasons
Theoretical and historical perspectives

Anthony Paré

As the chapters in this book make clear, writing groups in various configurations have proven to be successful support for people seeking to join the conversation in their scholarly disciplines. That comes as no surprise to thousands of teachers from primary to graduate school who, for many years, have created opportunities for students to share their writing with classmates. Like much else about teaching, this knowledge has been learned through practice, and teachers have not waited for, nor needed, research or theory to 'confirm' what they already understand. But a practice this successful deserves reflection, not only because it might tell us something more about writing as a human activity, but also because it can help us both justify and improve use of writing groups.

With that purpose in mind, this chapter explores some of the history of ideas that support group writing. It draws primarily on advances in English education over the past half-century or so and on the traditions of North American composition and rhetoric, but looks also to theory and research that justifies collaborative learning more broadly. The chapter considers the philosophical and psychological bases for a view of writing as a profoundly social act, reviews some of the literature that has reported on the social dynamics of writing, and traces the passage of that theory and research into the composition curriculum. Finally, the chapter considers the particular value of writing together during the doctorate, while students are preparing to join the intensely social practice of professional scholarly writing.

Anne Gere (1987) has written the definitive history of writing groups in the American tradition, tracing their academic and non-academic origins back to the early 1700s. Those deep roots are useful referents when explaining collaborative writing practices to colleagues or administrators, and Gere's book is highly recommended reading. However, for the purposes of this chapter, I will pick up the story at the moment when writing in groups was most recently re-discovered as a useful pedagogical practice—the 1960s. Gere argues, as others have (e.g., Dixon 1967; Moffett 1968; Muller 1967), that a sea change in language instruction can be traced to the Anglo-American Seminar on the Teaching of English at Dartmouth College in 1966 (usually referred to as the Dartmouth Conference). At that meeting, British and American educators met and shared their thoughts about needed educational reform. Much of the innovative thinking about language education that developed in the second half of the 1900s—including process writing, response to literature, language across the curriculum, and collaborative learning—was inspired by that meeting and the work that followed from it. What was common across all of these reforms was a change in focus from texts to students, from products to processes.

In writing instruction, attention began to turn from the formal features of exemplary texts to how writers moved from the blank page to the completed utterance. In the study of literature, the worship of the canon was gradually replaced by curiosity about how readers made sense of fiction and poetry. Across the disciplines, there was growing interest in how language was implicated in the individual's learning process. In each of these developments, there was a switch in emphasis from curricular content to the dynamics of student development.

In the UK, this new emphasis on language and development was most concentrated at the primary and secondary levels, and work from that era remains among the most powerful arguments for the central role of language in learning (e.g., Barnes 1976; Barnes *et al.* 1969; Britton 1970; Department of Education and Science 1975). The claim made in that work was simple but profound: language is the best way to engage students in the social and intellectual work necessary for true learning to occur. When employed as a tool of invention and discovery—that is, as a heuristic—language is not merely a medium for reporting thought: it actually encourages and enhances thought.

In a study that had an impact on language education in much of the English-speaking world, James Britton and his colleagues (1975) wrote of the importance of this sort of exploratory language, which they called 'expressive language'. Such language, they said, 'signals the self, reflects not only the ebb and flow of a speaker's thought and feeling, but also his assumptions of shared contexts of meaning, and of a relationship of trust with his listener' (10). That 'relationship of trust' was a crucial element: within a non-threatening and mutually supportive environment, the learner can take chances, consider possibilities, test out theories. Expressive writing, they argued, is 'thinking aloud on paper' (89), and is the ideal form of writing when someone is first exploring a topic or coming to grips with new ideas. Such writing is close to talk—that is, informal, context-bound, exploratory—and is best supported in classroom settings where talk is encouraged.

Across the Atlantic, North American teachers at all levels were encouraging students to exploit the creative power of language in their writing. The notion of *invention* was rescued from the classical rhetorical tradition to describe a phase in writing during which writers are busy exploring, discovering, and playing with ideas. The word 'process' entered American composition studies in 1965 (Rohman), and the notion became central to writing instruction throughout the 1970s and '80s. Teachers searched for topics and writing tasks that would engage students in matters that concerned them, rather than assigning the tired themes of traditional English courses. Accounts of the evolution of written texts described three phases or stages in the journey from blank sheet to completed utterance: pre-writing, writing, and revision. Stretching the writing act out over time allowed for attention to drafts, which were—in the oversimplified model that prevailed at the time—versions of an utterance that existed after writing but before revision. But what to do with all those unpolished gems? Here, the search for authenticity and teacher pragmatism merged: students were encouraged to share their drafts, to offer feedback, to talk about their writing, just as writers were known to do outside of school. Peer editing became the rage.

When theorists and researchers sought explanation and justification for this more open, social classroom, they found no shortage of arguments, from anthropology (e.g., Geertz 1983), sociology (e.g., Berger & Luckmann 1966; Gilbert & Mulkay 1984), literary theory (e.g., Fish 1980; Kristeva 1980; Bakhtin 1981), philosophy (e.g., Rorty 1979; Kuhn 1970), and psychology (e.g., Vygotsky 1978; Gergen 1982). What was common to all these accounts was an insistence on the social origin of beliefs, values, meaning, knowledge, language, and even cognition and consciousness. Human reality, from the everyday to the exotic, is shaped by historical and cultural forces. Those forces act within spheres of influence, from the close confines of the family to the specialized environment of disciplines to the all-encompassing authority of culture. Throughout the 1970s and 1980s, with a growing recognition of social activity as the seedbed of individual development, classrooms opened up and became more interactive and dynamic.

This deeply social view also influenced debates about human knowledge and knowing, and is central to what has been called cultural psychology (Cole 1996). The key notion here is that what and how we think are shaped by participation in realms of social interaction. Scratch a little in this theoretical soil and you find Vygotsky (e.g., 1978), whose theory of the sociogenesis of mind remains the foundation for ongoing efforts to create links between culture and cognition, and who had a major influence on English educators and composition theorists in the 1970s and 1980s. Vygotsky-inspired sociocultural research into situated learning (e.g., Lave & Wenger 1991), activity systems (e.g., Engeström *et al.* 1999), communities of practice (e.g., Wenger 1998), and distributed cognition (e.g., Hutchins 1995), for example, has amassed considerable evidence to demonstrate the profoundly social nature of human knowing. Even when acting alone, we are employing the language and conceptual tools we have internalized through participation in social activity. Moreover, human collectives—from small groups to world-wide research networks—can be seen as complexly organized activities that allow people to think together.

Questions about the source and authority of the meaning of literary texts also had an influence in the 1970s, particularly on English education, but also on composition and rhetoric. Scholars such as Stanley Fish (1980, 1976) and Louise Rosenblatt (1938, 1978) challenged the dominant New Critical assumption that meaning was in the text and accessible through the application of a method known as *close reading*. Such a reading attempted to ignore the reader's personal response to the text—regarded as idiosyncratic and unreliable—in favour of an interpretation that arose from careful attention to figurative language and the formal elements of the text. A reaction against that logocentric approach, known as *reader-response criticism*, argued that the meaning of texts was a negotiation—Rosenblatt called it a 'transaction'—between the reader and the text, with meaning as a co-constructed phenomenon. Anything resembling what might be called an 'authorized' meaning could be secured only by discussion among readers to determine what common or shared interpretation arose, with the understanding that such an interpretation would change over time or in different circumstances.

Another conversation in literary theory that looked beyond the text for sources of textual meaning focused on *intertextuality*, Kristeva's (1980) term to describe the ways in which texts are linked to each other by allusion, citation, imitation, parody, plagiarism, or other echoes of previous texts. Kristeva was drawing, in part, on Bakhtin's (1981) notion of *dialogism*, which refers to the same interconnectedness in literary texts that Kristeva was evoking, but encompasses *all* human language. For Bakhtin, every utterance is a link in a chain: each one responds to a prior utterance and anticipates one to come. Moreover, those utterances are drawn from a common store of language and thought, so that words are already saturated with meanings, with previous uses and associations.

In order to find an authoritative voice—to join the conversation as a participant rather than parrot—speakers and writers must turn the communal resource of language to their own ends. In Bakhtin's words:

> The word in language is half someone else's. It becomes 'one's own' only when the speaker populates it with his own intention, his own accent, when he appropriates the word, adapting it to his own semantic and expressive intention ... Language is not a neutral medium that passes freely and easily into the private property of the speaker's intentions; it is populated—overpopulated—with the intentions of others. Expropriating it, forcing it to submit to one's own intentions and accents, is a difficult and complicated process.
>
> (Bakhtin 1981: 293–4)

Because of its association with notions of an authentic or essential self, the concept of an individual writer's 'voice' was discredited by emerging social theories of writing (e.g. Faigley 1992), but those same theories struggled to make sense of what Bakhtin called the 'difficult and complicated process' of speaking for oneself while simultaneously deploying the linguistic and rhetorical resources of the collective.

As various disciplines made the shift in focus from the individual to the group in their attempts to understand human experience, the idea of *community* became central. In linguistics, the concept of *speech communities* arose, defined by Gumperz (1971) as 'any human aggregate characterized by regular and frequent interaction by means of a shared body of verbal signs and set off from similar aggregates by significant differences in language usage' (1971: 114). In literary criticism, Fish (1976) coined the term *interpretive communities* to describe cultural collectives that would draw on shared interpretive assumptions in their effort after literary meaning. Most influentially for those in writing theory and research, the term *discourse communities* (Swales 1990; see also Bizzell 1992; Porter 1992) was taken up as a useful way to draw boundaries around groups of people who employ language in similar ways to get collective work done. However, cautioned by Raymond Williams' (1976: 76) wry comment that community was a 'warmly persuasive word', a number of commentators pointed to the inevitable conflicts and inequity in all communal activity (e.g., Harris 1989), which led to a more critical view of the normative and conforming effects of social life.

In the field of North American composition and rhetoric, arguments for the social nature of language and knowledge were championed by Kenneth Bruffee (1973, 1984, 1986), who maintained that formal education's emphasis on testing, competition, and individual development failed to take advantage of the learning potential of social interaction. Under the banner of *collaborative learning*, he proposed classroom practices—such as peer editing and small-group discussion—that created the sort of social context in which students could teach and learn from each other: 'task must involve engaging students in conversation among themselves at as many points in both the writing and reading processes as possible' (Bruffee 1984: 642). Bruffee's argument was this: 'Collaborative learning ... assumes [that] learning occurs among persons rather than between a person and things' (1986: 787).

Other composition theorists of the period—notably, Donald Murray, Ken Macrorie, and Peter Elbow—made a similar case for the value of collaborative learning and, in particular, the use of peer response to writing. Their intention was to break the silence around the individual writer and to create a space for dialogue about work-in-progress. Such an exchange would allow writers to receive a reader's perspective while composing, and locate school-based writers and readers in the type of social dynamic that characterized nonacademic discourse. In Bruffee's words:

> social constructionist work in composition is based on the assumption that writing is primarily a social act. A writer's language originates with the community to which he or she belongs. We use language primarily to join communities we do not yet belong to and to cement membership in communities we already belong to.
>
> (Bruffee 1986: 784)

A more radical version of collaborative writing was proposed by others, including LeFevre (1987), Ede and Lunsford (1990), Faigley (1992), and Berlin (1987, 1982). In this account, which evokes Bakhtin, the writer is engaged socially before she opens her mouth to speak, even before anyone else is present. Her thoughts, her ways of thinking, and the language used to convey those thoughts are already social—deeply imbued with communal attitudes, values, and beliefs. While she writes, she invokes readers, imagining their response, anticipating their objections (Ede & Lunsford 1984). Moreover, the text has no meaning beyond the writer until there are actual readers, and then those readers don't merely *take* meaning, they *make* it. In other words, the written text doesn't become social only when the writer shares it, or talks about it; from start to finish, writing is a thoroughly collaborative activity.

Inspired by their own co-authoring experiences (Ede & Lunsford 1985, 1983; Lunsford & Ede 1992), and the difficulty that joint authorship caused their institutions when performance reviews occurred, Ede and Lunsford investigated the locations and variations of group and co-authorship across seven different professional fields by conducting surveys and interviews. In addition, they reviewed the literatures of a number of disciplines looking for signs of cooperative work. Their research (1990) described complex collaborations in every field they studied, including the production of corporate reports, which might reach publication with no authorship ascribed or with the name of a senior executive who had no actual hand in its production. But they also challenged the literary myth of single-authorship by uncovering the degree to which even novels result from collaboration.

In the academic disciplines, we are well aware now of the prevalence of multi-authorship in the sciences, but every social science or humanities journal article with a single author's name has almost certainly been reviewed by at least two anonymous readers as well as editors, and might well have been read and commented on by the author's colleagues before being submitted. And, of course, any article that adds to a discipline's ongoing conversation will include a list of previous texts with which it is in dialogue—the most literal meaning of intertextuality. Ede and Lunsford's findings matched those of the writing researchers who entered the nonacademic world in the 1980s looking for examples of situated writing (e.g., Faigley & Miller 1982; Odell & Goswami 1982, 1985).

That research into nonacademic writing offered immediate challenges to a view of writing as the work of solitary individuals. Knoblauch (1980) demonstrated the degree to which rhetorical goals develop from collective rather than individual intention, and Selzer (1983) explained how the audience in the workplace is not the writer's mental construct but, rather, the very real people with whom the writer works on a daily basis. Doheny-Farina's (1985) ethnography of a new company captured the complex ways in which key institutional texts are the product of collaboration among people at various levels and locations within an institution. Winsor reported what many workplace researchers came to understand:

> Collaborative writing at work doesn't just mean more than one person working on a report. It means that any individual's writing is called forth and shaped by the needs and aims of the organization, and that to be understood it must draw on vocabulary, knowledge, and beliefs other organization members share. Writing at work is firmly embedded in a social web.
>
> (Winsor 1989: 271)

The social view of writing that emerges from these accounts offers a damning critique of the individualism imposed on writers within most educational settings.

Given the profoundly social nature of knowledge and meaning-making, it is perverse that we continue to treat the student as isolated and separate. And yet, I still meet graduate students who have never shared their drafts with other students or with friends or family outside of school, and who reluctantly (and shyly) pass their texts to their classmates during peer-review sessions. Almost 50 years of arguments supporting a collaborative approach to learning, and still students compose alone.

More positively, these arguments for the sociocultural origins of knowledge and meaning offer a powerful justification for writing groups. Schools might treat students as individuals and measure their solo performances as evidence of ability, but we are in fact profoundly social creatures whose very ways of thinking and speaking depend on participation in collectives. When we write and read, we draw on shared resources and we reach meaning through complex collaborative processes. The broad picture of the individual writer as already and always socially engaged is convincing and has strong intuitive appeal to those of us who feel we found voice as writers only when we found community, but the argument in favour of writing groups becomes undeniable as we shift focus from the general case to the specific situation of doctoral writing.

As I have argued elsewhere (Paré 2011; Paré *et al.* 2011), students must make a significant rhetorical shift as they move into their doctoral studies. Before the doctorate, the student writer's role is generally to report on some sub-section of the literature within a subject area discipline. So, for example, the undergraduate anthropology student investigating the situation in post-colonial Africa must know the key texts, thinkers, theories, and debates concerning that topic. Any assessment of her as a learner would mean judging the degree to which she had heard and comprehended the conversation among professional anthropologists. She would not be expected to join that conversation as an actual participant—that is, as a practicing anthropologist—but she would be required to emulate the discourse of the academy:

> Every time a student sits down to write for us, he has to invent the university for the occasion—invent the university, that is, or a branch of it, like history or anthropology or economics or English. The student has to learn to speak our language, to speak as we do, to try on the peculiar ways of knowing, selecting, evaluating, reporting, concluding, and arguing that define the discourse of our community.
>
> (Bartholomae 1985: 134)

What makes the transition into doctoral work so difficult rhetorically is that students are suddenly expected to enter their disciplinary conversations; not only must they speak *like* us, as Bartholomae says, but now they must speak *to* and *with* us. Simply reporting the debate is no longer sufficient; doctoral students must join that debate, take a position, establish affiliations, and perhaps challenge or criticize others: 'A student can learn to command and reproduce a set of names, dates, places, and canonical interpretations (to "tell" somebody else's knowledge);

but this is not the same thing as learning to "think" (by learning to write) as an historian' (Bartholomae 1985: 145). The stakes go up during the doctorate, and a failure to be relevant or well-informed or logical no longer means just a poor grade; instead, it could mean the disastrous end of the doctorate, a failure to be published, or public condemnation by senior members of the community. This is the 'difficult and complicated process' to which Bakhtin (1981: 293–4) referred when he spoke about appropriating a social language to one's own ends.

Within the student's academic unit, this community judgement is first manifest by the supervisor, as Green (2005: 162) has noted: 'the supervisor represents, or stands in for, the Discipline itself, and also the Academy'. Beyond that, there may be a local committee and external reviewers for the dissertation and then working scholars to evaluate manuscripts submitted to journals and grant applications for funding agencies. As Aitchison (2009; and see Chapter 4 in this volume) has argued, writing groups can recreate the social dynamics of peer review and prepare writers for the difficult task of hearing, weighing, and exploiting critical feedback. Before doctoral education, students have likely seen teacher feedback as justification for their grade, since the teacher was the terminus for the paper; but feedback in doctoral education becomes the grounds for revision. It isn't the end of the process, but the beginning of a different stage in the process.

Opening one's mouth to speak during the doctorate and beyond becomes fraught with danger. The writer's identity, her status in the community, her relations with others, her graduation and job prospects, her very livelihood are now on the line and at risk. Why, then, would we not offer students as many opportunities as possible to work socially, to test ideas out in safe, collaborative settings, to hear others' comments when the stakes are still low, and to (literally) join the disciplinary conversation? The image of the solitary scholar working alone by the light of a flickering lamp has always been misleading, but it has now become ridiculous. Knowledge does not develop from inspiration or individual genius, it comes from the hard work of collective action—action that proceeds through and is made possible by language.

The chapters in this book offer a range of possibilities for writing groups and activities that best occur within a context of frequent, rich social interaction. Such support for doctoral students can begin well before words are put on paper, when they are reading in their respective literatures and first forming opinions and positions in their disciplinary debates. Ideally, of course, the graduate seminar is just such an environment: an opportunity for students to share their responses to common readings, to engage in discussion, to question and confirm each other's interpretations, to try out emerging analyses. Where such gatherings are not possible—where course work is limited or non-existent, for example—students might be encouraged to form reading groups or, as they are often called in medical education, 'journal clubs'. Whatever their designation and structure, the point of these meetings would be to allow students to employ the discourse of their chosen fields, to test out their voices in the debates of the day, and to shape relevant arguments.

And doctoral students' own writing can be supported by others from the beginning of the thinking process, before actual writing starts, when they can be encouraged to speak about their emerging ideas while they are still vague and ill-formed. Nothing aids clarity so much as attempts to articulate something that remains scrambled or inchoate in our minds. Moreover, the questions that students pose to each other in such sessions anticipate the confusion readers might experience when the text is finally realized. One strategy that I have found useful in courses is to have students prepare proposals or abstracts for end-of-term papers, as working academics must do for conference papers, for example. Working in pairs or small groups, the students discuss the abstracts, question each other, and recommend changes; the original abstract may bear little resemblance to the eventual paper, but the talk that accompanies it helps launch the students' thinking.

Perhaps no activity more powerfully locates doctoral students within their community than conference attendance, especially small conferences or conferences where organization into special interest groups allows for smaller sessions and familiar faces. At least, that was certainly true for me and for many colleagues with whom I've spoken. The authors that students have been reading are suddenly there, in the flesh, available for questioning, and breaks and meal times are filled with discussion and networking. This experience of the collective effort at work during conferences extends the notion of conversation—of 'writing groups'—beyond the small circle of classmates and into the broader disciplinary community. And, of course, presenting a paper at a conference, and receiving feedback, is both exhilarating and profoundly formative (as well, perhaps, as terrifying).

In my experience, it takes some time for doctoral students to see themselves as participants in the disciplinary conversation, and—as we know—many fail. They have been held out so long, and trained as listeners rather than speakers; as a result, entering the debate seems presumptuous, rude, and risky. Some lack confidence in their own voice, and find it hard to believe they have anything of interest to say; others continue speaking in their student voice, and are easily identified as outsiders. The voice they seek is not discovered by gazing within but, rather, by speaking out in situations of authentic discourse, where others take up their contributions and respond. It is only in and through that engagement that a person can develop a sense of membership and authority. Those who have extensive experience in writing groups have a good chance to see academic writing as what it really is, or really can be: a dialogue among colleagues. As educators, our responsibility is to help doctoral students find their place in that discussion. Oakeshott captures this nicely:

> As civilized human beings, we are the inheritors, neither of an inquiry about selves and the world, nor of an accumulating body of information, but of a conversation, begun in the primeval forests and extended and made more articulate in the course of centuries. It is a conversation which goes on both in public and within each of ourselves ... Education, properly speaking, is an initiation into the skill and partnership of this conversation in which we

learn to recognize the voices, to distinguish the proper occasions of utterance, and in which we acquire the intellectual and moral habits appropriate to conversation.

(Oakeshott 1962: 199)

I noted at the start of this chapter that those of us who teach have seen the general value of collaborative work and the specific benefit of writing groups. We *know* that membership in discourse communities cannot be taught or conferred, it must be earned, and it can only be earned through authentic social engagement. Unfortunately, much about contemporary higher education works against this practice. Testing and credentialing regimes isolate the individual and too often detach learning from collective practice. Rising concerns about attrition and times-to-completion have led to efficiencies that resist the slow but natural process of experiential learning; the pressure to publish likewise hurries the developing writer. Resources are being drained from teaching initiatives to support research activity. However, theories of human knowing and meaning—such as those summarized in this chapter—and our own practical knowledge confirm that writing groups provide a safe and supportive environment for the transition from student to participant. The chapters in this book offer multiple examples of how writing groups can work, and they reassure us that we are doing the right thing.

References

Aitchison, C. (2009) 'Writing groups for doctoral education', *Studies in Higher Education*, 34: 905–16.

Bakhtin, M. M. (1981) *The Dialogic Imagination: Four Essays* (ed. M. Holquist, trans. C. Emerson and M. Holquist), Austin, TX: University of Texas Press.

Barnes, D. (1976) *From Communication to Curriculum*, Harmondsworth, UK: Penguin Books.

Barnes, D., Britton, J. and Rosen, H. (1969) *Language, the Learner and the School*, Harmondsworth, UK: Penguin Books.

Bartholomae, D. (1985) 'Inventing the university', in M. Rose (ed.) *When a Writer Can't Write: Studies in Writer's Block and Other Composing Process Problems*, New York: Guilford Press.

Berger, P. and Luckmann, T. (1966) *The Social Construction of Reality*, London: Penguin.

Berlin, J. (1982) 'Contemporary composition: the major pedagogical theories', *College English*, 44: 765–77.

—— (1987) *Rhetoric and Reality: Writing Instruction in American Colleges, 1900–1985*, Carbondale, IL: Southern Illinois University Press.

Bizzell, P. (1992) *Academic Discourse and Critical Consciousness*, Pittsburgh, PA: University of Pittsburgh Press.

Britton, J. (1970) *Language and Learning*, Harmondsworth, UK: Penguin Books.

Britton, J., Burgess, T., Martin, N., McLeod, A. and Rosen, H. (1975) *The Development of Writing Abilities*, London: Macmillan Education.

Bruffee, K. (1973) 'Collaborative learning: some practical models', *College English*, 34: 579–86.
—— (1984) 'Collaborative learning and the "conversation of mankind"', *College English*, 46: 635–52.
—— (1986) 'Social construction, language, and the authority of knowledge: a bibliographical essay', *College English*, 48: 773–90.
Cole, M. (1996) *Cultural Psychology: A Once and Future Discipline*, Cambridge, MA: The Belknap Press of Harvard University Press.
Department of Education and Science (1975) *A Language for Life* (The Bullock Report), London: HMSO.
Dixon, J. (1967) *Growth Through English*, Reading, UK: National Association for the Teaching of English.
Doheny-Farina, S. (1985) 'Writing in an emerging organization: an ethnographic study', *Written Communication*, 3: 158–85.
Ede, L. S. and Lunsford, A. A. (1983) 'Why write ... together?', *Rhetoric Review*, 1: 150–8.
—— (1984) 'Audience addressed/audience invoked: the role of audience in composition theory and pedagogy', *College Composition and Communication*, 35: 155–71.
—— (1985) 'Let them write—together', *English Quarterly*, 18: 119–27.
—— (1990) *Singular Texts/Plural Authors: Perspectives on Collaborative Writing*, Carbondale: IL: Southern Illinois University Press.
Engeström, Y., Miettinen, R. and Punamäki, R. L. (1999) *Perspectives on Activity Theory*, Cambridge: Cambridge University Press.
Faigley, L. (1992) *Fragments of Rationality: Postmodernity and the Subject of Composition*, Pittsburgh, PA: University of Pittsburgh Press.
Faigley, L. and Miller, T. P. (1982) 'What we learn from writing on the job', *College English*, 44: 557–69.
Fish, S. (1976) 'Interpreting the variorum', *Critical Inquiry*, 2: 465–85.
—— (1980) *Is There a Text in This Class? The Authority of Interpretive Communities*, Cambridge, MA: Harvard University Press.
Geertz, C. (1983) *Local Knowledge*, New York: Basic Books.
Gere, A. R. (1987) *Writing Groups: History, Theory, and Implications*, Carbondale, IL: Southern Illinois University Press.
Gergen, K. J. (1982) *Toward Transformation in Social Knowledge*, New York: Springer-Verlag.
Gilbert, N. and Mulkay, M. (1984) *Opening Pandora's Box: A Sociological Analysis of Scientists' Discourse*, Cambridge: Cambridge University Press.
Green, B. (2005) 'Unfinished business: subjectivity and supervision', *Higher Education Research and Development*, 24: 151–63.
Gumperz, J. J. (1971) *Language in Social Groups*, Stanford, CA: Stanford University Press.
Harris, J. (1989) 'The idea of community in the study of writing', *College Composition and Communication*, 40: 11–22.
Hutchins, E. (1995) *Cognition in the Wild*, Cambridge, MA: The MIT Press.
Knoblauch, C. H. (1980) 'Intentionality in the writing process', *College Composition and Communication*, 31: 153–9.
Kristeva, J. (1980) *Desire in Language: A Semiotic Approach to Literature and Art*, New York: Columbia University Press.
Kuhn, T. S. (1970) *The Structure of Scientific Revolutions*, Chicago: University of Chicago Press.

Lave, J. and Wenger, E. (1991) *Situated Learning: Legitimate Peripheral Participation*, Cambridge: Cambridge University Press.
LeFevre, K. B. (1987) *Invention as a Social Act*, Carbondale, IL: Southern Illinois University Press.
Lunsford, A. and Ede, L. (1992) 'Collaborative authorship and the teaching of writing', *Cardoza Arts and Entertainment Law Journal*, 10: 681–702.
Moffett, J. (1968) *Teaching the Universe of Discourse*, Boston, MA: Houghton-Mifflin.
Muller, H. J. (1967) *The Uses of English*, New York: Holt, Rinehart & Winston.
Oakeshott, M. (1962) *Rationalism in Politics and Other Essays*, New York: Basic Books.
Odell, L. and Goswami, D. (eds) (1982) 'Writing in non-academic settings', *Research in the Teaching of English*, 16: 201–23.
—— (1985) *Writing in Nonacademic Settings*, New York: Guilford Press.
Paré, A. (2011) 'Publish and flourish: joining the conversation', in A. Lee and V. Mallan (eds), *Connecting the Local, Regional and Global in Doctoral Education*, Kuala Lumpur, Malaysia: Universiti Putra Malaysia Press.
Paré, A., Starke-Meyerring, D. and McAlpine, L. (2011) 'Knowledge and identity work in the supervision of doctoral student writing: shaping rhetorical subjects', in D. Starke-Meyerring, A. Paré, M. Horne, N. Artemeva, and L. Yousoubova (eds.), *Writing in Knowledge Societies*, Fort Collins, CO: The WAC Clearinghouse and Parlor Press. Available online: http://wac.colostate.edu/books/winks/ (accessed 16 August 2012).
Porter, J. (1992) *Audience and Rhetoric: An Archaeological Composition of the Discourse Community*, New Jersey: Prentice Hall.
Rohman, D. G. (1965) 'Pre-writing: the stage of discovery in the writing process', *College Composition and Communication*, 16: 106–12.
Rorty, R. (1979) *Philosophy and the Mirror of Nature*, Princeton, NJ: Princeton University Press.
Rosenblatt, L. (1938) *Literature as Exploration*, New York: Appleton-Century.
—— (1978) *The Reader, the Text, the Poem: The Transactional Theory of the Literary Work*, Carbondale, IL: Southern Illinois University Press.
Selzer, J. (1983) 'The composing process of an engineer', *College Composition and Communication*, 34: 178–87.
Swales, J. M. (1990) *Genre Analysis: English in Academic and Research Settings*, Cambridge: Cambridge University Press.
Vygotsky, L. S. (1978) *Mind in Society: The Development of Higher Psychological Processes*, Cambridge, MA: Harvard University Press.
Wenger, E. (1998) *Communities of Practice: Learning, Meaning, and Identity*, Cambridge: Cambridge University Press.
Williams, R. (1976) *Keywords: A Vocabulary of Culture and Society*, New York: Oxford University Press.
Winsor, D. (1989) 'An engineer's writing and the corporate construction of knowledge', *Written Communication*, 6: 270–85.

Chapter 3

Pick-n-Mix

A typology of writers' groups in use

Sarah Haas

Introduction

There is a growing body of research indicating that writers' groups are beneficial to research writers. Participation in groups enables writers to increase both quantity and quality of texts. Writers' group members write more (Faulconer *et al.* 2010; Lee & Boud 2003; Murray & MacKay 1998a; Murray & Newton 2009; Lonka 2003) because belonging to a community increases motivation (Aitchison & Lee 2006; Cafarella & Barnett 2000; Cuthbert & Spark 2008; Ferguson 2009; Clark *et al.* 2000) and confidence (Cuthbert *et al.* 2009; Faulconer *et al.* 2010; Murray & Newton 2009), while decreasing anxiety (Grant 2006; MacLeod *et al.* 2012) and isolation (Aitchison & Lee 2006; Murray & Newton 2009). Higher-quality text is produced because writers both receive feedback (Elbow & Belanoff 1989a, 1989b), and give it (Aitchison 2010; Cuthbert *et al.* 2009; Washburn 2008; Galligan *et al.* 2003; Faulconer *et al.* 2010; Catterall *et al.* 2011). The community situation of a writers' group helps demystify the process of writing (Ferguson 2009), enabling writers to understand this process better (Murray 2012), and thus to fear it less (Badley 2006). Such community interaction around writing leads to the development of meta-language (Aitchison 2003) for talking about writing processes. In turn this talk increases writers' metaconscious awareness of their own processes, further decreasing anxiety, and increasing self-efficacy and self-regulation (Castello *et al.* 2009).

Research on writers' groups comes not only from writing development disciplines, but also from law (Burke 1991), from medicine (Grzybowski *et al.* 2003; Salaz-Lopez *et al.* 2012), from the sciences (Ferguson 2009; Hay & Delaney 2007), and from teacher education (Page *et al.* 2012). The problem with writers' groups, however, became clear when Claire Aitchison and I gave a workshop at the Writing Development in Higher Education (WDHE) Conference in London (Aitchison & Haas 2010).

Claire introduced the focus of our workshop with, 'It is generally agreed that writers groups are a bloody good idea, but if you want to go from that good idea to an actual functioning writers' group, where do you start?' The audience nodded their agreement. We introduced various writers' group activities, and pointed out how these activities are beneficial to writers, thinking that this would give people a solid starting point. At the end of what seemed a successful workshop, however, one participant raised his hand and apologetically said, 'I'm sorry, but I still really don't know what a writers' group *is*. What do you actually *do* in a writers' group?' Several others echoed his confusion. The audience seemed to want a recipe for a writers' group.

The problem, however, is that there *is* no fixed understanding of what constitutes a 'writers' group'. All groups involve writers coming together to support each other, and all groups share the common goal of improving both process and product of writing—but no two groups are alike. One successful writers' group might function completely differently from another. This flexibility is essential, as different groups have different needs. If there were only one size of writers' group, it would be unlikely to fit all—or even most.

While flexibility is essential, the main drawback of the lack of a formalized structure is that, without a 'recipe' to follow, those with little experience, wanting to reap the benefits of writers' groups, can be at a loss as to where to start or how to proceed.

This chapter responds to the question 'What is a writers' group?' by offering a typology derived from the literature on writers' groups. The typology identifies and categorizes elements (here called 'dimensions' and 'variables') in order to identify what *can* be combined to form a successful writers' group.

The typology (Table 3.1 below) is organized into 11 dimensions. Within each dimension lie variables and sub-variables. To illustrate the value of the model, I will use it here to describe a group with which I am currently involved. The numbers in brackets represent the dimensions in the table.

> Our writers' group is a continuous (9), near-peer led (3), interdisciplinary (2) group with weekly (7), face-to-face (4) meetings lasting two hours (8). We meet in the late afternoon (5) in our faculty library (6) to support each other in our individual projects (1); our main activities are setting goals and working together in a typing pool (10). As we are quite social, we normally go out for a drink and a game of pool after our writing is finished (10). In between our weekly meetings, individual members work on goals set at the end of each meeting (11).

The next section introduces the typology in full, explaining each dimension, along with its variables and sub-variables. All dimensions and variables in the typology are reported in literature on *successful* writers' groups. Please note that this is *not* an evaluation. Advantages and disadvantages must be assessed in light of the needs of specific writers' groups and the preferences of its members.

The typology

This typology is an update of an earlier version (Haas 2012), adjusted to reflect both new literature on writers' groups, as well as my own data collected from Writer Development courses which I facilitate in Denmark, Belgium, Japan, the US and the

UK. As more research is published, I expect further growth and change. Currently, there are 11 dimensions and 69 variables/sub-variables in the typology (Table 3.1).

Table 3.1 Typology of writers' groups

	Dimension	Variables	Sub-variables

1 Purpose (of group)
- Generally provide mutual support to increase quantity/quality of writing of members
- Specific activity common to members
    - *Research assessment*
    - *Funding bid*
    - *Joint article*
- Other purpose
    - *Education*

2 Membership
- Number of participants
- Discipline
    - *Interdisciplinary*
    - *Discipline-specific*
- Progress on project/experience writing
    - *Same level of experience/stage of completion*
    - *Varying levels of experience/stages of completion*
- Selection/recruitment
    - *Invited*
    - *Compulsory*
    - *Volunteer*

3 Leadership
- No leader
- Start-up leader
- Peer-led
    - *Rotating leader*
    - *Static leader*
- Expert-led
    - *Writing expert*
    - *Language expert*
    - *Subject expert*
    - *Experienced (published) academic writer*

4 Contact
- Face-to-face
- Remote

5 Time (of day)

	Dimension	Variables	Sub-variables
6	**Place (of meeting)**		
		• Institutional setting	
		• Away from institution	
			• Home
			• Other place away from institution
7	**Frequency (of meeting)**		
8	**Length (of meeting)**		
9	**Duration (of groups)**		
		• Limited	
		• Continuous	
10	**In-meeting activities**		
		• Naming the group	
		• Setting/re-examining group ground rules	
		• Goal-setting	
		• Writing	
			• *Freewriting*
			• *Generative writing*
			• *Writing to prompts*
			• *Self-directed writing*
		• Reading (each others' writing)	
		• Feedback/response	
		• Discussions	
			• *About writing*
			• *About feedback*
			• *About the meetings themselves*
		• Other research-related activities	
			• *Searching for literature*
			• *Reading research literature*
			• *Working with data*
		• Social element	
11	**Between-meeting activities**		
		• Goal-setting	
		• Self-directed writing	
		• Publishing	
			• *To the group or individual group members*
			• *To authority*
		• Responding to co-members' writing	
		• Between-meeting membership communication	
		• Reflective journals	
		• Other research-related activities	
			• *Searching for literature*
			• *Reading research literature*
			• *Collecting/working with data*

Dimension 1: Purpose

As mentioned previously, the underlying goal of any writers' group is for writers to provide mutual support to each other. The support is intended to help members increase both quantity and quality of written output, to help ensure work gets done in a timely manner, and to make research writing a more enjoyable, less lonely experience than it is stereotypically thought to be. Some groups do, however, have more specific purposes. Some writers' groups are formed so that members can work on a project—a funding bid, for example, the production of a joint article, or for the completion of research assessment exercises. Writers' groups are also used within postgraduate education, focusing on 'transferable skills' (Cuthbert *et al*. 2009; Ferguson 2009). My own data from the Writer Development courses includes one group who shared the aim of submitting their theses within three months' time.

Dimension 2: Membership

Membership, that is, who is in the writers' group, varies in four ways: number; discipline; experience or progress; and selection or recruitment.

There is no agreed optimum number of members for a writers' group. While the working definition for this book stipulated 'three or more people', my own data includes a 'group' of two members who successfully supported each other in their PhD writing for over two years. Elbow (1973) suggests seven as a good number, while the Writing Center at the University of Central Florida cautions that group effectiveness might be lost if there are more than five members.

While it seems to be the norm that groups have fixed members, with a set maximum, some of the participants from the Writer Development course set up a group with a floating membership: instead of breaking into smaller groups, all 20 participants from the course joined the same group. They set a weekly time, day, and place for meetings. The agreement was that the meetings would operate on a set of ground rules. Any member who was available could attend the meetings at any time, so long as the rules were kept. There was no upper limit to the number of people who could join the group. I was sceptical at first, but at the end of a three-month period, the members reported on what can only be considered a successful group: there had always been at least five members present at each meeting, and never more than eight. Every member in the group attended at least twice, and all members reported benefiting from being a part of the group. Furthermore, the group continued beyond its obligatory three months, lasting for over a year, until most of the participants had submitted their theses. Given the success of such a floating membership, I added the possibility to the typology.

The second variable in membership is academic discipline. Writers' groups seem to be equally successful if they are multi-disciplinary (Aitchison 2003; Cuthbert *et al*. 2009; Galligan *et al*. 2003) or have members from a single discipline (Clark *et al*. 2000). Multi-disciplinary groups offer the advantage of having readers outside one's own field, so that discussions centre on writing rather than on subject matter. Conversely, single-discipline groups benefit from being able to discuss content as well as writing.

Along with discipline, differing levels of experience with writing, and in academia, seem to have no impact on group success. Some writers' group facilitators recommend that groups can be enriched by including members of varying academic levels, or having varying experiences of publishing (Galligan *et al.* 2003). In these groups, less-experienced members can draw on the knowledge of the more experienced, and more experienced members can benefit from supporting the less-experienced. There is evidence too that writers' groups are equally successful when the members are similarly experienced or in the same year in their program of study (Haas 2011). These groups pose no problems of 'seniority', or of less experienced members feeling intimidated by more experienced members.

How people become members of the group is the next variable. Outside of the North American undergraduate context where writing groups often feature in Freshmen Composition and Rhetoric courses, voluntary group membership is most common, although occasionally members are hand-picked (Faulconer *et al.* 2010). Murray (2002) considers the possibility of compulsory groups for university staff members and Paré describes a credit course for graduate students where writing groups operate within the curriculum (Aitchison & Paré 2012). Girgensohn (2010) has semi-compulsory groups, requiring students who have attended a writing retreat to subsequently attend a writers' group meeting at least twice.

Dimension 3: Leadership

One of the best-known types of writers' group is the 'Teacherless Writing Class' proposed by Elbow (1981), which has no leader at all. On the other hand, some groups have a start-up leader, where an expert facilitator will attend the first few meetings before leaving the members to their own devices (Guerin *et al.* 2013). Groups can be peer led, either with one established peer leader, or a rotating leader (Fingar 2002). Quite common is an expert-led group, where the leader can have expertise in running writers' groups, in language, in the discipline of the members, or in academic writing (Murray & MacKay 1998a, 1998b; Aitchison 2009a; Aitchison & Lee 2006; Badley 2006). Some leaders (for example, Lee & Boud 2003; Haas 2011) position themselves as 'near-peer' leaders (Murphey 2001), having slightly more experience than other members, but work along with the group.

Dimensions 4–9: Contact, Time, Place, Frequency, Length, and Duration

Contact in writers' groups has traditionally required people to be physically located in the same space, meeting and talking face-to-face. However, online writing groups are becoming common (Faulconer *et al.* 2010; Rosenthal 2003; also see Chapter 15 in this volume). Virtual groups can be ultra-organized (Waite

2012), or very low-maintenance. An example of a simple, yet effective virtual group was started by a Writer Development participant who lived remotely from the rest of her classmates: everyone exchanged Skype details; then anyone who wanted company for writing would log in to Skype, send out a message declaring intention to work, and see if anyone would join. When other members were recruited, the group worked in one-hour intervals, first typing hourly goals into the text chat feature on Skype, and agreeing on a starting/ending time. At the end of the hour, writers would report on how the hour had progressed, and make plans/goals for the next hour. This group still functions—three years later.

Timing of meetings will vary according to the needs of participants and their ability to fit writing in and around study, work and domestic lives. Thus meetings may fall during office hours or after hours, over weekends or during holiday breaks.

Where the group meets also depends on member preferences. Some writers require silence; others find that a lively setting enhances productivity. Some groups meet at the workplace (Faulconer *et al.* 2010). Other prefer a private space, such as a member's home (Haines *et al.* 1997). Girgensohn (2010) tells of a group who met in a cemetery, explaining that it was peaceful and quiet.

Frequency and duration. The literature indicates voluntary writing groups typically meet fortnightly for approximately two hours (Aitchison, 2009a; Murray & MacKay 1998b; Teaching & Learning Unit 2010). However, groups have successfully met weekly, for one hour at a time (Washburn 2008). The PhD writers from the Writer Development courses have organized weekly or bi-weekly meetings, ranging from two-hour to all-day meetings.

Lifespan. Some groups are short-term, having a limited lifespan—for example, 9–10 weeks (e.g., Cuthbert & Spark 2008); some groups are ongoing and can continue for years (Aitchison 2009b). The Writer Development groups start out with a mandatory three-month lifespan, but many of them continue well beyond this.

Dimension 10: In-meeting activities

Possibly of the greatest interest to new, or would-be, writers' group members is what actually happens when writers meet in groups—Dimension 10 of Table 3.1. For easy reference, Dimension 10 is presented again in Table 3.2.

The activities of writers' groups can generally include: group-forming/maintaining activities; writing; reading; and talking.

If starting out new, some find it important to name their group. I prefer the term writ*ers'* groups, as opposed to writ*ing* groups to put the emphasis on the person rather than the activity, and to indicate that activities other than writing can go on in groups. 'Academics Anonymous', and 'W(h)ining Women Writers' are two examples of groups who put importance on naming.

It is essential that groups negotiate and agree on explicit ground rules or rules of engagement for meetings. Some are strict, such as no talking or moving around during writing times (Murray & Newton 2009); others are more liberal, such as the

Table 3.2 What happens in a writers' group

	Dimension	Variables	Sub-variables
10	**In-meeting activities**		
		• Naming the group	
		• Setting/re-examining group ground rules	
		• Goal-setting	
		• Writing	
			• *Freewriting*
			• *Generative writing*
			• *Writing to prompts*
			• *Self-directed writing*
		• Reading (each others' writing)	
		• Feedback/response	
		• Discussions	
			• *About writing*
			• *About feedback*
			• *About the meetings themselves*
		• Other research-related activities	
			• *Searching for literature*
			• *Reading research literature*
			• *Working with data*
		• Social element	

group with just one rule—that 'someone has to bring cake'. After the initial set-up, regularly revisiting ground rules can help ensure the efficacy and sustainability of the group.

Writing activities can be broken down in to *scribbling* and *scribing* (Badley 2011). Scribing is the careful structuring of text with a reader in mind. Scribbling is unmonitored, low-stakes, writer-centred text (Haas 2011) and includes freewriting, generative writing, and writing to prompts. Although scribbling is not intended for a reader, it is recognized as a necessary part of the writing process (Elbow 1981), and is thus a common activity in writers' groups (Li 2007; Murray & MacKay 1998a, 1998b; Murray & Newton 2008).

Freewriting is writing without stopping, without editing, and without any specific topic; generative writing is similar to freewriting, but writers stick to one topic—often one gleaned from their freewriting (Boice 1987; Lonka 2003; Murray & MacKay 1998a, 1998b; Murray & Newton 2008). Writing to prompts (Murray 2012) is another way to scribble, where the writer starts out with the beginning of a sentence (a prompt), or with several prompts, and then finishes the prompts in a certain number of words, or continues writing for a certain amount of time (Murray 2011).

Some writers' groups, similar to Murray's and Newton's structured retreat (2009), gather together simply to write in the company of other writers. In this 'typing pool' kind of group (Murray 2011; and Chapter 7 in this volume), each writer will be working on his/her own project, and making his/her own decisions about what to write, but for a certain amount of time everyone is writing (as described in Chapter 15 in this volume). I call these 'self-directed' writing sessions, to distinguish them from, for example, facilitator-led writing-to-prompts sessions.

Along with writing during meetings, participants can give feedback on or respond to each others' work (Elbow 1973; Fingar 2002; Gere 1987; Reeves 2002; Schneider 2003). Elbow provides an overview in his 'map of writing in terms of audience and response' (2000: 29). In some groups, writers read their writing out loud and get immediate response (Elbow 2000); alternatively, writing is sent beforehand and group time is spent giving feedback (Teaching and Learning Unit 2010). Some writers' groups are, essentially, feedback groups, as meeting time is spent solely on giving/receiving feedback (Teaching and Learning Unit 2010).

In addition to feedback, group members can engage in other kinds of talk. Meta-discussions about writing, feedback, and the group meetings themselves (Aitchison & Lee 2006; Elbow & Belanoff 2003) have been found to be an essential part of group activity. Writer Development participants have observed that a social element can emerge organically, with shared jokes, suggestions for social outings or invitations to each others' homes arising after only a few meetings (see, for example, Thesen, Chapter 11 in this volume).

Some writers' groups focus exclusively on writing. Activities such as searching for literature, reading, working with data, must be done outside meetings because they can be displacement activities that prevent writers from getting writing done. Some Writer Development course members, however, allowed other research-related activities in their groups, provided that people who engaged in them would also spend at least 15 minutes of every working hour writing (usually to prompts) about the activities they had done. The group saw this as a way to incorporate writing into the entire research process, rather than to see it as an add-on at the end (Badley 2010). They also saw it as a way to allow members who were working on other things, but not necessarily needing to do any writing at the moment, to still attend meetings and be part of the community.

Writers in groups can write together, read each others' writing, and talk to each other. An activity that spans writing and talking is goal-setting (Murray 2011). Writers write down goals, and report them to (an)other writer(s). Murray recommends setting short, medium, and long-term goals, as well as setting goals for 'snacking'—writing for very short periods of time (Murray & Newton 2008). Goals can be set for tasks to be accomplished during the meeting itself (short-term goals), or set at the end of the meeting, to be accomplished by the next meeting (medium-term goals). It is possible for writers' groups to function as 'goal groups'. Academics Anonymous is one such group, meeting Fridays and focusing solely on reporting progress and setting goals.

Dimension 11: between-meeting activities

Along with working on goals set at group meetings, between-meeting activities include self-directed writing, publishing (to group members, supervisors, periodicals), and keeping reflective journals. Reflective journals are 'dialogues in [writers'] heads' (Elbow 1981: 25); Elbow suggests that writers pay attention to and make notes on what they think about writing, how they feel, what difficulties they encounter, and how they deal with them to facilitate the writing process. Along with various writing activities, members can spend between-meeting time engaging in other necessary research-related activities such as data collection/analysis, or searching for/reading literature.

The above discussion of the typology demonstrates how writers' groups can take many different forms, and how the term 'writers' group' can have as many different meanings as there are groups. The typology offers an overview of multiple ingredients that *can* constitute a successful group. The next section will discuss how the typology has been put to use by PhD writers from Writer Development courses.

Pick-n-Mix: the typology as a tool for setting up sustainable writers' groups

While I can envision several possible uses of the typology, one particularly pleasing application is as a tool that can help non-specialists set up sustainable writers' groups. This has been done as part of Writer Development courses run for PhD students at a large European university where I worked. This section will give a brief overview of the course, explain the procedures for using the typology as such a tool, and briefly discuss the results of the intervention.

The Writer Development course was started in 2009 due to a perceived need for more writing support for PhD students. While there were copious courses available on how to write (focusing on language and text construction), none were available on how to get writing *done*. The Writer Development course was designed to fill that gap, drawing on the productivity benefits of both writers' retreats and writers' groups. The participants on the courses are PhD candidates at any stage of completion. There is no separation of discipline, and up to 15 PhD researchers can register for any of five yearly courses. The courses consist of two writing retreats spaced two months apart; between retreats, students meet in student-designed, student-led writers' groups.

The retreats themselves are three-day residential workshops, taking place in youth hostels. The concept behind them is that they would serve as an extended writers' group meeting. For three days, participants would be under the guidance of a start-up leader, and would experience a sampler of some typical writers' group activities. After getting a taste of procedures and benefits of writers' groups, participants could then go on to set up and run their own groups, thus allowing PhD candidates to benefit from writers' groups at a lower cost than if all groups were run by a specialist leader.

Initially, these retreats closely followed Murray's structured retreat and typing pool models. After the completion of the first course, however, it was retrospectively perceived by the participants that protected space alone was not enough: they needed guidance. In addition, there were some eyebrows raised at spending money and allowing students to earn credits simply by going away to 'do something they could do at home'. It was thus decided that there should be some traditional course components to supplement the protected time and typing pool. Consequently, the current model for the Writer Development retreats incorporates whole-group discussions, small-group tasks, and one input session per day from the facilitator. The input session on the last day of the first retreat is where the typology is used. This emerged only after some trial and error, however.

For the first three courses, I simply told participants, at the end of the first retreat, to sort themselves out and meet in writers' groups until the next retreat. They had just spent three days experiencing first-hand what writers' groups had to offer. That, along with the enthusiasm they displayed for community writing, led me to believe they were convinced of the value of writers' groups, as well as equipped to function in them. When the participants came back to the second retreat, however, and reported on their groups, it became clear that things were not as I had imagined. Of the eight groups formed from the first three courses (39 participants in all), only two had met more than once, and three of them had not met at all. Since the pattern was clear in all three courses, I decided intervention was necessary.

The first intervention, implemented in the next two Writer Development cohorts, was to follow Girghenson's example, and make it compulsory that participants meet in writers' groups at least twice. I also introduced writers' group logs (see Table 3.3). Participants were to keep records of their writers' group meetings, including logistical information such as time, place, length, attendees, and activities. Along with the quantitative data, participants were also asked to write a short reflection of their experience of each meeting, including thoughts on how satisfactory they found it. (The participant whose log appears in Table 3.3 devised a four-point rating scale for satisfaction.) These logs were collected at the second retreat.

Discussions showed that making the groups compulsory had had some effect, but still not quite enough. All six of the groups (from two cohorts) did indeed meet twice. Only one group met more than twice and it continued beyond the second retreat. The goal of sustainable student-run groups was not being achieved.

To see if I could find where the problem lay, I examined some audio recordings of discussions, along with the data collected in the writers' group logs. From the discussions, it seemed that 'inconvenience' was the main cause of the groups not working out: people reported busy schedules, inability to find a time to suit everyone, and lack of a good place to meet as the main reasons the writers' groups did not work. These were not convincing answers, however. Many successful writers' groups consist of busy members with conflicting schedules and less than idyllic meeting places. While there was no overriding theme in the writers' logs that would suggest the true reason why groups weren't working, five comments

Table 3.3 Writer's log sample

Writers' group meeting date, time, and place	What we did during the meeting	My rating of this meeting	My thoughts/feelings/reflections/gripes/raves about this meeting	Who attended this meeting
April 20, 2008 14:00–18:00 My house	**Unloading** (writing to prompts I had made to get them thinking about the parts of their dissertations, and dissertation presentations). **Structuring** they all got the structures and content of their presentations decided, and some of them even got some.... **Polishing** done.	★★★	It was okay today. I thought everyone got some unloading done, and everyone seemed to feel a lot better when they left. We all seemed a bit overwhelmed at the idea of a dissertation, and didn't know where to start. You could almost feel the relief in the room after we did the writing to prompts for about 20 minutes. Berna even said, "that felt good." And after that, everyone was able to make their dissertation presentations for next week. I was worried that they wouldn't like the writing to prompts I suggested. Some of them before said they just hated freewriting, so I was a little nervous about suggesting we do freewriting before we worked on our presentations, but it turned out okay. Better than okay, really, so I gave it 3 stars of 4.	Berna, Sam, Nadine, George, Julia, Di

pointed me toward my next intervention. Four of the comments suggested that members were operating at cross-purposes regarding logistics and procedures of the meetings: one member preferred to meet during working hours, while others in his group preferred after hours. In another group, one member wanted to give and receive feedback, while her co-members just wanted to get together to write. It seemed possible, then that 'convenience' was not as significant a factor in sustaining writers' groups as the *compatibility* of member preferences—regarding both group logistics and in-group procedures.

The fifth comment said simply, 'we didn't really know how to go about it'. I inquired further, and got an answer similar to the question posed at the beginning of this chapter: 'We just really don't know what a writers' group is, or what we are supposed to do in our groups'. It became clear that simple exposure to or experience of some of the possibilities of writers' groups was not enough information for these candidates to form their own groups. More explicit direction was needed.

The second intervention addressed the two factors I had identified as possible barriers to sustainability: the lack of an explicit explanation of what to do in writers' groups, and the failure to emphasize the importance of member compatibility as far as logistics and group procedures were concerned. These factors were attended to via a presentation of the typology, followed by some scribbling and then discussion.

I presented the typology visually, as a 'Pick-n-Mix' (Figure 3.1) showing each dimension in a different coloured block. After introducing some established benefits of writers' groups, I went through each dimension and explained the

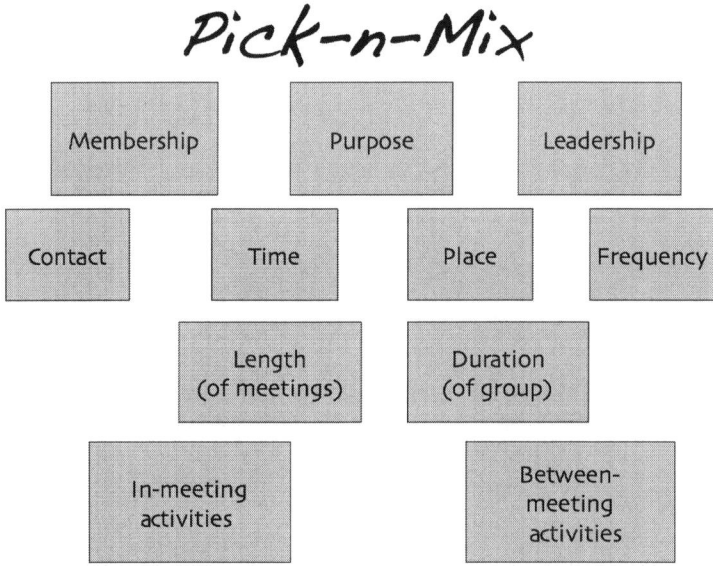

Figure 3.1 'Pick-n-Mix' typology.

variables therein, demonstrating how writers' groups could choose (Pick) variables and sub-variables, combining (Mixing) them to form customized groups fitting individual needs and preferences. It was pointed out that the groups from the Writer Development courses would have to work within some parameters: the groups would necessarily be compulsory, interdisciplinary groups, lasting at least two months, meeting at least twice, and, after having had a start-up leader, they would have to go on to be peer led or leaderless. Outside these requirements, however, group members would have complete autonomy for picking and mixing other dimensions/variables according to their needs and preferences.

After the Pick-n-Mix presentation, I asked the participants to think carefully, and to explicitly, and honestly, state what they would like in a writers' group, attending to each of the components that were optional to them. We had a 10-minute session of writing to prompts, after which everyone in turn summarized their preferences and participants were given the opportunity to organize themselves into groups, seeking out members with similar preferences/needs, and making their plans from there.

Since this intervention, I have had eight further Writer Development courses. From these have emerged 19 writers' groups. Only two of those 19 decided to stop after they had fulfilled the minimum requirements of two meetings and most of the groups met four or more times. The two-meeting minimum requirement is important for facilitating connections and building momentum. Thirteen of the groups continued after the course was finished, four of them enduring for over two years.

These results seem to suggest that the typology presented here, conceptualized as a Pick-n-Mix, was successfully used as a tool to help non-specialists set up sustainable writers' groups. The intervention of (1) emphasizing that all writers' groups are different, (2) using the typology to itemize possibilities and (3) having participants state explicitly what they prefer has made a difference for the sustainability of writers' groups, and seems to have served as a pre-emptive strike against early breakdown of groups.

Conclusion

There is very little doubt that writers' groups are beneficial to research writers and that being a member of a group of writers can improve both the process and product of writing. It is thus understandable that the popularity of writers' groups is growing for researchers. Because writers' groups necessarily need to be flexible in order to cater to different needs and preferences, there is no single, fixed way to 'do' a writers' group. Variety is necessary, as well as enriching, but it is also frustrating and confusing for the uninitiated. This chapter offers a typology of writers' groups that provides an overview of the different factors that have been reported in the literature to constitute successful groups. In addition, the typology, when presented as a Pick-n-Mix, has been shown to be a beneficial tool in setting up student-led writers' groups. It serves to give the bigger more informed picture of what is possible, so that would-be members can make explicit their own needs and preferences, and seek out members with compatible preferences, increasing the likelihood that groups will be sustainable. The success of the typology as a tool for new groups leads me to envision some other uses, for those who are already familiar with, or experts in, writers' groups.

The typology has potential for use as a descriptive or explanatory tool. Existing writers' groups might use it to become aware of how they operate, by concisely describing what variables/sub-variables constitute their group (as I have done in the beginning of this chapter). They could then use the description to review the operation of their group and discuss any desired changes. As it has been shown that periodic revisiting of group goals and procedures can keep a group healthy, the typology, used in this way, could contribute to sustaining already existing writers' groups.

As mentioned earlier, the research on writers' groups is situated across different disciplines. This variety greatly enriches our understanding; however, it could be further enriched if we had a common framework around which to situate discussions of writing group pedagogies. The typology, as it is now, is an answer to *what* writers' groups are; with adjustment it could include *how* and *why*, perhaps enabling further usage for research of socially situated peer learning groups.

It is exciting to see the research on writers' groups growing. It is gratifying to see more research writers recognizing the possibilities of writers' groups. I see the typology in this chapter as a potentially useful tool for both theoretical and practical use. I also view the typology as a pilot of sorts: it is my hope that both researchers and writers' group members will take the typology and use it—adjusting it, adding to it, updating it—as our knowledge, and use, of writers' groups continues to grow.

References

Aitchison, C. (2003) 'Thesis writing circles', *Hong Kong Journal of Applied Linguistics*, 8(2): 97–115.

—— (2009a) 'Research writing groups and successful thesis writing', in J. Higgs, D. Horsfall and S. Grace (eds) *Writing Qualitative Research on Practice*, Amsterdam: Sense Publishers.

—— (2009b) 'Writing groups for doctoral education', *Studies in Higher Education*, 34(8): 905–16.

—— (2010) 'Learning together to publish: writing group pedagogies for doctoral publishing', in C. Aitchison, A. Lee and B. Kamler (eds) *Publishing Pedagogies for the Doctorate and Beyond*, London: Routledge.

Aitchison, C. and Lee, A. (2006) 'Research writing: problems and pedagogies', *Teaching in Higher Education*, 11(3): 265–78.

Aitchison, C. and Haas S. (2010) 'Establishing and maintaining successful writing groups for research students', Workshop given at WDHE conference, London.

Aitchison, C. and Paré, A. (2012) 'Writing as craft and practice in the doctoral curriculum', in A. Lee and S. Danby (eds), *Reshaping Doctoral Education: International Approaches and Pedagogies*, London: Routledge.
Badley, G. (2006) 'Using writing groups to transform university teachers into scholar-writers', *Proceedings of EATAW conference*, Athens, June.
—— (2010) 'Academic writing as shaping and re-shaping', *Teaching in Higher Education*, 14(2): 209–19.
—— (2011) 'Academic scribbling: a frivolous approach?', *Teaching in Higher Education*, 16(2): 255–66.
Boice, R. (1987) 'Is released time an effective component of faculty development programs?', *Research in Higher Education*, 26(3): 311–26.
Burke, B. (1991) 'Legal writing (groups) at the University of Montana: professional voice lessons in a communal context', *Montana Law Review*, 373. Available online: http://scholarship.law.umt.edu/faculty/20 (accessed 10 January 2014).
Caffarella, R. and Barnett, B. (2000) 'Teaching doctoral students to become scholarly writers: the importance of giving and receiving critiques', *Studies in Higher Education*, 25(1): 39–52.
Castello, M., Inesta, A. and Monereo, C. (2009) 'Towards self–regulated academic writing: an exploratory study with graduate students in a situated learning environment', *Electronic Journal of Research in Educational Psychology*, 7(3): 1107–30.
Catterall, J., Ross, P., Aitchison, C. and Burgin, S. (2011) 'Pedagogical approaches that facilitate writing in postgraduate research candidature in science and technology', *Journal of University Teaching and Learning Practice*, 8(2): 1–7.
Clark, W. M., Jankowski, P. J., Springer, M. and Springer, N. P. (2000) 'Moving beyond nouns and verbs', *Journal of Feminist Family Therapy*, 11(2): 49–54.
Cuthbert, D. and Spark, C. (2008) 'Getting a GRiP: examining the outcomes of a pilot program to support graduate research students in writing for publication', *Studies in Higher Education*, 33(1): 77–88.
Cuthbert, D., Spark, C. and Burke, E. (2009) 'Disciplining writing: the case for multi-disciplinary writing groups to support writing for publication by higher degree by research candidates in the Humanities, Arts and Social Sciences', *Higher Education Research and Development*, 28(2): 137–49.
Elbow, P. (1973) *Writing Without Teachers*, New York: Oxford University Press.
—— (1981) *Writing With Power: Techniques for Mastering the Writing Process*, New York: Oxford University Press.
—— (2000) *Everyone Can Write*, New York: Oxford University Press.
Elbow, P. and Belanoff, P. (1989a) *Sharing and Responding*, New York: Random House.
—— (1989b) *A Community of Writers: A Workshop Course in Writing*, Boston: McGraw Hill.
—— (2003) *Being a Writer: A Community of Writers Revisited*, New York: McGraw Hill Higher Education.
Faulconer, J., Atkinson, T., Griffith, R., Matusevich, M. and Swaggerty, E. (2010) 'The power of living the writerly life: a group model for women writers', *NASPA Journal About Women in Higher Education*, 3(1) 207–35.
Ferguson, T. (2009) 'The "write" skills and more: a thesis writing group for doctoral students', *Journal of Geography in Higher Education*, 33(2) 285–97.

Fingar, J. (ed.) (2002) *Pickin' Fleas: Writers Grooming Writers. The Athens Writers' Group*, Athens, OH: Friends of the Athens Public Library.

Galligan, L,. Cretchley, P., George, L., McDonald, K. and Rankin, J. (2003) 'Evolution and emerging trends of university writing groups', *Queensland Journal of Educational Research*, 11(1): 1928–41.

Gere, A. R. (1987) *Writing Groups: History, Theory, and Implications*, Carbondale: Southern Illinois University Press.

Girgensohn, K. (2010) Keynote address at EATAW conference, Limerick.

Grant, B. M. (2006) 'Writing in the company of other women: exceeding the boundaries', *Studies in Higher Education*, 31(4): 483–95.

Grzybowski, S. W., Bates, J., Calam, B., Alred, J., Elwood, J., Andrew, R., Rieb, L., Harris, S., Wiebe, C., Knell, E. and Berger, S. A. (2003) 'Physician peer support writing group', *Faculty Development*, 35(3): 195–201.

Guerin, C., Xafis, V., Doda, D. V., Gillam, M., Larg, A., Luckner, H., Jahan, N., Widayati, A. and Xu, C. (2013) 'Diversity in collaborative research communities: a multicultural, multidisciplinary thesis writing group in Public Health', *Studies in Continuing Education*, 35(1): 65–81.

Haas, S. (2011) 'A writer development group for Master's students: procedures and benefits', *Journal of Academic Writing*, 1(1): 88–99.

—— (2012) 'Writers' groups', in K. Draheim, F. Liebetanz and S. Vogler-Lipp (eds), *Schreiben(d) lernen im Team – Ein Seminarkonzept für innovative Hochschullehre*, Wiesbaden: VS Verlag.

Haines, D. D., Newcomer, S. and Raphael, J. (1997) *Writing Together: How to Transform Your Writing in a Writing Group*, New York: Perigee.

Hay, I. and Delaney, E. J. (2007) 'Who teaches, learns: writing groups in geographical education', *Journal of Geography in Higher Education*, 18(3): 317–34.

Lee, A. and Boud, D. (2003) 'Writing groups, change and academic identity: research development as local practice', *Studies in Higher Education*, 28(2): 187–200.

Li, L. Y. (2007) 'Exploring the use of focused freewriting in developing academic writing', *Journal of University Teaching and Learning Practices*, 4(1): 40–53.

Lonka, K. (2003) 'Helping doctoral students to finish their theses', in G. Rijlaarsdam, (series ed.), L. Bjork, G. Bräuer, L. Rienecker and P. Stray Jorgensen (volume eds) *Studies in Writing, Vol. 12, Teaching Academic Writing in European Higher Education*, Amsterdam: Kluwer Academic.

MacLeod, I., Steckley, L. and Murray, R. (2012) 'Time is not enough: promoting strategic engagement with writing for publication', *Studies in Higher Education*, 37(6): 641–54.

Murphey, T. (2001) 'Reported belief changes through near peer role modeling', *TESL-EJ*, 5(3): 1–15.

Murray, R. (2002) 'Writing development for lecturers moving from further to higher education: a case study', *Journal of Further and Higher Education*, 26(3): 229–39.

—— (2011) *How to Write a Thesis* (3rd edn), Maidenhead: Open University Press.

—— (2012) 'Social writing', in L. Clughen, L. and C. Hardy (eds) *Writing in the Disciplines: Building Supportive Cultures for Student Writing in UK Higher Education*, Bingley, UK: Emerald.

Murray, R. and MacKay, G. (1998a) 'Supporting academic development in public output: reflections and propositions', *International Journal for Academic Development*, 3(1): 54–63.

—— (1998b) 'Writers' groups for researchers and how to run them', UCoSDA Briefing Paper 60, Committee of Vice-Chancellors and Principals of the Universities of the United Kingdom, Staff Development Agency, 1–6.

Murray, R. and Newton, M. (2008) 'Facilitating writing for publication', *Physiotherapy*, 94(1): 29–34.

—— (2009) 'Writing retreat as structured intervention: margin or mainstream?', *Higher Education Research and Development*, 28(5): 541–53.

Page, C. S., Edwards, S. and Wilson, J. H. (2012) 'Writing groups in teacher education: a method to increase scholarly productivity', *SRATE Journal*, 22(1): 29–35.

Reeves, J. (2002) *Writing Alone, Writing Together*, Novato, CA: New World Library.

Rosenthal, L. (2003) *The Writing Group Book: Creating and Sustaining a Successful Writing Group*, Chicago: Chicago Review Press.

Salas-Lopez, D., Deitrick, L., Mahady, E. T., Moser, K., Gertner, E. J. and Sabino, J. N. (2012) 'Getting published in an academic-community hospital: the success of writing groups', *Journal of General Internal Medicine*, 27(1): 113–16.

Schneider, P. (2003) *Writing Alone and With Others*, New York: Oxford University Press.

Teaching and Learning Unit (2010) *Writing Groups—Why and How?*, Teaching and Learning Unit of Social Sciences, University of Copenhagen.

Waite, M. (2012) *A collaborative and virtual writing group for postgraduate dissertation students and lecturers in the Faculty of Health and Life Sciences*. Proposal for Brooks Claim for Excellence Fellowship.

Washburn, A. (2008) 'Writing circle feedback: creating a vibrant community of scholars', *Journal of Faculty Development*, 22(1): 32–9.

Part II

Theory and reflection

Chapter 4

Learning from multiple voices
Feedback and authority in doctoral writing groups

Claire Aitchison

Introduction

Feedback has long been recognized as a powerful tool for learning to write, and expert peer review is an established feature of research scholarship. These two practices come together in writing groups in ways that are not well understood. What happens when novice researchers in writing groups receive feedback from multiple sources? How do they interpret, prioritize and respond to different critiques given by their peers? And how do they position peer feedback *vis-a-vis* that from writing group facilitators, supervisors and external readers? These questions are especially weighty for doctoral scholars learning to prepare research texts, such as the examinable dissertation and related publications, for the gaze of the examiner and for scholarly reviewers who will be making judgements about the quality of their research and their contribution to knowledge.

Unlike undergraduate scholarship, which requires the student to prove their critical understanding of a given body of knowledge, the doctoral candidate is additionally required to apply this knowledge base in the construction of *new* knowledge. This task of constructing knowledge is highly individuated, occurring iteratively over time through intimate connections with others, in, and through, the construction of the doctoral texts (Paré *et al.* 2011). These 'knowing others' will include the omnipresent voices from the scholarly literature, and the voices of supervisors, reviewers and a perhaps a raft of other readers, all of whom help shape the text and the intellectual and personal development of the doctoral scholar.

Viewed in this way, doctoral writing necessitates a broader than sentence-level appreciation of text and text-making to include social and individual dimensions. Novice scholars become certain kinds of disciplinary subjects as their doctoral texts are written into being. This process is beautifully explored by Bronwyn James (2013) who combines Systemic Functional Linguistics (Halliday 1994), Butler's performativity (1997) and Grosz's notion of 'difference' (2005) for a unique window into the transformative aspects of writing. Such perspectives see writing as social practice, rather than simply a set of skills brought to bear on the creation of text. Taking up this perspective, the process of writing is inherently interactive and mutually constitutive: writers and their writing are influenced by, and in turn influence, specific social networks.

Thus knowledge making is socially constructed and doctoral writing is dialogic (Bakhtin 1981), intertextual and multivoiced. This kind of writing involves high-stakes learning about the textual norms and expectations of the discipline—and a key aspect of becoming a certain kind of scholar is the experience of the author attempting to appropriate, integrate and claim ownership of their own ideas in relation to those of others. With obvious parallels for doctoral writers, Thompson (2006) examines undergraduate student struggles to become legitimate academic authors as they appropriate from, and claim ownership of, domain knowledge sourced from the literature. She notes how the traditional division between the production and consumption of text/knowledge in the academic environment maintains the separation between the expert scholar (the producer) and the student/novice (the consumer). The doctoral scholar must traverse these divisions, being a consumer but also a producer of knowledge, and thus their struggles for originality, voice and identity are amplified.

Doctoral student writers face the difficult task of integrating existing knowledge into their unique research project. They must do this in relation to writing about the literature and disciplinary knowledge, their research approach and findings, and in relation to the resultant knowledge claims they make. Importantly too, along the way as they engage in this highly complex writing, they receive ongoing feedback from at least one supervisor, if not from an entire panel, thus experiencing an additional layer of influence on their texts and textual practices. Scholars who publish during their candidature invite even further sets of feedback on their writing when they submit their work to conference and journal reviewers, for example.

For students who participate in writing groups, there is yet another layer of influence on their text and textual practices—that which comes from their writing group peers and facilitators.

My interest here is to move beyond interrogations of sentence-level intertextuality to examine more broadly the interplay of multiple knowers and their influence on the construction of doctoral texts as occurs in doctoral writing groups. In doing this, I seek to better understand the nuances that distinguish 'feedback' from 'review' and how these activities work together in writing groups.

The voices of others: peer review and feedback

When an author receives feedback on their writing, that feedback has the potential to influence further iterations of the author's text. In educational contexts, formal teacher feedback has long been recognized as a powerful tool for learning. Relatively more recently, (see Paré, Chapter 2) pedagogical approaches such as collaborative learning, peer learning, peer editing, reciprocal peer review, and so on, have explicitly endorsed student-to-student feedback. This kind of practice, where peers work together on their written texts, has elements of both traditional teacher feedback and of scholarly peer reviewing.

Outside of academia, peer review is a common tool used by 'expert peers' for assessing the work of industry colleagues, for example, in the allocation of funding or performance awards. Peer review by 'expert peers' is also a deeply entrenched practice within academic scholarship for purposes such as assessing grant applications and publication merit. This kind of peer review has been defined as 'the evaluation of proposed publications, presentations, or research projects by ... experts in the discipline, whereby the most highly valued form of this practice, double-blind peer review, involves concealing the identity of the authors and peer reviewers' (Starke-Meyerring 2010: 340).

According to Starke-Meyerring (2010), expert academic peer reviewing originated in emerging scientific societies, such as the Royal Society of London, for the purpose of regulating, censoring and protecting reputation. She describes how, over time, this practice has verified and shaped academic knowledge by normalizing behaviours and genres, thus producing 'orthodoxies, values, norms and epistemological commitments, ... [and] disciplinary knowledge making practices' (2010: 341). Scholarly peer review has also been put to work globally by institutional stakeholders for the distribution of funds, for reputation building and for the regulation of promotion for individuals and institutions.

Expert peer review in the academy has been criticized as a conserving influence which militates against the unorthodox, is often ineffective for identifying inaccuracies or fraudulent claims, has minimal effect on improving publication quality and perpetuates bias (Starke-Meyerring 2010: 342; UK Parliament 2011). Nevertheless, in academic life peer review is endemic, and as such is regarded as a key competency for doctoral researchers (Donmoyer 2011) with direct benefits for learning the writing and publication practices of the discipline (Thomson *et al.* 2010) and for keeping abreast of new knowledge.

As with expert peer review, feedback is a well-established practice in higher education, also often dependent on tacit knowledge, with its own ritualized practices and mythologies, foremost amongst which is that feedback is widely, if not uncritically, regarded as beneficial to learning. Unlike expert peer review, feedback is positioned within teaching and learning as pedagogy (formative feedback) and for measurement (summative feedback). Feedback is generally intended to inform students on their performance and thus enable improved and accelerated learning (Nicol & MacFarlane-Dick 2006).

There is a belated but growing literature on feedback in higher education with research clustering around the more 'technical' aspects of assessment criteria, experiences of feedback and language use in feedback (Adcroft 2011). Focusing on undergraduate education, much research indicates persistent disenchantment by both students and academics (Nicol 2010). Student dissatisfaction with written teacher comments on student writing include criticism that teacher comments are difficult to understand, lack specifics on how to improve, are difficult to act on (Carless *et al.* 2011), unhelpful, inconsistent and rarely timely (Nicol 2010). Further aggravating the problem, research indicates alarmingly different perceptions of feedback: 'whilst both academics and students share the same view that feedback is important in clarifying criteria and standards, they share little else' (Adcroft 2011: 416). Adcroft's research of undergraduate and postgraduate students in the faculties of law and management showed that academics value feedback primarily for its contribution to learning and for improving performance and changing behaviour, but that students don't necessarily share this view.

The scant literature on feedback on doctoral student writing (Aitchison *et al.* 2012; Cadman & Cargill 2007; Caffarella & Barnett 2000; Can & Walker 2011; Eyres *et al.* 2001; Knowles 1999; Paré *et al.* 2009; Stracke & Kumar 2010) shares many parallels with research on undergraduate student feedback. Like that research, key foci have been to examine student experiences of feedback (mainly from supervisors and other faculty) and analysis of written and spoken feedback. A common theme arising is of general dissatisfaction with feedback practices across disciplines. Concerns which have been highlighted include insufficiently detailed or unexplained feedback (Aitchison *et al.* 2012; Paré *et al.* 2009), low quality and/or contradictory feedback (Caffarella & Barnett 2000) and timeliness of feedback (Cadman & Cargill 2007).

A number of studies have reported on affect, particularly regarding how feedback influences student confidence and the role of confidence and perception in the uptake of feedback. Palmer and Howell (2008) talked about the 'emotional toll' of giving and receiving graduate student peer feedback, and how graduates feel underprepared and lacking in confidence to provide feedback on a peer's writing. Supervisor lack of confidence and skill in regard to providing feedback on writing has also been reported (Aitchison *et al.* 2012; Paré *et al.* 2009).

Attitudinal aspects seem to play an important role in regard to receptiveness towards feedback. Studies have shown how the perceptions and attitudes of the author towards the feedback giver can influence the uptake of feedback, irrespective of the quality of the feedback itself. Feedback was more likely to be taken seriously when the receiver perceived that the feedback giver 'cared' (Can & Walker 2011; Eyres *et al.* 2001). Furthermore, Can and Walker showed that, from the student perspective, a range of factors trumped content knowledge as desirable attributes *vis-a-vis* feedback: students sought feedback providers who 'exhibit high quality thinking, organizational, analytical and general writing skills' (2011: 526).

Such studies have enabled us to build a picture of 'good feedback practices', again showing many parallels with undergraduate feedback research. Good feedback in doctoral education has been shown to include a preference for in-depth comments (Can & Walker 2011) that include specifics and stimulate critical thinking (Eyres *et al.* 2001). Additionally, feedback needs to be appropriate to the stage of writing; for example, Kumar and Stracke (2007) found that students appreciate feedback on broader structural and conceptual aspects and may resent sentence level, editorial corrections on early stages writing. Cadman and Cargill

(2007) point to how feedback should vary according to changing supervisor positions as disciplinary experts, colleagues and gatekeepers. Paré and colleagues (2009) interpret supervisor feedback according to their roles as implied, disciplinary and implicated readers. Feedback that was perceived as dialogue was more favourably received and more effective, and opportunities to talk about written feedback with the feedback provider are highly valued (Aitchison 2009; Li & Seale 2007; Knowles 1999; Paré *et al.* 2009). Quick turnaround times, reliability and care, especially when combined with high quality thinking and general writing skills, are also highly ranked (Can & Walker 2011).

The peer review that goes on in doctoral writing circles shares features of both expert peer review and the teaching and learning approaches to feedback, but there are also important distinctions. Where doctoral writing groups are voluntary associations, then unique power relations, purposes and practices characterize the relationship between givers and receivers of feedback. Feedback on doctoral writing is unlikely to be an institutionally sanctioned aspect of the curriculum or of assessment; nor does it carry the formal weight or imprimatur of publishers' peer review. In writing circles, peers are colleagues, in that relationships between them are more horizontalized (Boud & Lee 2005); readers and writers are known to each other, often quite intimately; and feedback is given face-to-face within a relationship of mutually agreed purposes with benefits to both parties (Aitchison & Lee 2006; Lee & Boud 2003). Some group members may be in the early stages of candidature, others nearing completion; disciplinary, research and writing expertise will be differentiated, thus the usual boundaries of authority and expertise are disrupted.

More than ever before, doctoral students are purposefully writing themselves into becoming publication-ready (Aitchison *et al.* 2010), and in pursuit of this objective they value opportunities to practice scholarly reviewing skills, including critiquing the writing of others, and interpreting and responding to expert peer review. Feedback within writing groups has elements of both expert peer review and feedback, serving educational purposes for the improvement of writing, as well as enabling participants to practice scholarly reviewing.

Empirical work

In this chapter I draw on recent research conducted in an ongoing interdisciplinary doctoral writing circle which I facilitate. At the time, the group had a core of eight regular members (two men, six women), approximately half of whom had been attending for over a year. The group included visual artists, social scientists and scholars from business, education, science and anthropology. Three people had English as a second language. The group met for two and half hours fortnightly to discuss the writing of two members which had been circulated a week prior. It was a well-established practice that submitting authors indicated what particular aspects of the writing they were seeking feedback on.

The purpose of the research was to investigate how authors negotiated and incorporated multiple different responses into their writing. The study involved collecting the original manuscripts which were circulated to writing group members, the written peer feedback received by the authors on these manuscripts, an audio recording of the writing group discussion of these manuscripts, the resultant reworked manuscript, and interviews with the volunteering author.

Prior to interviewing the authors, I had already examined and compared the original text which was submitted to the group for review, copies of the peers' written reviews consisting of handwritten or 'track change' comments, and the transcription of the group discussion. This process enabled me to identify differences between what was discussed together in the group and the individual written feedback given by peers. It allowed me to locate where changes had been made in the reworked text, and crosscheck this against the reflections and perspectives raised by the authors in interview. In this chapter I draw primarily from the interviews with the authors in which they reflect on the process of receiving and incorporating feedback into the reworking of their manuscripts, with specific examples from the texts.

Managing feedback: take up and rejection of peer feedback

Authors in the writing group were able to receive feedback every six to eight weeks. For writers, this meant receiving up to eight individual written reviews as well as an hour's discussion on their text. Participation in writing groups is an additional commitment for already busy doctoral students, but when the authors in this research project were asked, every one said they had received the feedback they wanted—plus additional, unrequested feedback.

Other than one person who was new to the writing circle, everyone had developed processes for managing feedback. This usually involved taking notes during the writing group discussions and then, after the meeting, following a series of steps which involved: collating the individual peer feedback with notes from the discussions; examining each point 'page by page' and checking it against the original text; assessing the value or relevance of each comment; and deciding if, and how, to incorporate suggestions into the reworking of the original text.

It was particularly interesting to note how group members came to make judgements about the trustworthiness of their peers' feedback. While there was unanimous agreement that feedback was good ('I think any feedback is good … especially in my situation where you don't get feedback [regularly] and it's good to get feedback from people who don't know your work because they can help clarifying things'), in actual fact, the authors had developed sophisticated strategies for filtering feedback. These filtering strategies were usually based on judgements about the knowledge base and experience of the reviewer (*vis-a-vis* their discipline, methodology, or style), the frequency of comments (i.e., the greater the number of comments on a particular aspect, the more likely the author would take note) and how they imagined their supervisor would respond.

One of the strongest themes to emerge from the interviews was how writing groups allowed for 'just-in-time' and needs-based feedback achieved in tandem with the developing confidence, skill and agency of both feedback givers and receivers. As one interviewee said:

> when people haven't been so long in candidature, they often criticize the grammar ... sentence level, and to me a bit superficial ... Then those who have been in candidature for longer they are more likely [to be] asking questions or looking at structures, seeing things from a different angle and more in depth.

The more long-standing members of the writing group reflected on how, over time, they had become more skilled at making these judgements: 'When I first started, I was just taking feedback from everyone, but now ...'; 'After a few months in the writing circle you can make good judgements about the people around you ... Not because they are incompetent, but probably because they're from another discipline ...'; 'when you are at an advanced stage you are more into the process, you know better than someone else which part needs to be explored'.

The developing agency of more long term members to direct feedback in order to get what they needed, when they needed it, was evidenced by one participant who said: 'It really depends what I asked for. If I asked for general [feedback], it can go anywhere'. Newer members of the writing circle were more conservative in their requests, most frequently seeking feedback on sentence-level matters and asking 'Does it make sense?'. More senior members asked for commentary on argument, integration of claims and evidence in discussion of data and responses to experiments in writing style. Multilingual scholars were always interested in feedback on sentence-level grammar and punctuation.

One of the strongest reasons for rejecting feedback centred on an author's judgement of the authority and capacity of the feedback giver or reviewer. This was often based on an assessment of the peer's knowledge of the discipline. For example, where a peer had suggested a change that didn't make sense, one interviewee said, 'I know that they're not in the discipline ... So if they decide to change sentences ... I don't take that piece of feedback because I understand that it sounds right to them, but it's not'.

Personality and personal preference also influenced the take-up or rejection of feedback. For example, one person said they found another member's manner off-putting—'I was taken aback'—but even here, the substance of the criticism was evaluated for its relevance: 'it's not simply the opinions of the people here, it's got to be filtered by you, and perhaps even put by a supervisor'.

Peer feedback: written and spoken

The sociality of writing groups is repeatedly cited as one of the most valued aspects of membership (Aitchison 2009): it also has very specific implications for an enriched feedback cycle. The peer feedback of writing groups operates in contrast to the flat, one-way feedback typical of 'undergraduate teacher feedback' and expert peer review because it involves multiple written reviews as well as real-time author and reviewer negotiation and discussion of feedback: 'The combination of having the physical meeting and the written feedback is essential', and 'they are the perfect combination'. In addition, authors have numerous opportunities to seek further feedback throughout the life of the manuscript.

An analysis of the writing group conversations alongside the written feedback to authors revealed a greater attention to specific, sentence-level issues in written feedback, while more holistic and ideas-centred feedback arose in the group discussions: 'Sometimes people don't bother to say there was a comma missing ... the discussion is more about the ideas, the structure, the flow'. On the other hand, writing groups have the flexibility to adapt as required: 'during the conversations we can have broad or specific feedback'.

One example of how written and conversational feedback work in a complementary fashion was illustrated in one feedback cycle, where only two of the five peers had made written comment on the use of a particular word in a table heading. Although the discussion began with reference to the word 'Meaning', a broader exchange followed about the presentation of data in tables and alternatives for presenting associated interpretive information. Much of the hour's discussion revolved around these matters and everyone participated, offering suggestions for alternative formats and placements of information. In this example, as in others, a seemingly inconsequential issue identified in written feedback took on greater significance through discussion, influencing changes beyond the suggested word substitution originally identified.

As the submitting author said, the value of this combined feedback was that it alerted her to a potential issue: 'the discussions helped clarify real issues'. Her strategy was to filter these concerns and suggestions through the lens of her discipline; her peers had identified a problem but didn't have the disciplinary knowledge to propose an acceptable solution. In the end her reworked paper contained significant changes including fewer, more simply presented tables ('the feedback confirmed the fact that it was too much'), but with increased commentary elsewhere ('I've put words in between them as well'), the addition of a legend and more discipline-specific presentation and terminology.

A cacophony of voices: managing authority and influence

Even in facilitated writing groups, peer learning is the predominant mode of learning, but it does not occur in isolation. Doctoral writers are part of a larger network of relations including supervisors, other disciplinary scholars, institutional departments and policies, all of whom have some investment and influence on doctoral writing texts and practices. The data in this study revealed the interaction of voices from within the writing group and beyond.

It was common in the interviews with authors to hear them reflect on these multiple influences on their texts. Feedback was filtered by the receiver based on judgements about the authority of the reviewer and the needs of the author. For example, writing group facilitators were seen to be language experts and their views in this regard were valued more highly, sometimes even over those of the supervisor: 'when it comes from you, [the facilitator] then it's 99%'. One writing group member explained how his wife was part of his circle of reviewers. Following feedback from the writing group and a subsequent discussion with his supervisors, he asked his wife to read the troublesome section, and when 'she told me back exactly what I'd written', he was satisfied. As a candidate well into his doctorate, he had a clear understanding of how to seek and use feedback from a variety of sources according to his needs.

Another writing group author explained how she managed multiple influences on her text when she described how she struggled with the levels of headings in her doctoral writing, 'trying to make them compliant to the APA guidelines'. When her writing group colleagues told her it wasn't necessary to follow the rules so strictly, she said this knowledge had been a great relief to her: 'after that I felt more confident to explore other options', including checking authoritative sources such as the APA Manual, institutional policy and looking at other cross-disciplinary theses. Another spoke about needing to resolve differing views, specifically the different opinions of her supervisor and a journal article reviewer who had been described by her supervisor as 'really picky'.

For most participants, reconciling the views of their supervisors and those of their writing group colleagues was a key task. Interviewees reported that it was not uncommon for supervisors to ask about the views of the writing circle when there was a piece of text or an issue in dispute. On occasions supervisors had suggested an author seek the views of the writing circle. The views of supervisors were, not surprisingly, the most influential, but even still, these were not taken up automatically nor in isolation. More experienced writing group participants had found a way to incorporate the voices of their peers and supervisors:

> [in the writing circle] we came up with suggestions … I adopted them and then they sat there, sort of, part of the working document, and then … it was sent to my supervisors and they also identified this is an issue. Then they had a little bit of a brainstorming themselves … So then I expanded on that … Then when I was reviewing the chapter myself, just a couple of weeks ago, I used the same ideas …

The supervisor–writing group relationship was generally complementary where students and supervisors had established good practices for maximizing the different possibilities of these sources of feedback:

> usually the writing circle is more about grammar, structure and flow. My supervisor is more concerned with the content. What happens is when someone in the writing circle says something that makes me question how I am writing—or questions my ideas or content, then I go to my supervisor…

For writing group members the supervisor was omnipresent: 'the supervisor is always behind, over my left shoulder', but not omnipotent: 'You get guidance, but you still need to have the ownership of it'. Writing group members used supervisors as a filter for screening the acceptability of peer commentary, and also as a guide when offering feedback to colleagues: 'My supervisor says …'. In some cases feedback recipients were clear about the authority of the supervisors over the views of their peers: 'so if someone gave me the advice to use the third person, I don't take it on board because I know my supervisor doesn't want it'. Frequently peer feedback prompted further consultation with their supervisors: 'if I was really perturbed I would go back to my supervisor and talk to him about it and then I would probably make up my own mind'; 'Yeah, I'd get some good feedback from the writing circle, then I make changes and then my supervisor saw and accepted it. I find the circle a good environment or good first step before taking it to the supervisors'. Balancing supervisory and writing group feedback could also bring tension:

> It works for me … but my supervisor is quite worried about having so much feedback from so many different people, but for me, everyone knows how much my writing has improved since I joined two years ago. Everybody, it's just unanimous and I do believe it [too].

Multidisciplinary groups are valued by students, but at certain points in candidature they can potentially confuse, even overwhelm students struggling to find their own voice amongst numerous different perspectives. In the main, however, this context seemed to help students become acutely aware of their own disciplinary and methodological requirements through the processes of negotiating these different perspectives. The safe and reciprocal feedback space of the writing group enabled them to appropriate, borrow and experiment with alternatives, but also, ultimately, to learn how to reject or integrate numerous perspectives to create a unified and authentic voice:

> we all have a unique way of talking and writing—one type of sentence works really well for one particular person, but that may not be how … that wouldn't sit well with the rest, it would stand out too much. Sometimes I just use the idea and change it myself.

The project of knowledge construction mostly, but not always seamlessly, benefited from multiple diverse feedback.

Conclusions

The literature tells us that good feedback is not routine in higher education. We also know from work on doctoral student writing and feedback that timely, appropriate, needs-based, dialogic, higher order feedback is valued by students.

For most doctoral writers there is one primary source of feedback on writing, that is, from their supervisor(s). Increasingly, however, students now also submit their work to wider audiences inviting expert peer review via conference participation and scholarly publication. We know from the literature that there is unevenness in the quality, quantity and timeliness of feedback from these two sources. We know that doctoral students depend on feedback to progress their thinking and identity formation and for the progress of the doctoral project itself. Feedback on writing is also used for monitoring doctoral progression and developing the examinable and associated research documentation. And yet, where we do know of their views, it would appear that doctoral students continue to experience frustrations around feedback from these sources. Any number of online forums and doctoral-related blogs are testimony to these frustrations.

This chapter documents the feedback experiences of students in a writing group, showing most clearly the desire of doctoral students for feedback on their writing, especially when it occurs in socially supportive and collegial environments. It shows the kind of feedback that students receive from peers and how they reconcile this with feedback from other sources, including supervisors. In particular this small study builds a picture of how students actually sift through the variety of information impinging on their text work, how they juggle these influences and with growing confidence move from being passive recipients of the views of others to active, purposeful seekers and implementers of feedback. It shows too how students develop quite sophisticated strategies for attributing authority and appropriateness to the feedback they receive, as a first step in a process of integrating multiple voices into a text which they make their own.

As with other students in the university, doctoral students seek to learn through feedback on their writing: indeed, this is their *raison d'être* for joining or forming writing groups (Aitchison 2009). Writing group community practices include elements from both traditional educationally focused feedback and expert peer review. In writing groups participation is agentic in that scholars set their own deadlines for submitting their work for review and they direct review by indicating what kind of feedback they are looking for. But unlike blind expert peer review, they know their reviewers and, in addition to receiving written feedback, they engage in collegial dialogue with their reviewers, even collaborating with them in text construction and reconstruction. Unlike expert peer review, which is blind and temporal, these scholars develop intimate knowledge of their reviewers over time, coming to appreciate their strengths and weaknesses as writers and reviewers, and as particular kinds of disciplinary scholars. This intimate knowledge of their peer reviewers facilitates the agency, direction and uptake of feedback by writing group members. Unlike traditional classroom-based teacher feedback, writing group peer feedback is not imbued with power nor sanctioned influence. Each receiver of feedback must learn how to assess the value of the critique they are given.

Writing group feedback is ongoing, formative and iterative. It is a deeply social practice that is mutually advantageous, and, at its best, combines the best elements of scholarly peer review and traditional feedback, thus facilitating the construction of knowledge through the process of writing and rewriting through iterations of feedback from multiple sources.

References

Adcroft, A. (2011) 'The mythology of feedback', *Higher Education Research and Development*, 30(4): 405–19.
Aitchison, C. (2009) 'Writing groups for doctoral education', *Studies in Higher Education*, 34(8): 905–16.
Aitchison, C. and Lee, A. (2006) 'Research writing: problems and pedagogies', *Teaching in Higher Education*, 11(3): 265–78.
Aitchison, C., Kamler, B., & Lee, A. (eds) (2010) *Publishing Pedagogies for the Doctorate and Beyond*, London: Routledge.
Aitchison, C., Catterall, J., Ross, P. and Burgin, S. (2012) '"Tough love and tears": learning doctoral writing in the sciences', *Higher Education Research and Development Journal*, 31(4): 435–47.
Bakhtin, M. M. (1981) *The Dialogic Imagination: Four Essays* (ed. M. Holquist, trans. C. Emerson and M. Holquist), Austin, TX: University of Texas Press.
Boud, D. & Lee, A. (2005) '"Peer learning" as pedagogic discourse for research education', *Studies in Higher Education*, 30(5), 501–16.
Butler, J. (1997) *Excitable Speech: A Politics of the Performative*, New York: Routledge.
Cadman, K. and Cargill, M. (2007) 'Providing quality advice on candidates' writing', in C. Denholm and T. Evans (eds) *Supervising Doctorates Downunder: Keys to Effective Supervision in Australia and New Zealand*, Camberwell, Victoria, Australia: ACER Press.
Caffarella, R. S. and Barnett, B. G. (2000) 'Teaching doctoral students to become scholarly writers: the importance of giving and receiving critiques', *Studies in Higher Education*, 25: 39–54.
Can, G. and Walker, A. (2011) 'A model for doctoral students' perceptions and attitudes toward written feedback for academic writing', *Research in Higher Education*, 52(5): 508–36.
Carless, D., Salter, D., Yang, M. and Lam, J. (2011) 'Developing sustainable feedback practices', *Studies in Higher Education*, 36(4): 395–407.
Donmoyer, R. (2011) 'Why writers should also be reviewers', in T. Rocco and T. Hatcher (eds) *The Handbook of Scholarly Writing and Publishing*, San Francisco, CA: Jossey-Bass.

Eyres, S. J., Hatch, D. H., Turner, S. B. and West, M. (2001) 'Doctoral students' responses to writing critique: messages for teachers', *Journal of Nursing Education*, 40(4): 149–55.

Grosz, E. (2005) 'Bergson, Deleuze and becoming', *Parallax*, 11(2): 4–13.

Halliday, K. (1994) *An Introduction to Functional Grammar* (2nd edn), London: Edward Arnold.

James, B. (2013) 'Researching student becoming in higher education', *Higher Education Research and Development*, 32(1): 109–21.

Knowles, S. (1999) 'Feedback on writing in postgraduate supervision: echoes in response—content, continuity and resonance', in A. Holbrook and S. Johnston (eds) *Supervision of Postgraduate Research in Education*, Coldstream, Victoria: Australian Association for Research in Education.

Kumar, V. and Stracke, E. (2007) 'An analysis of written feedback on a Ph.D. thesis', *Teaching in Higher Education*, 12(4): 461–70.

Lee, A. and Boud, D. (2003) 'Writing groups, change and academic identity: research development as local practice', *Studies in Higher Education*, 28(2): 187–200.

Li, S. and Seale, C. (2007) 'Managing criticism in Ph.D. supervision: a qualitative case study', *Studies in Higher Education*, 32(4): 511–26.

Nicol, D. (2010) 'From monologue to dialogue: improving written feedback processes in mass higher education', *Assessment and Evaluation in Higher Education*, 35(5): 501–17.

Nicol, D. and MacFarlane-Dick, D. (2006) 'Formative assessment and self-regulated learning: a model and seven principles of good feedback practice', *Studies in Higher Education*, 31(2): 199–218.

Palmer, B. and Howell, C. (2008) 'Using reciprocal peer review to help graduate students develop scholarly writing skills', *The Journal of Faculty Development*, 22(2): 163–9.

Paré, A., Starke-Meyerring, D. and McAlpine, L. (2009) 'The dissertation as multi-genre: many readers, many readings', in C. Bazerman, A. Bonini and D. Figueiredo (eds) *Genre in a Changing World*, Fort Collins, CO: The WAC Clearinghouse and Parlour Press.

—— (2011) 'Knowledge and identity work in the supervision of doctoral student writing: shaping rhetorical subjects', in D. Starke-Meyerring, A. Paré, N. Horne, N. Artemeva and L. Yousoubova (eds) *Writing in the Knowledge Societies*, Fort Collins, Colorado: The WAC Clearinghouse and Parlour Press. Available online: http://wac.colostate.edu/books/winks/ (accessed 10 January 2014).

Starke-Meyerring, D. (2010) 'Between peer review and peer production: genre, wikis, and the politics of digital code in academe', in C. Bazerman, R. Krut, K. Lunsford, S. McLeod, S. Null, P. Rogers and A. Stansell (eds) *Traditions of Writing Research*, New York: Routledge.

Stracke, E. and Kumar, V. (2010) 'Feedback and self-regulated learning: insights from supervisors' and PhD examiners' reports', *Reflective Practice: International and Multidisciplinary Perspective*s, 11(1): 17–30.

Thompson, C. (2006) 'Dialogism and social computing: academic authorship in cyberspace', in J. McConachie, M. Singh, P. A. Danaher, F. Nouwens and G. Danaher (eds) *Changing University Learning and Teaching: Engaging and Mobilising Leadership, Quality and Technology*, Teneriffe, Qld, Australia: Post Pressed.

Thomson, P., Byrom, T., Robinson, C. and Russell, L. (2010) 'Learning about journal publication: the pedagogies of editing a "special issue"', in C. Aitchison, B. Kamler and A. Lee (eds) *Publishing Pedagogies of the Doctorate and Beyond*, London: Routledge.

UK Parliament (2011). *Peer Review* Commons Select Committee, Science and Technology. Session 2010–11, 17 March. Available online: http://www.publications.parliament.uk/pa/cm201011/cmselect/cmsctech/writev/856/m55.htm (accessed 19 July 2013).

Chapter 5

Writing groups as critical spaces for engaging normalized institutional cultures of writing in doctoral education

Doreen Starke-Meyerring

Like all practices of doctoral education, doctoral writing, including writing groups, exists in institutional environments, which—as much research on writing has documented internationally (e.g., Thaiss *et al.* 2012)—are stubbornly consistent in one respect: they tend to keep writing marginalized and shrouded in silence. Doctoral education, where research writing constitutes the central activity of doctoral scholars, is no exception (Kamler & Thomson 2006; Lee & Aitchison 2009). As Lee and Aitchison (2009) put it, attention to writing remains 'in some senses reactive and often intellectually poorly resourced' with 'questions of textuality and of rhetoric submerged and marginal' (87).

These institutional environments are not necessarily the invention of those who currently work in them—doctoral scholars, supervisors, academic developers, administrators, and others. Rather, having evolved historically, these institutional environments emerged long before the recent surge in pressures on doctoral education for faster degree completion with more extensive research funding and publication records (Lee & Boud 2009). Along with their historically evolved assumptions, these institutional environments continue to guide our practices, programs and policies, including those related to doctoral writing. Passed on from generation to generation, and reproduced in our daily practices, these historically evolved assumptions have become normalized or 'common sense'; this is simply 'how things are done'. In the rush of daily tasks, these inherited normalized assumptions easily escape collective research-led reflection.

The purpose of this chapter, therefore, is to take a step back—to pause and reflect on these inherited institutional environments in which doctoral writing (and specifically writing groups) are situated, to de-familiarize and de-normalize them by reconsidering them through the perspectives and experiences of doctoral scholars. This need for reflection on the situatedness of doctoral writing groups in institutional environments is particularly important because in many ways doctoral writing groups have emerged out of the need to 'squeeze out' writing in institutional environments that continue to marginalize and shroud writing in silence despite growing pressures on doctoral writers and supervisors (see Aitchison and Guerin, Chapter 1 in this volume). How, then, do these institutional environments influence doctoral writing and writing groups in particular? How are they experienced by doctoral writers? What insights do these experiences offer to our understanding of the roles of writing groups in doctoral education? And in what ways can doctoral student experiences with writing groups help us re-think institutional environments for doctoral writing?

For this purpose, the chapter draws on data from a larger ongoing program of research examining writing practices in doctoral education at Canadian research-intensive universities. Although the study collected a number of data sets, including data from surveys and interviews with faculty and administrators, here I am particularly interested in the perspectives of doctoral scholars in order to understand their experiences with research writing, and specifically the roles writing groups play in these experiences. The data are drawn from a survey of 3,000 doctoral scholars across disciplines and across the 11 most research-intensive universities in Canada, as well as from extended (1–3 hour) follow-up interviews with 60 doctoral scholars across disciplines and universities about their experiences with research writing. The interviews were largely open-ended, as my interest has been in the lived institutional experiences of doctoral scholars with writing as they play out in daily interactions, the assumptions about writing that doctoral scholars encounter in their daily interactions, and the consequences those assumptions have for their writing.

Accordingly, the chapter begins with a brief review of the insights doctoral scholars have previously shared into the roles institutional environments play in their writing, then explores their experiences with writing groups, and examines in more detail the ways in which institutional environments influence the efforts of doctoral scholars to form writing groups. The chapter concludes by offering critical insights into how these experiences of doctoral scholars help us re-think and re-imagine institutional environments for doctoral writing, and explore new directions for understanding, studying and facilitating doctoral writing.

Arhetorical institutional cultures of research writing and their implications for doctoral writing

Much research on writing at any level in higher education in many locations has invariably observed that writing and writing pedagogy tend to remain shrouded in silence and marginalized. Of concern here is that this silencing of writing also shrouds (and at the same time is produced by) what doctoral scholars in their accounts of their research writing experiences revealed as highly arhetorical institutional cultures of research writing, which consistently deny the rhetorical nature of research writing (Starke-Meyerring 2011).

A rhetorical understanding of doctoral writing means recognizing writing as a site of long-term socialization or 'disciplining' of doctoral scholars into the discourses and genres of their fields—the repeated discursive practices that have evolved in specific research cultures through repetition over time (Miller 1984; Bazerman 1988; Bawarshi & Reiff 2010). These discourses and their specific genres do the knowledge work of the research cultures in which they have evolved: they regularize and regulate what can, must, or must not be said, thought, or acknowledged; what and whose knowledge (e.g., indigenous knowledge, practitioner knowledge, etc.) or evidence counts or not; which conversations to take up and how; how to work out and position one's contribution amidst competing epistemological, ontological, and ideological factions of a given research culture; whom doctoral scholars are being asked to become as researchers through their writing; what disciplinary orthodoxies are to be reproduced; and much more (Starke-Meyerring 2011).

More specifically, research into writing has produced a number of insights into this rhetorical dimension that have deep implications for doctoral writing. First, perhaps most importantly, understanding writing as rhetorical means that doctoral writing is highly socio-culturally situated; that is, it is specific to the research cultures whose work it does. Accordingly, a dissertation in history, for example, differs from one in sociology, anthropology, or even physics, not just in its subject matter or its specific terminology, but in its ways of arguing, considering evidence, articulating research questions, projecting an authorial presence, and so on.

Second, these particular discursive practices constitute the work of these research cultures; that is, different research cultures have evolved different ways of writing because they pursue particular kinds of knowledge goals. In short, writing is epistemic (Starke-Meyerring & Paré 2011). A reflective authorial presence or particular uses of the active or passive voice, for example, may be highly valued in a dissertation in anthropology for specific epistemic purposes, but perhaps less so or differently in physics. It is impossible, therefore, to separate research writing from the disciplinary knowledge-making practices and the relationships and activities that sustain those knowledge-making practices (Bazerman 1988; Bazerman & Prior 2005). As Thomson and Kamler (2010) emphasize, writing is knowledge work—it *is* research and vice versa.

Third, the particular genres of a discipline evolve historically through repetition. A doctoral scholar will hardly be the first person to write a dissertation in their field; rather, the particular range of expectations of what a dissertation in a given field is to look like, sound like, and what it is to do, have evolved over time. However, because they have evolved through constant repetition over generations, those expectations become normalized, tacit, 'just the way things are done' (Paré 2002), and are often assumed to be universal or 'simply good writing'.

Fourth, as much research on writing has documented, of course, it is impossible for doctoral scholars to be familiar with the unique discursive practices and research conversations that have evolved historically long before they enter their programs and research cultures. Rather, the discursive practices of a given research culture are learned over time—through the gradual, and ideally critical, exploration of and increasingly mentored participation in research cultures and their discursive practices (Bazerman & Prior 2005; Dias *et al.* 1999).

Fifth, from a rhetorical perspective, the discourses and genres into which doctoral scholars are to be socialized are not neutral (Coe *et al.* 2002). Rather, they are saturated with assumptions, regularities, norms and values, for example, whose knowledge and positionalities or what evidence are considered credible and acceptable, whose are not, and what audiences and purposes are acceptable or even imaginable. Although this political nature of writing is normalized through repetition and hence shrouded from attention, writers may have good reasons to resist the demands genres place on their identity (Turner 2003).

However, the daily interactions around research writing described by doctoral scholars (Starke-Meyerring 2011) revealed institutional cultures that were saturated with arhetorical and non-research-informed assumptions about writing. Participants encountered assumptions about writing as a universal skill presumably able to be thought of as separate from disciplinary knowledge-making practices and that doctoral scholars should simply be equipped with upon entering their doctoral programs. These arhetorical assumptions about writing as a generic skill invariably gave rise to deficit views of doctoral writers as 'lacking writing skills' and therefore as in need of remediation and fixing. Viewed as separate from disciplinary knowledge-making practices, this 'remediation' was imagined to have to happen elsewhere—outside the disciplinary knowledge-making practices in which the students were learning to participate—such as in a writing centre or in a writing course. Accordingly, doctoral scholars encountered writing as a non-question in their daily interactions with supervisors and others—not a site of dialogue and inquiry into the knowledge-making practices of their field.

This arhetorical nature of institutional research writing cultures produced a decidedly consequential paradox for doctoral student writers. On the one hand, the demands placed on doctoral scholars were, of course, deeply rhetorical: students were expected to perform in the highly contextual and historically evolved discursive practices of their research cultures. On the other hand, given the non-research-based assumptions about writing as a universal skill, these discursive practices remained shrouded in silence and therefore difficult to access for doctoral scholars.

This paradox of having the rhetorical nature of their work denied in institutional cultures, while at the same time being asked to enter the deeply rhetorical research cultures and conversations of their fields, produced a number of significant consequences for doctoral scholars (Starke-Meyerring 2011). For example, students reported finding their writing stifled, being sent on wild goose chases in a search for external remediation of their presumed writing deficits, feeling disoriented and left in the dark, afraid of sharing and submitting drafts to supervisors and others, encountering an atmosphere of normalized and universalized assumptions about writing that rendered asking questions about writing—and hence about the very knowledge-making practices in which they are expected to participate—as a risky business. Rendered as a generic skill in arhetorical institutional cultures, writing became a site of chance learning and anxiety, with dialogue about disciplinary knowledge-making practices difficult to come by. Given this paradox, what roles then do writing groups play in the institutional lived experiences of doctoral scholars, and how do institutional environments affect doctoral writing groups?

The roles of writing groups in the experiences of doctoral scholars with research writing

To explore the experiences of doctoral scholars with writing groups, it seems helpful to begin with some sense of the overall role writing groups may play in their doctoral experience, specifically, the support they seek as well as the support they receive from writing groups and other sources. How prominent are writing groups in the doctoral students' experiences? Two questions in the survey—questions about the various sources of support doctoral scholars have sought out and received—offer some initial insight into this concern (see Figures 5.1 and 5.2 and Table 5.1).

In terms of support received, the responses were similar, which suggests that doctoral scholars do receive support from the sources they sought out.

Table 5.1 below shows the breakdown of where writing support was sought and received.

As the data suggest, despite their well-established pedagogical value (e.g., Aitchison 2009; Aitchison & Lee 2006; Guerin *et al.* 2013; Lee & Boud 2003), writing groups as such do not seem to feature prominently in student accounts of resources in their research writing work. This, of course, does not mean that relationships with supervisors, professors and peers are not important for

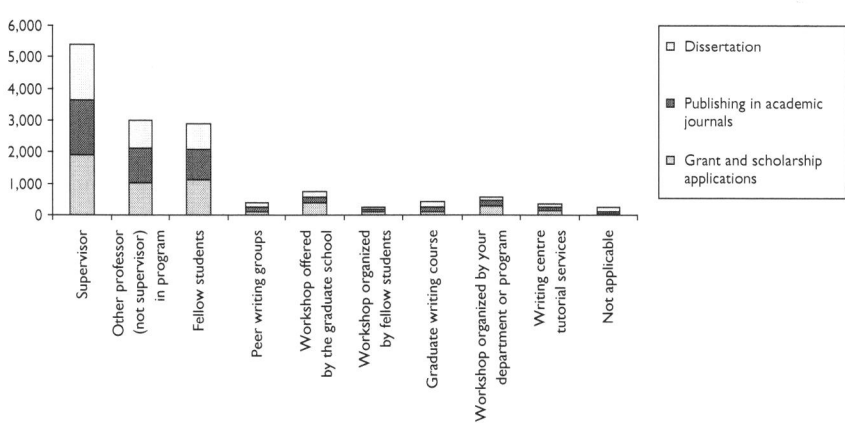

Figure 5.1 Writing support sought by doctoral students for different writing projects.

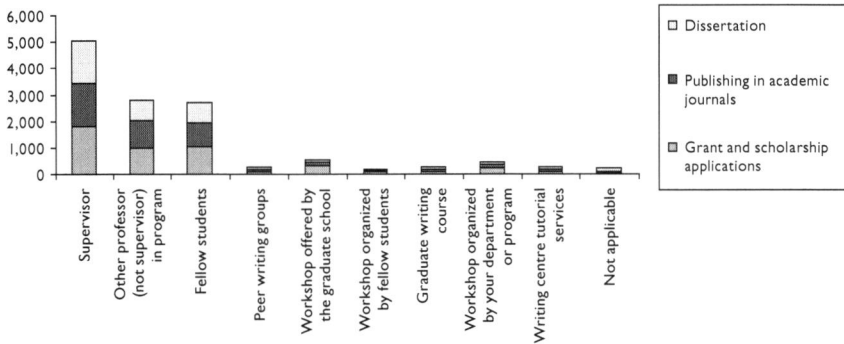

Figure 5.2 Writing support received by doctoral students for different writing projects.

Table 5.1 Support sought and received by doctoral students for different writing projects

Source of writing support	Writing support sought (n = 2,367)	Writing support received (n = 2,342)
Supervisor	2,282 (96.4%)	2,218 (94.7%)
Other professor (not supervisor) in program	1,674 (70.7%)	1,603 (68.4%)
Fellow students	1,626 (68.7%)	1,544 (65.9%)
Peer writing groups	263 (11.5%)	197 (8.4%)

doctoral writing; quite the contrary, the data indicate that they are central to doctoral writing. The centrality of supervisors, of course, reflects their rhetorical role as long-time members of the research cultures doctoral scholars are entering—a role that includes mediating and facilitating access to disciplinary discourses and networks (Green 2005) and facilitating doctoral scholar positioning within them (Paré *et al.* 2011). As an active, long-term member of the student's research culture, the supervisor is well familiar with the nuances of the genres and of the impact different rhetorical choices may have, what must be said, where and how. Not surprisingly, a typical comment by doctoral scholars in open-ended sections of the survey was: 'My supervisor is key; no one else knows the research as well and can offer guidance that is as relevant.' However, with writing silenced in institutional environments, the work of supervising doctoral writing is often underestimated, leading the student to add: 'I just wish I could have gotten more guidance from him.'

Not surprisingly, relationships with peers also played an important role. Most frequently, these were identified as research lab colleagues or friends.

However, these relationships and the support mechanisms they provide did not seem to be identified as writing groups. Insights into why that might be the case emerged from the interview data with doctoral scholars, with two observations arising. First, doctoral scholars may well organize into groups to discuss writing, without necessarily identifying these arrangements as 'writing groups', because for them writing may be inseparable from their academic life, positionalities, and the related politics of writing in institutions. As the section below explains, such groups hold particular potential for learning, for exploring alternative discourses, or for dealing with racialized and gendered experiences around research writing, but they may be overlooked and lack institutional support. Second, saturated with arhetorical assumptions about writing, institutional environments may present particular challenges for doctoral student efforts to develop and sustain writing groups. I now explore each observation in more detail.

Sociality, relationships and community: when writing groups work, but lack institutional support

Writing was experienced as an inseparable part of the academic experiences and relationships of doctoral scholars, which are largely shaped by their positionalities, the politics of these positionalities and of writing in institutions. Accordingly, doctoral scholars may set up support groups or peer mentoring groups around those shared positionalities and experiences, for example, to deal with issues of racialization and gender on campus in which experiences with writing are, of course, central. One participant provided a particularly revealing account of such a group, its situatedness in peer relationships and community, and in the institutional environment:

Participant: It was a space of like building scholarship and just learning, um, learning to support each other in the writing and surviving academia ... and uh, it was quite painful—it was very painful because people really talked about the isolation. People talked about dropping all the time.... And ... we would always talk about our dilemmas in writing and ... about our struggles as graduate students....
Researcher: Can you provide an example of those dilemmas?
Participant: Yeah. I remember one student, she was in English and um she was of Chinese descent and she wrote her paper and the teacher gave her like an 'A' or something and he said it was a really good paper; it was really an 'A+' paper, but because she was of Chinese descent, she couldn't truly ever write—you know, English—to the full extent of an 'A+'. And I remember her coming in the room and being very, very upset about it. She had, you know, she was at that time I assume in her 20's and

	she had come here, ... she was just a baby when she had come here ... So those were kind of some of the things people would talk about, and then, it was about building community and learning to be there.
	... [the group also helped] to develop another type of knowledge also because we were reading things that weren't in the classroom. We were learning about authors that we were each bringing in, but so a lot of kind of the critical thinking I have came from those networks. A lot of knowing how to write came from those networks; it didn't really come ...
Researcher:	In what sense?
Participant:	In the sense, so we had a library, we built our own little women of color library, and it was housed in the [name of a university office], ... so we were starting to understand new scholars coming out ... we would read each other's work, and I mean there were some of the most brilliant women and the things they were writing was just—and they had no faculty support because nobody understood what the hell they were talking about.
Researcher:	Wow, ok. ... Can you say a little bit about, you know, ... what the group was doing, what it was talking about and how that then influenced your writing ...?
Participant:	Yeah, yeah, like once we did a series on ... writing about disability studies as women of color .... I remember reading, um, [the work of a US writer and civil rights activist], right? So we were kind of learning different types of narrative writing, different types of auto-biography, learning, how do you, in a scholarly way bring your voice, in an informed way while fully kind of substantiating and referencing, right? ... Um, so, it's just, you know, you learn things just like in any kind of community that is not mainstreamed, because when it is mainstreamed, it leaves a lot of ... I learned about how much we leave out when we're kind of not looking at different knowledge systems and [when] the traditional things are being reproduced.
Researcher:	So this group is going on now?
Participant:	No, no, it ended. It ended because the university shut down the [office where this group was housed], closed it down completely.... I think I need to add that there's a whole backlash, ... we don't ... have those spaces anymore.... students of color just really do not have places to go on campus, you know? You see the pain, the turmoil, the lack of mentors ...

This participant's account provides a number of important insights into writing groups in doctoral student experiences. First, it helps us understand where, how and why doctoral writing, including conversations about writing, happen in institutional environments. It raises a number of questions about how we conceive of writing groups, where we look for them, how we support them, and what roles community and positionality play in their emergence. They may not be called 'writing groups', but rather, as in this case, a support network for women of color. Regardless, they perform many of the functions and facilitate the kinds of conversations about research writing that are vital to doctoral education.

This account also suggests that writing groups are dynamic and fluid, grounded in the activities, communities and relationships that sustain doctoral writing. Writing here is not experienced as separate or separable from, but rather as quite rhetorical—as constitutive of these positionalities, relationships and activities. As the participant emphasized, 'it was about building community and learning to be there'. Her account illustrates how talk about writing grew organically out of a need for community building, a social exigence for coping with institutional environments that marginalize writing as a central site where issues of racism and gender are experienced. The participant's account raises questions about the extent to which these issues might come up in writing groups that are set up as separate from community building, as well as the shared experiences and trust these generate for potentially sensitive discussions about writing to take place.

Second, the insights shared by this participant also raise important issues of identity and the politics of writing involved in learning to write. As illustrated, doctoral scholar communities can explore alternative discourses and ways of writing that reflect the positionalities from which they write and the concerns they wish to address. These concerns are otherwise stifled in an environment that remains silent on writing and offers little space for innovative writers who explore human experiences outside the canon of their research cultures. The group allowed for the important work of writing to push sedimented knowledge systems—work that we know historically has been performed by new groups who enter higher education, such as the shifts in disciplinary discourses described by Gesa Kirsch (1992) in her study of women entering and writing in higher education.

Arhetorical assumptions and lack of community: when writing groups don't work

While some doctoral scholars see the communities they develop to deal with the constraints of institutional environments shut down, others struggle hard to set up writing groups—sometimes as a replacement for a lack of research sociality or community. Indeed, the difficulty of establishing writing groups was a common theme in the accounts of doctoral scholars. Doctoral scholars offered two insights in particular: that relationships and communities are central to sustaining writing groups; and that arhetorical assumptions may hinder talk about writing.

l Without the necessary relationships and communities, writing groups may be difficult to sustain

In particular, participants who reported experiencing a strong sense of isolation in their doctoral work went to great lengths to establish writing groups, but found them difficult to initiate and maintain, to the extent that they almost wished writing groups were 'forced' as a way of dealing with the isolation they were experiencing. The following exchange with a participant in the social sciences illustrates this difficulty:

Participant: I did try to get a few people together to do a writing group ... Um, not many takers. ... It's hard to um, ...and we're all on a different schedule so with the work and .... everything; it's very hard to share, like pieces and I find—I would like to have someone read my writing; however, I find I'm disturbing them like asking them to do something on top of their workload. So yeah. I think that's a concern. So if there's a structure I think that's already in place, I think it would be easier.

Researcher: What kind of structure do you think would be useful?

Participant: If there is a structure where people from disciplines that are very similar, just meet when you enter the program and you're part of this little group, writing group, and perhaps meet once a month and just share a small piece of what you're doing perhaps in your classroom or anything outside with that group and you follow each other for the duration of the program, I think that would help. And you develop a better sense of what the other person is trying to do because you've been following their work for a while ... Something like that, I mean, ... it's forcing the people to participate at the beginning, but I think in the end it will help. Not sure.

The participant has a strong sense that there is a sociality in place that distributes workloads, occupies space and time, and so on, therefore rendering a writing group an add-on to that existing sociality, an imposition on an existing workload—something that would need to be grafted on or 'forced'.

Another participant from the humanities, who experienced a strong sense of isolation, cements this idea of writing groups as difficult to establish and sustain when community is lacking:

Participant: At various points, I've tried to run writing groups. I find them—they're super hard to do.

Researcher: What did you find hard? That's interesting.

Participant: Um, people don't commit to them; they don't come ... Just to have any kind of sense of momentum beyond a few meetings was really hard, but I've done them.

Researcher: Do you have a sense of what you might attribute that to—that sense that the momentum gets lost?

Participant: I think a lot of it is that people are too busy ... And it's just like whoever was supposed to schedule the meeting never sent the email out and just did not pick up the ball ... But I've also tried to initiate them and had very little response as well. ... When I've done them and like at least for the like couple of months that they've managed to last, I found them super helpful, you know. Usually someone would present, you know, a short like five to ten pages of whatever they were working on and get feedback and everyone else could talk a bit about where they were at, and, ... the one person would get sort of detailed content based feedback, and everyone else could get a bit of process sort of support kind of like 'Where are you at? What are you working on? How's that going?' ... That worked pretty well when it was happening; it just didn't last. ...

I know my supervisor has said repeatedly to me, 'cause I've been like 'yeah I'm really just sitting here alone in my apartment writing'. She's been like, 'oh yeah, so and so and so and so and so and so are also complaining about that; I don't know why you guys don't talk to one another'. But ... I'm like, well it's cause that one person I've never talked to ever before. I know their name, I've never met them; this other person I kind of know and don't really like; or this other person, you know—they're not people I see regularly or have connections with.

As this participant illustrates, although writing groups may be experienced as helpful, they may be difficult to sustain without the necessary relationship and community. This is particularly the case if writing groups must be grafted onto existing socialities, where collaborative approaches to writing do not feature prominently in the research culture, and where time and space have already been allocated. The last comment in particular illustrates the centrality of sociality, relationships and community; when these are thought of as separate from writing groups, they seem difficult to sustain. What is particularly significant here is that, although doctoral scholar isolation in this particular research environment seems to be recognized as a widespread problem, the blame and responsibility seems to be placed squarely on the student for not being able to alter that isolating research environment.

2 Arhetorical assumptions about writing may render talk about writing difficult

An institutional culture saturated with arhetorical assumptions may render talk about writing and feedback difficult, inadvertently leading to student impressions of writing groups as unhelpful. Two types of difficulties in particular were identified by participants: (1) arhetorical assumptions about writing groups that led to generic expectations of feedback; and (2) a lack of research and theory or 'language' for talking about writing. I now turn to the accounts of participants to explore each of these challenges.

Arhetorical assumptions about writing groups led to confusing expectations about writing and feedback specifically, and thus to conclusions that writing groups may not be helpful. One participant in the social sciences who had made several attempts at forming writing groups and then ended up forming a writing partnership with one friend describes the following experience:

> Well, we're just in the same program, but the field is a bit different. But still I understand what she writes. I can still give some feedback. The problem with the writing groups was that some people are just not in the field, so I could not give feedback. I remember trying to give feedback on a paper about clouds, or other things and I was like, 'What the hell', I did not have any clue?! I just, like, one friend and exchange things. It's not easy also to find people that understand what you want... The feedback has to be pretty deep. Like, I really want something related to the content of what I write, rather than really like just the way it looks.

The participant's account of her experience interacting with colleagues about writing raises the question of who can usefully provide what kinds of readings and responses to what kind of writing and how.

This question surfaced quite frequently, most notably in accounts of attempts at forming writing groups across disciplines. Another participant, a doctoral scholar in the humanities, who also had tried numerous times to organize a writing group, shares a similar experience. In the group of four to five doctoral scholars, members came from different types of research cultures, including the natural sciences and the humanities:

Participant: It's been helpful, sometimes more than others. Right now, there's more science students involved and ... their writing projects are very different so—I don't find the science students as helpful in terms of giving feedback just 'cause they don't—their writing process is just really different. Like, they're like 'I did research or I programmed something and now I have to ... describe this in my publications', and I'm like, 'no, that's really not what I do, and they really don't get it'.

... So it's sort of helpful. I mean it's helpful just to talk to other people who are like trying to write stuff but it's—
Researcher: Um-hum. So it's helpful at the process level?
Participant: Yeah. When we've had discussions with the arts students, it's more useful. Like if someone in one of the sciences brings in a draft, I can

> kind of read it and like look at grammar and stuff, but I can't give a lot of useful feedback to them, and they don't tend to be able to give super useful feedback on my drafts either. There's too big a disciplinary gulf.

These participants raise the question about the extent or ways in which writing groups can be productive across disciplines or research cultures when members are unfamiliar with those research cultures, the particular discursive practices, values, expectations and conversations that have evolved in those research cultures. Perhaps even more importantly, without a research-informed introduction to research writing, writing group members may not even be aware of research cultures and their roles in shaping writing; rather, with writing perceived as a universal skill, they may perceive their ways of writing as universal. Accordingly, what is identified as helpful is not a particular rhetorical knowledge-making goal that would benefit from the reading and response of colleagues in a particular field; rather, the driving force is 'trying to write stuff'. In other words, the driving force is trying to 'squeeze out' writing in institutional environments that silence and stifle writing.

If writing is thought of arhetorically, as a generic skill, however, writing practices and experiences are essentialized and homogenized, and accordingly, the expectation is that anybody can be expected to give useful feedback on anything. As indicated in the participants' accounts, such experiences may inadvertently lead doctoral scholars to believe that that such disciplinary boundary work may not be useful, despite research to the contrary (Guerin *et al.* 2013).

These challenges deriving from arhetorical assumptions about writing are closely linked to concerns about the lack of a 'language' or research and theory-led ways for conceptually understanding and discussing writing. In an arhetorical non-research-led institutional culture of research writing, students rarely encounter theoretically informed dialogue about writing. As the survey of doctoral supervisors in the study showed, more than 99 per cent lacked any introduction to the supervision of doctoral writing. It would not seem surprising then that faculty teaching doctoral seminars in their fields would likewise lack opportunities for research-led introductions to research writing. Accordingly, even in coursework, doctoral scholars may encounter writing groups that are experienced as unrewarding, as this participant explains with regard to her experience with writing groups in a doctoral seminar:

> I didn't really find it very helpful. It was ... I think because being the first time reviewing other people you know, so then in reviewing I think we focused a lot more on the structure and the format and the ... not really on the idea, so it didn't push my thinking further but I don't know, add a linking word here or like, um, 'your paragraph—it doesn't flow well; perhaps you can add a sentence on this to?'... So it didn't—it's not on the idea that I was trying to think about, it was still on the structure about writing.

As the participant explained further, there was no introduction to research writing as knowledge work and the ways in which writing groups might operate to push that knowledge work.

As the examples here illustrate, without any research-informed conceptual introduction to research writing, faculty and doctoral scholars may be left with little else other than to reproduce the arhetorical assumptions about writing that saturate institutional environments. As all three accounts suggest, writing group members may have little to guide them in exploring the rhetorical work 'grammar and stuff' are to perform in the written work as a whole, let alone the rhetorical situatedness of the work that shapes decisions about such textual choices. Or they may miss opportunities to have their thinking pushed, which arguably, of course, is what academic knowledge work is all about.

Conclusion

As the experiences shared in this chapter indicate, writing groups in many ways respond to traditional arhetorical cultures of writing in institutions where writing is assumed to be merely a generic skill—an assumption that stifles dialogue to explore the research cultures, discourses and genres in which writing is situated and shaped. Accordingly, doctoral writing groups emerge as efforts of 'trying to write stuff' under difficult conditions where writing is regularly 'squeezed out.'

This institutional situatedness of doctoral writing groups has a number of implications for those of us tasked with facilitating them. First and foremost, the student experiences in many ways strengthen the main argument of this book: that approaches to research writing in doctoral education must be research-led to help students understand why they find themselves in the situations they do; how research writing works to produce particular kinds of knowledge; what politics are involved; and how writing groups might work to push that knowledge work as well as the sedimented knowledge systems doctoral scholars are entering. In other words, research education and its central activity—writing—must be grounded in research and theory. Clearly, inherited assumptions about writing are no longer tenable.

Second, writing groups may need to be viewed more broadly and more rhetorically, that is, more as situated in the disciplinary locations, politics, communities and relationships that sustain a diverse range of practices and experiences with research writing. We may need to rethink where we look for them, how we support them, and most importantly, how we facilitate them in the locations where disciplinary knowledge-making activities take place. Rather than focusing on creating new writing groups apart from the communities, relationships and disciplinary locations where research writing does its work (that is, rather than grafting them onto research environments), we might work with these communities towards the kinds of research socialities, collaboration, mentoring and research-informed dialogue about writing that facilitate participation in the conversations of those research cultures. If writing groups do need to be created as 'add-on' structures, attention to community and trust building over time, positionalities, and the politics of writing seem to be paramount. Most importantly, it seems that the experiences of doctoral scholars shared here urge us to make sure that the concept of writing groups does not reflect arhetorical, homogenizing and essentializing assumptions about writing as universal. Rather, we need to ensure that writing groups allow for and thrive off the rich diversity of writing practices and experiences in different disciplines and from different positionalities.

Third, and perhaps most importantly, the doctoral student experiences with writing groups shared here urge us to take a step back and to consider the limits and perhaps even possible risks involved in creating doctoral writing groups. As Aitchison (2009) alerts us, despite their rich pedagogical value, 'writing groups cannot be a panacea for the challenges to contemporary research education' (915). Indeed, the doctoral student experiences reported here raise a number of questions. Created under pressure to make doctoral writing happen in institutional cultures that marginalize writing, do writing groups run the risk of becoming *ad hoc*, add-on spaces where doctoral writing is kept apart from the research cultures doctoral scholars are entering? Or can writing groups strengthen the participation of doctoral scholars in the socialities of their research cultures? Do writing groups run the risk of becoming band-aid solutions for the larger systemic institutional problem of lack of attention to writing and arhetorical deficit views of doctoral writing? Or can they serve as critical spaces for re-thinking normalized institutional cultures of research writing where institutional change can be pushed?

Given the rich insights doctoral scholars have shared here, doctoral writing groups most certainly can serve as such critical spaces. However, their experiences also show that such change must be research and theory driven, as well as deeply grounded in understanding the experiences of doctoral scholars, who are most consequentially influenced by institutional cultures of writing. In short, as researchers, supervisors, academic developers and administrators, we have a lot of listening to do; if the accounts of doctoral scholars presented here are any indication, there may be no better, more generative, more inspiring, and more thought-provoking space for doing so than doctoral writing groups.

References

Aitchison, C. (2009) 'Writing groups for doctoral education', *Studies in Higher Education*, 34(8): 905–16.
Aitchison, C. and Lee, A. (2006) 'Research writing: problems and pedagogies', *Teaching in Higher Education*, 11(3): 265–78.

Bawarshi, A. S. and Reiff, M. J. (2010) *Genre: An Introduction to History, Theory, Research, and Pedagogy*, West Lafayette, IN: Parlor Press & WAC Clearinghouse. Available online: http://wac.colostate.edu/books/bawarshi_reiff/ (accessed 14 January 2014).

Bazerman, C. (1988) *Shaping Written Knowledge*, Madison: University of Wisconsin Press.

Bazerman, C. and Prior, P. (2005) 'Genre, disciplinarity, interdisciplinarity', in J. Green, R. Beach, M. Kamil and T. Shanahan (eds) *Multidisciplinary Perspectives on Literacy Research* (2nd edn), Cresskill, NJ: Hampton Press.

Coe, R., Lingard, L. and Teslenko, T. (eds) (2002) *The Rhetoric and Ideology of Genre: Strategies for Stability and Change*, Cresskill, NJ: Hampton Press.

Dias, P., Freedman, A., Medway, P. and Paré, A. (1999) *Worlds Apart: Acting and Writing in Academic and Workplace Contexts*, Mahwah, NJ: Erlbaum.

Green, B. (2005) 'Unfinished business: subjectivity and supervision', *Higher Education Research and Development*, 24(2): 151–63.

Guerin, C., Xafis, V., Doda, D. V., Gillam, M. H., Larg, A. J., Luckner, H., Jahan, N., Widayati, A. and Xu, C. (2013) 'Diversity in collaborative research communities: a multicultural, multidisciplinary thesis writing group in public health', *Studies in Continuing Education*, 35(1): 65–81.

Kamler, B. and Thomson, P. (2006) *Helping Doctoral Students Write: Pedagogies for Supervision*, London: Routledge.

Kirsch, G. (1992) *Women Writing the Academy: Audience, Authority, and Transformation*, Carbondale, IL: Southern Illinois University Press.

Lee, A. & Boud, D. (2003) 'Writing groups, change, and academic identity: research development as local practices', *Studies in Higher Education*, 28(2): 187–200.

—— (2009) 'Framing doctoral education as practice', in D. Boud and A. Lee (eds) *Changing Practices of Doctoral Education*, London: Routledge.

Lee, A and Aitchison, C. (2009) 'Writing for the doctorate and beyond', in D. Boud and A. Lee (eds) *Changing Practices of Doctoral Education*, London: Routledge.

Miller, C. (1984) 'Genre as social action', *Quarterly Journal of Speech*, 70: 151–67.

Paré, A. (2002) 'Genre and identity: individuals, institutions, and ideology', in R. Coe, L. Lingard and T. Teslenko (eds) *The Rhetoric and Ideology of Genre*, Cresskill, NJ: Hampton.

Paré, A., Starke-Meyerring, D. and McAlpine, L. (2011) 'Knowledge and identity work in the supervision of doctoral student writing: shaping rhetorical subjects', in D. Starke-Meyerring, A. Paré, N. Artemeva, M. Horne and L. Yousobova (eds) *Writing in Knowledge Societies*, West Lafayette, IN: Parlor Press and WAC Clearinghouse Online. Available online: http://wac.colostate.edu/ (accessed 14 January 2014).

Starke-Meyerring, D. (2011) 'The paradox of writing in doctoral education: student experiences', in L. McAlpine and C. Amundson (eds) *Supporting the Doctoral Process: Research-based Strategies*, New York: Springer.

Starke-Meyerring, D. and Paré, A. (2011) 'The roles of writing in knowledge societies: questions, exigencies, and implications for the study and teaching of writing', in D. Starke-Meyerring, A. Paré, N. Artemeva, M. Horne and L. Yousobova (eds) *Writing in Knowledge Societies*, West Lafayette, IN: Parlor Press and WAC Clearinghouse. Available online: http://wac.colostate.edu/books/winks/chapter1.pdf (accessed 14 January 2014).

Thaiss, C., Bräuer, G., Carlino, P., Ganobcsik-Williams, L. and Sinha, A. (eds) (2012) *Writing Programs Worldwide: Profiles of Academic Writing in Many Places*, Anderson, SC, and WAC Clearinghouse: Parlor Press. Available onlne: http://wac.colostate.edu/books/wpww/ (accessed 10 January 2014).

Thomson, P. and Kamler, B. (2010) 'It's been said before, and we'll say it again—research *is* writing', in P. Thomson and M. Walker (eds) *The Routledge Doctoral Student's Companion*, London: Routledge.

Turner, J. (2003) 'Academic literacies in post-colonial times: hegemonic norms and transcultural possibilities', *Language and Intercultural Communication*, 3(3): 187–97.

Chapter 6

Transparent transactions
When doctoral students and their supervisors write together

Michelle Maher

Writing for one's discipline, and the mentoring of that writing, are intertwined within the tapestry of doctoral education. Contributing to the published dialogue of one's discipline underpins the transformation from student to scholar. In turn, facilitating that transformation is a defining act of doctoral mentoring. In this chapter, I explore how writing group participation can support the development and mentoring of disciplinary writing in faculty supervisors and their students. I contend that writing groups can provide a protected space within which both students and faculty can feel psychologically safe to make transparent their struggles to write, as well as their strategies for writing success. I situate my exploration of these ideas within a voluntary writing group of novice and advanced students, recent degree recipients, and new and experienced doctoral supervisors associated with a doctoral program in higher education administration at a research-intensive university in the United States. I frame my consideration of disciplinary writer and writer supervisory development using the conceptual lens of cognitive apprenticeship, which 'focuses on intellectual skills and practices ... makes thought visible through formal representations (e.g., writing), and ... expects teachers and learners to think explicitly about what they're doing' (Walker *et al.* 2008: 109).

Our writing group

In contrast to the purposeful development of some writing groups profiled in this book, ours began unexpectedly. Facing a fast approaching deadline, a faculty member decided to devote a full weekend day to writing. During a casual conversation, she spontaneously invited a doctoral student for whom she served as dissertation supervisor to join her at her home to write. Each wrote in relative isolation, in different sections of the house. Discussion over lunch provided an opportunity to share morning writing accomplishments and ideas to counter writing difficulties. At day's end, both were surprised at how much each had accomplished. Focused writing time, coupled with 'real time' dialogue about writing progress and the companionship of a nearby writer boosted productivity.

Informal faculty member discussion around this rather unexpected productivity spurt created spaces for contemplation about writing (and its relative absence) within the doctoral program. Why didn't disciplinary writing, and discussion about it, happen more often? As might be expected at a research-oriented university, high expectations about writing for publication were clearly communicated through annual performance review guidelines. However, in view of ever-expanding teaching and service duties, these guidelines seemed increasingly ill aligned with daily faculty practice. Doctoral students, most of whom were enrolled part-time and employed full-time, also juggled competing obligations associated with work and family. To complicate matters further, many lived and worked a considerable distance from campus. Disciplinary writing, especially writing undertaken for peer-reviewed publication, was not embedded in the programmatic culture for either faculty members or their students.

What if, faculty wondered, the day-long writing productivity of the doctoral member and her student could be replicated on a larger scale? What if, once each month, a different faculty member hosted a day-long writing session for all programmatic faculty and doctoral students? Would anyone attend? If so, would their attendance facilitate or slow their writing progress? Invitations were sent to all program faculty and doctoral students, and soon monthly day-long writing sessions became a regular part of the milieu. Attendance varied, but ranged on average from four to six participants, including both students and faculty. The writing sessions were christened '*Write On!*' to capture and sustain the shared initial enthusiasm. To accommodate a geographically dispersed doctoral student population, session locations rotated throughout the geographic region.

On a scheduled *Write On!* day, participants arrived at the host's home with all personal material needed for a full day of writing. The session officially began with each writer identifying specific writing goals for the day. Our definition of 'writing' was expansive and included not only putting words to paper, but reading relevant literature, a critical precursor to effective disciplinary writing (Boote 2012; Kamler & Thomson 2006; Kiley & Wisker 2009). Data analysis and interpretation were also welcomed activities. Revising written text was honored as a crucial part of the writing process. Lunch was a collective affair during which goal updates were shared over sandwiches, while day's end provided each participant an opportunity to describe their accomplishments and intended next steps. As the routine became familiar, students began volunteering to host writing sessions in their homes.

While *Write On!* served the needs of many faculty and student writers, it did not attract all who were invited. Some faculty and students declined to participate, finding it more comfortable to write without the benefit of companionship. Faculty and students, like all writers, vary in their need for support and accountability during the writing process (Johnson & Mullen 2007), and writing group participants respected the decision of those who did not join them. For students electing to participate, however, the writing group sessions provided specific positive outcomes. As I and two *Write On!* student participants earlier reported (Maher, Fallucca & Mulhern Halasz 2013), students identified the community of peer support networks, faculty interaction, and the ability (and courage) to 'own' the writing group strategy and reproduce it outside of the official writing sessions as distinctive benefits of engagement. In this chapter, I use quotations drawn from data collection for the earlier effort to showcase *Write On!* participants' voices.

Transparency and writing practices

My purpose in this chapter, however, goes beyond recounting our writing group's processes and perceived outcomes. Instead, I seek to explore faculty and student writing group experiences through the lens of cognitive apprenticeship. I select this framework because it provides a robust structure within which to reflect on how the accomplishment of cognitively difficult tasks, such as writing for one's discipline, can be made more transparent to disciplinary novices. I contend that cognitive transparency around the development of disciplinary writers is critical for several reasons. First, the broad context within which disciplinary writing occurs within the everyday practices of doctoral education is riddled with inaccurate and potentially damaging assumptions. For example, students are often expected to be fully formed disciplinary writers upon graduate program entry (Sallee *et al.* 2011). Similarly, supervisors are often expected to be fully informed of writing pedagogies upon joining the faculty post-doctoral graduation, although they usually receive no formal training in this area (Lee & Aitchison 2009).

Second, disciplinary writing is, in a word, difficult, even for those for whom it is 'supposed' to be easy. Wendy Belcher, in her reflections on a decade of teaching writing to graduate students and their faculty supervisors, memorably describes a dinner party conversation with an academic:

> One professor confessed that he could write only if he chained himself to his chair. I said, 'Well, you don't really mean chained,' and he laughed and said, 'No, no, I don't chain myself. I belt myself. Take my belt out of a few loops, thread it through the chair, and buckle back up. Stay there for hours that way.' He must have seen something in my face, because he then added defensively, 'Well, I am British, you know.'
>
> (Belcher 2009: 184)

Given this approach to disciplinary writing, it is not surprising that literature in this area is replete with descriptions of pain and suffering. For example, in their attempt to identify characteristics of the disproportionately few prolific contributors to higher education literature, Hunter and Kuh (1987) observed, 'Like "birthing," the knowledge production process [to produce substantial numbers of publications] is very difficult and sometimes painful...' (456). Doctoral students fare no better. In exploring doctoral students' perceptions of writing,

Aitchison *et al.* (2012) offered the understated finding: 'Overall, strikingly few students spoke about the joy of writing' (4). Further, the difficulty many doctoral students experience as they write is compounded because their faculty supervisors may struggle to articulate their problem-solving strategies around writing, as writing expertise is often automated (Aitchison *et al.* 2010; Paré 2011). Thus, because candid dialogue about the difficulty of disciplinary writing is scarce in the academy, I have found that doctoral students often internalize writing difficulty as their own personal deficit; they begin to believe that they are the *only one* who has *ever* had *this much difficulty* with writing.

Finally, disciplinary differences around the practice of research and writing hold the potential to exacerbate the difficulties noted above. Within science and engineering fields, for example, research activities, and the written account of this research, are likely to be collective endeavours between faculty advisors and their students. Student participation in multiple member research teams of faculty, graduate and undergraduate students, and possibly post-doctoral fellows, is common (Cumming 2009; Parry, 2007; Pole *et al.* 1997). Together, team members represent differing layers of expertise around a communal area of investigation, and as such might serve as a community of practice (Lave & Wenger 1991). Opportunities to ask—and have answered—questions about the research process and writing, a constitutive part of research (Norris & Phillips 2003), are likely abundant. Further, faculty–student co-authorship is a common disciplinary practice in science and engineering doctoral education (Maher *et al.* 2013), allowing for transparency about the writing process throughout the successive iterations of the developing manuscript. Strategies for 'brokering' the communication between editors and writers (Kamler 2010) may be on display as faculty and students collaborate to move the manuscript through the editorial process.

While science and engineering doctoral students often experience research and writing activities as collaborative efforts, doctoral students in other fields, such as education, usually experience these activities in relative isolation (Becher & Trowler 2001). In our department, this isolation was too often reflected in the attrition of students who had completed all degree requirements except a dissertation, mirroring a pattern observed at national level (Nerad & Miller 1996). Students were often left to learn the intricacies of disciplinary writing on their own. Those who were able to complete their dissertation study rarely published from this work, either by themselves or with a faculty co-author.

It was within this setting that the writing group described earlier took hold and flourished. Students and their faculty supervisors were eager for a change to the status quo, and for many, writing group participation facilitated this change. In the following section, I identify and describe 'transparent' writing group practices that appeared to expedite the development of disciplinary writing, and the mentoring of this writing, among our students and faculty. First, however, I provide a brief overview of the cognitive apprenticeship framework that serves as the conceptual underpinning for these practices.

The cognitive apprenticeship model in theory and practice

The cognitive apprenticeship model (Brown *et al.* 1989; Collins *et al.* 1991) was originally applied to the K–12 schooling process. However, it is now increasingly applied to the study of doctoral education (e.g., Austin 2009; Gabrys & Beltechi 2012). Its introduction theoretically advanced the consideration of differences between traditional and cognitive apprenticeships. Traditional apprenticeships, practised from ancient times, provide a mechanism for learning to perform easily observable psychomotor tasks, such as sewing or carpentry. The 'master' first models how the task is accomplished, with the 'apprentice' carefully observing. As Austin (2009) noted, 'The modeling needs to reveal the procedures as well as the 'tricks of the trade' or techniques used in accomplishing the work' (176). Then it is the apprentice's turn to try their hand at the task under the watchful eye of the master, who coaches their efforts through feedback and scaffolds increasingly sophisticated attempts at more difficult parts of the work. Cognitive apprenticeship follows the steps of traditional apprenticeship, but extends these steps to include the steps of articulation and reflection. The master facilitates the apprentice's efforts to articulate their own cognitive processes, and to query, reflect on, and refine these processes as they solve problems related to their cognitive task. Thus, as Walker and his colleagues (2008) note, apprenticeship of this nature is '"cognitive" because it focuses on intellectual skills and practices, because it makes thought visible through formal representations (e.g., writing), and because it expects teachers and learners to think explicitly about what they're doing' (109).

In theory, cognitive apprenticeship is by nature a highly personal and potentially powerful pedagogical strategy. In disciplinary writing practice, however, its power is dependent upon the alignment of many factors. For example, does the faculty supervisor know how to model the development of a piece of disciplinary writing at a level accessible to novice writers? Is the supervisor able to clearly articulate key writing strategies? Given the quickened pace and ever expanding nature of faculty work (Austin & McDaniels 2006; McAlpine & Amundsen 2011), does the novice disciplinary writer receive timely supervisory feedback on writing efforts? Is the supervisory feedback at a level that effectively scaffolds students' attempts at the more difficult parts of disciplinary writing? The list of questions can be continued. Clearly, however, the successful operationalization of cognitive apprenticeship around disciplinary writing is not a given. Thus, I contend that by situating cognitive apprenticeship practices within regularly offered writing sessions, we can more predictably harness their power. In the next section, I describe how the key cognitive apprenticeship practices of modeling, coaching, scaffolding, articulation and reflection were enacted in our writing group, serving to make transparent the process of disciplinary writing.

Modeling

As noted earlier, in fields such as education, disciplinary writing is often undertaken in isolation. While isolation in itself may not inhibit writing progress, it does effectively remove the opportunity to see—literally—others enact their writing practice. In the absence of this opportunity, students (and faculty), especially those new to disciplinary writing, may mythologize others—others are faster, smarter, more organized and better writers than oneself. Conversely, observing others as they write, seeing their struggles and their response to those struggles, and witnessing their 'tricks of the trade' demystifies the writing process. It further opens possibilities for dialogue around disciplinary writing and the mentoring of this writing on several levels.

In our writing group, modeling of disciplinary writing occurred between more and less experienced student writers, faculty and student writers, and more and less experienced faculty writers. Less experienced writers deeply valued being able to see more experienced writers 'in action'. These observations allowed students to visualize themselves as becoming more experienced writers, motivating and encouraging their efforts toward this goal:

> You see the level of intensity with other people, and it is like, 'Oh my gosh, maybe I am not intense enough. Maybe I need to be more intense.

> There is something very important about being in a roomful of people where you can see what they are working on, and you can see that they have gone beyond where you are, and that it is possible. And that they are no different than you are, and they struggle with the same things that you struggle with, but they have managed to get to that next place. And that is *very* important, because then it is no longer theoretical or conceptual, it is very real and concrete and practical. You say to yourself, 'Here is someone who is actually revising their research proposal or writing the analysis of their research work'. It is like, 'Oh, it can really happen'.

> I've had the opportunity to be with students who were in a different place in the program; they were writing the dissertation, and I could see what those research activities looked like. I remember someone who was working on data analysis, and she had most of a dining room table spread out with things. She was talking about her research. That is a place that I will get to. It is fine to hear about it in an abstract way in a class, but it is something else to see in action.

Student writers also appreciated the opportunity to see faculty at work both as writers, and as writing mentors to each other. As students writers recalled:

> It was really important that [faculty] were there [at the writing sessions]. It meant a great deal to me personally to see [faculty] with their own writing

because it gave me a vision of what my life could also be like. I am a practitioner, and I wanted to do a Ph.D. forever. Part of what I had hoped to do is become more of a scholar and researcher, and I didn't know then what that really meant. What does that work look like? And this is something that you can really do and so, honestly, watching [faculty] do that, and be engaged in that process, has been important and helpful for me.

I returned to school after almost twenty years in the fields of student affairs and academic affairs. I came back because I felt like I didn't have the research tools. I didn't have the skills to know what sort of research I should be doing in my practical life as an academic advisor, a student affairs professional. So *Write On!* sessions were a great way to see. In fact, at a writing session, a faculty member who hosted had another faculty member, a newer professor, who was there. The two of them had been collaborating on a national research paper, so they were there together meeting talking about their progress. Just to see; hey, that's really interesting.

More experienced student writers, some now doctoral recipients, were cognizant of their roles as writing models. As one recent doctoral recipient recounted:

I am still writing. I didn't just write my dissertation and say, 'Done! I am never going to do any writing ever again'. That sets an example that once you are done, you should continue to write and get stuff out there.

Coaching and scaffolding

Beyond the opportunity to observe others' disciplinary writing in action, our writing group provided the context within which novice writers could hone their skills in a psychologically safe environment. Questions about disciplinary writing that might have remained unasked in other contexts could be posed within our writing group:

The students who participated in *Write On!* sessions were the ones I turned to when I had questions. I'm not sure I would have been comfortable asking those questions of others.

Even though it is a set of individualized journeys, we're all in it together. You can bounce something off each other. You realize that someone else had the same question or same problem and it is not a big deal.

Feedback, a key component of coaching and scaffolding, was abundantly shared between student writers. Comments such as, 'We could break for lunch and be able to give each other feedback' and 'We talked at lunch and got ideas from other people' were common in their descriptions of writing group activities. It seemed particularly salient to students that they could receive immediate peer feedback on writing questions and concerns:

> It was helpful for me to know that people were at different phases of this [dissertation writing process], and if at any moment you wanted to ask someone something, you could, and I did, and it was awesome. You got immediate feedback, you had an immediate conversation, and you got yourself immediately unplugged or out of a bottle neck that you had been in with an issue or a topic, and it was very freeing, from that respect.
>
> When you are doing it [writing] alone, it's in such an isolated fashion. You didn't have anybody to bounce ideas off of. Faculty are really busy. I would email them and they would email me back and I would get a little feedback. With the writing sessions, you get feedback right there. You are around people who were going through the same kind of stuff. That made writing seem like it was doable, when before it was like, 'I don't know if I'll ever climb this mountain'.

Other students found that sharing their own writing struggles with peers served to scaffold their writing development:

> I think that working with other students and sharing ideas with them enabled me to expand my ideas. Sometimes, it opened my mind a little bit. I think sometimes I get into a box, *per se*, about the way that things had to be done or written. In talking to other students, that helped me get out of that. In terms of exchanging ideas, and I think that is how it helped me the most.
>
> I was really struggling at first with how to introduce the study, and a student said, 'Well, forget about that. Why don't you start with your lit review? You have to figure out who is out there, who is doing what anyway'. So I stopped stressing about chapter one, although that is not what the textbook said to do, and I worked on finding authors and a good solid review of the literature. I got that from a conversation I had with someone at *Write On!* who was having the same problem with not knowing where and how to start. She said, 'Well, this is what I did, and it seems to be working for me, and I think when you do your lit review and begin to review the literature, it is going to give you the foundation you need for chapter one' and I went, 'Yes, that makes sense. It doesn't have to be happening in any particular order; do what works best for you'.

Student writers of all experience levels valued the opportunity to receive immediate faculty feedback:

> I would get written feedback from my faculty supervisor, but at the writing session, I could converse with her about it. So I could say, 'Right here you said this, but what did you mean?' So I think that really helped me shape my writing.

> It was productive to be able to sit down with faculty and focus on a particular section that needed revision, or questions that needed honing. It was definitely constructive in terms of being able to progress, keeping inching forward. I think that was helpful in teaching me that having a community of people who are in the same situation is really helpful, because you sometimes progress through things that can be isolating.

Articulation and reflection

Writing group participation also provided ample opportunity for students to articulate their thinking to peers and faculty. It allowed students to query, reflect on and refine their thinking as they solved problems related to their disciplinary writing. For example, one student recounted:

> We would support each other and, when necessary, we would give recommendations like, 'Do you really want to do that? Are you sure?' We would say to each other, 'This is what I'm doing, does it make sense to you?'

The ability to clearly articulate the cognitive processes underlying disciplinary writing was typically seen only in more experienced disciplinary writers. Novice writers grappled to find a topic of interest and to determine if or how possible topics fit their nascent professional identity. Once an initial commitment was made to a topic, writers were consumed by exploring the literature to determine where they could meaningfully add to the disciplinary dialogue. Questions of dissertation manuscript form and function usually followed. It was not until writers had a firm grasp of the relevant literature and a reasonable sense of their study's purpose and structure that they felt confident posing and responding to questions such as, 'Do you really want to do that? Are you sure?' However, the practice of articulation and reflection, though perhaps enacted mainly by experienced writers, was beneficial to all writers. Observing more experienced writers respond to these probing questions served to sharpen and deepen novice writers' reflections on the developing written account of their study.

Closing reflections

As I reflect on my characterization of our writing group and participant interactions offered above, I realize it touches on interconnected issues of the role of mentoring and of power relationships in the creation of disciplinary writers. In this writing group, relationships among faculty and students were horizontalized (Boud & Lee 2005) to a greater extent than typically occurs within an academic context. In terms of doctoral supervisor–student mentoring, this type of relationship presents both benefits and, possibly, limitations. Doctoral supervision, especially around writing, is often regarded as a 'private pedagogical space' (Manathunga 2005: 17). It is entirely possible that writing sessions such as ours would have failed to evolve as they did had one or more associated faculty felt threatened by the flattening of power relationships around the 'private pedagogical space'. Further, it is entirely possible that our writing sessions would have failed to evolve as they did had students not shown the level of maturity and earnestness that they abundantly did. In terms of cognitive apprenticeship, the lines between 'master' and 'apprentice' were lightly drawn.

However, given that the creation of disciplinary writing has the power to unleash many emotional responses, not every participant interaction within writing groups, horizontalized or otherwise, will always be positive. Writing groups, like all human groups, are organic entities. In general, their behavioral patterns derive from the actions, interactions and reactions of group members. We were lucky that *Write On!* and *Mini Write!* sessions were mostly free of the many issues that can erupt when people congregate. Going forward, to rely less on luck and to model the creation and maintenance of positive writing group norms, our writing groups will hold up-front, candid discussions of 'ground rules'. Ground rule discussions will explore topics such as appropriate feedback content and delivery, sensitivity to others' writing struggles and clarification of appropriate topics to scaffold writing progress. These focused discussions can not only deter possible problems, but strengthen our reflection on the process of creating both text and identities as writers. Further, as a peer reviewer of this chapter suggested, I plan to entice writing group members to follow a blog on disciplinary writing, or even collectively review one of the many excellent books available on disciplinary writing, such as Kamler and Thompson's (2006) *Helping Doctoral Students Write* or Aitchison, Kamler and Lee's (2010) *Publishing Pedagogies for the Doctorate and Beyond*. Every offering of these writing groups provides opportunities for exploration and improvement.

This chapter explored the use of a student and faculty writing group through the lens of cognitive apprenticeship. While students and faculty pursued individual writing activities, together they created a community in which the often tacit cognitions and private actions underpinning disciplinary writing became transparent. In the process, students and faculty writing practices served as visible models, exposing the 'tricks of the trade' that demystified the writing process. Additionally, both students and faculty served as writing coaches, providing feedback and scaffolding writing efforts. Finally, the writing group prompted students and faculty to articulate and reflect upon the cognitive processes underlying disciplinary writing.

In closing, I suggest that these student and faculty writing groups offer a way to conceptualize the cognitive apprenticeship of disciplinary writing writ large by underscoring the practice of 'cascading mentoring' proposed by Golde and colleagues (2009). Cascading mentoring, originally conceptualized in a research lab setting, occurs when 'post-doctoral fellows mentor senior graduate students, senior graduate students mentor junior graduate students, and junior graduate students mentor undergraduates' (Golde *et al.* 2009: 57). Cascading mentoring or multiple mentoring easily applied to our writing group interactions, in which senior faculty mentored junior faculty and more experienced student writers mentored their less experienced peers. However, in a true horizontalized cognitive apprenticeship, the cascade flows both ways. As a participant in these writing groups, I mentored and was mentored, as is common in life's most rewarding undertakings.

References

Aitchison, C., Kamler, B. and Lee, A. (2010) 'Introduction: why publishing pedagogies?', in C. Aitchison, B. Kamler and A. Lee (eds) *Publishing Pedagogies for the Doctorate and Beyond*, New York: Routledge.

Aitchison, C., Catterall, J., Ross, P. and Burgin, S. (2012) '"Tough love and tears": learning doctoral writing in the sciences', *Higher Education Research & Development*, 31(4): 435–47.

Austin, A. E. (2009) 'Cognitive apprenticeship theory and its implications for doctoral education: a case example from a doctoral program in higher and adult education', *International Journal for Academic Development*, 14(3): 173–83.

Austin, A. E. and McDaniels, M. (2006) 'Preparing the professoriate of the future: graduate student socialization for faculty roles', in J. C. Smart (ed.) *Higher Education: Handbook of Theory and Research*, Dordrecht: Springer.

Becher, T. and Trowler, P. (2001) *Academic Tribes and Territories: Intellectual Inquiry and the Culture of Disciplines* (2nd edn), Buckingham, UK: Open University Press.

Belcher, W. L. (2009) 'Reflections on ten years of teaching writing for publication to graduate students and junior faculty', *Journal of Scholarly Publishing*, 40(2): 184–200.

Boote, D. N. (2012) 'Learning from the literature: some pedagogies', in A. Lee and S. Danby (eds) *Reshaping Doctoral Education: International Approaches and Pedagogies*, New York: Routledge.

Boud, D. and Lee, A. (2005) 'Peer learning as pedagogic discourse for research education', *Studies in Higher Education*, 30(5): 501–16.

Brown, J. S., Collins, A. and Duguid, P. (1989) 'Situated cognition and the culture of learning', *Educational Researcher*, 18(1): 32–42.

Collins, A., Brown, J. S. and Holum, A. (1991) 'Cognitive apprenticeship: making things visible', *American Educator: The Professional Journal of the American Federation of Teachers*, 15(3): 6–11, 38–46.

Cumming, J. (2009) 'The doctoral experience in science: challenging the current orthodoxy', *British Educational Research Journal*, 35(6): 877–90.

Gabrys, B. J. and Beltechi, A. (2012) 'Cognitive apprenticeship: the making of a scientist', in A. Lee and S. Danby (eds) *Reshaping Doctoral Education: Instructional Approaches and Pedagogies*, New York: Routledge.

Golde, C. M., Conklin Bueschel, A., Jones, L. and Walker, G. E. (2009) 'Advocating apprenticeship and intellectual community: lessons from the Carnegie Initiative on the Doctorate', in R. G. Ehrenberg and C. V. Kuh (eds) *Doctoral Education and Faculty of the Future*, Ithaca, NY: Cornell University Press.

Hunter, D. E. and Kuh, G. D. (1987) 'The "Write Wing": characteristics of prolific contributors to the higher education literature', *The Journal of Higher Education*, 58(4): 443–62.

Johnson, W. B. and Mullen, C. A. (2007) *Write to the Top! How to Become a Prolific Academic*, New York: Palgrave Macmillan.

Kamler, B. (2010) 'Revise and resubmit: the role of the publication brokers', in C. Aitchison, B. Kamler and A. Lee (eds), *Publishing Pedagogies for the Doctorate and Beyond*, New York: Routledge.

Kamler, B. and Thomson, P. (2006) *Helping Doctoral Students Write*, New York: Routledge.

Kiley, M. and Wisker, G. (2009) 'Threshold concepts in research education and evidence of threshold crossing', *Higher Education Research and Development*, 28(4): 431–41.

Lave, J. and Wenger, E. (1991) *Situated Learning: Legitimate Peripheral Participation*, Cambridge: Cambridge University Press.

Lee, A. and Aitchison, C. (2009) 'Writing for the doctorate and beyond', in D. Boud and A. Lee (eds), *Changing Practices of Doctoral Education*, New York: Routledge.

McAlpine, L. and Amundsen, C. (2011) *Doctoral Education: Research-Based Strategies for Doctoral Students, Supervisors and Administrators*, Dordrecht: Springer.

Maher, M., Fallucca, A. C. and Mulhern Halasz, H. (2013) 'Write On! through to the PhD: using writing groups to facilitate doctoral degree progress', *Studies in Continuing Education*, 35(2): 193–208.

Maher, M., Timmerman, B. E., Feldon, D. F., Strickland, D. C. (2013) 'Factors affecting the occurrence of faculty–doctoral student coauthorship', *Journal of Higher Education*, 84(1): 121–43.

Manathunga, C. (2005) 'The development of research supervision: turning the light on in a private space', *International Journal for Academic Development*, 10(1): 17–30.

Nerad, M. and Miller, C. M. (1996) 'Increasing student retention in graduate and professional programs', in J. G. Haworth (ed.) *Assessing Graduate and Professional Education: Current Realities, Future Prospects*, San Francisco, CA: Jossey-Bass.

Norris, S. P. and Phillips, L. M. (2003) 'How literacy in its fundamental sense is central to scientific literacy', *Science Education*, 87: 224–40.

Paré, A. (2011) 'Speaking of writing: supervisory feedback and the dissertation', in L. McAlpine and C. Amundsen (eds) *Doctoral Education: Research-based Strategies for Doctoral Students, Supervisors and Administrators*, Dordrecht: Springer.

Parry, S. (2007) *Disciplines and the Doctorate*, Dordrecht: Springer.

Pole, C. J., Sprokkereef, A., Burgess, R. G. and Lakin, E. (1997) 'Supervision of doctoral students in the natural sciences: expectations and experiences', *Assessment and Evaluation in Higher Education*, 22(1): 49–63.

Sallee, M., Hallett, R. and Tierney, W. (2011) 'Teaching writing in graduate school', *College Teaching*, 59(2): 66–72.

Walker, G. E., Golde, C., Jones, L., Conklin Bueschel, A. and Hutchings, P. (2008) *The Formation of Scholars: Rethinking Doctoral Education for the Twenty-first Century*, San Francisco, CA: Jossey-Bass.

Chapter 7

Doctoral students create new spaces to write

Rowena Murray

Introduction

The thinking for this chapter started with my eavesdropping on conversations among doctoral students. I heard them talking about how they were going to continue writing after retreats. We always have semi-formal conversations about this at the end of the retreats, and I began to notice that students were arranging to meet to write after retreats, sometimes continuing to meet regularly for months and years. Many of them attended multiple retreats and organized mini-retreats (a day or half-day) between retreats.

Drawing on doctoral students' accounts, this chapter describes how they adapted practices learned at structured writing retreats to work in 'micro-groups' (groups of five or less). They met to write in a range of settings and at different times. In these micro-groups they not only produced writing but also constructed writing practices. This was not about creating one writing space; instead, students were developing the capacity to construct a range of different spaces for writing.

This chapter provides a new twist in the debate about writing groups and retreats (Aitchison 2009; Lee & Boud 2003; MacLeod *et al.* 2012; Moore 2008; Murray & Moore 2006; Murray 2013; Murray *et al.* 2012): it describes the capacity for constructing diverse writing spaces that provide coherence for doctoral writing and argues that this may be less about the 'spaces' where students write and more about the people with whom they choose to write.

This chapter begins by describing what micro-groups do, then explores an emerging theme of coherence, in terms of the behavioural, cognitive and social coherence that writing micro-groups bring: behavioural coherence in terms of consistency in the act of writing, cognitive coherence in terms of focus and concentration, and social coherence from writing in groups that accept and thereby sustain the behavioural and cognitive framework. Finally, this chapter concludes that micro-groups are associated with the experience of coherence in writing, which, in turn, can sustain a disposition towards writing. I argue that developing the capacity to write in many different spaces should be an important component of doctoral pedagogy (Aitchison *et al.* 2010; Murray 2011).

It started with structured writing retreat

The structured writing retreat model involves writing for fixed periods of time (Murray & Moore 2006; Murray & Newton 2009). In this 'typing pool' model, everyone writes in the same room, and there are short discussions to set and review writing goals. Participants are usually from different disciplines, and a facilitator (who is also writing) keeps the group to the program (Murray *et al.* 2012). In response to participants' feedback, the program has been adapted, so that there are a few minor changes from previous published versions.

Structured writing retreat program

Day 1

5.00–5.30pm	Introductions, writing warm up, writing plans
5.30–6.30	Writing

Day 2

9.15–9.30am	Discussion: planning and goal setting
9.30–11.00	Writing
11.00–11.30	Break
11.30–12.30	Writing
12.30–1.30	Lunch
1.30–3.00	Writing
3.00–3.30	Break
3.30–5.30	Writing

Day 3

9.15–9.30am	Discussion: planning and goal setting
9.30–11.00	Writing
11.00–11.30	Break
11.30–12.30	Writing
12.30–1.30	Lunch
1.30–3.00	Writing
3.00–3.30	Break
3.30–4.00	Taking stock of outputs and outcomes, new goals

The benefits of this model are that it makes writing the primary task, prevents anti-task behaviour and contains writing-related anxiety (MacLeod *et al.* 2012). Participants say they are more focused, creative and productive at structured writing retreats than in other environments. For doctoral students there are potential benefits in exposing writing-in-progress, comparing writing experiences and concepts and developing conversations with others who are engaged in writing (Murray & Newton 2009). However, the potential for taking practices learned at a retreat into other spaces, and thereby extending its benefits, is often limited (MacLeod *et al.* 2012; Murray & Cunningham 2011).

During breaks and free time in the retreat program and at final review sessions between 3.30 and 4.00 at the end of retreats, participants spontaneously began to arrange meetings to continue writing after retreats. They planned to use the structured retreat program, or segments of it, to construct a range of different writing sessions: an hour, 90 minutes, a half day or full day, at different times of the day and in many different places. While they did not always use the same timeslot, they always wrote with the same people, drawing on the pool of people who had attended structured writing retreats. This could, therefore, be seen as a spin-off of structured retreat—micro-groups of writers, regularly meeting in all sorts of spaces and making progress with their theses outside of retreat and away from departments.

Because this was happening so regularly (as far as I could tell from recurring conversations), and because the micro-groups seemed to be working so well (as far as I could tell from reports of outputs, doctoral completions and growing confidence in the ability to produce writing), I decided to find out more about these micro-groups. What exactly were they doing? How were they using the structured writing retreat approach? Did all the micro-groups work in the same way, or were they different? If so, why? How did they relate micro-groups to other writing spaces?

Gathering information from/on micro-groups

I emailed four questions to 35 people I had heard talking about meeting to write after retreat, most of whom were doctoral students. I focused on subjects I had heard them discussing and explained that I would write about their responses for this chapter.

> I'm doing some research on writers' groups for a chapter I'm writing for an edited collection called *Writing Groups for Doctoral Education and Beyond: Innovations in Practice and Theory*. If you have a few minutes, can you tell me how you use writing groups?
>
> 1 How would you describe what you do? How often do you meet? Where? Always with the same people? How many? Always for the same amount of time?
> 2 How do you describe what you do to other people who are not in writing groups?
> 3 What do you like most about writing in groups? What do you like least?
> 4 Is writing different when you write in a group, even in a group of 2 or 3 people?

I know some of you use groups to extend the retreat effect, and some use retreat timeslots in your groups—OK to talk about retreats too. Similarly, many of you are writing articles and theses—again, OK to talk about both.

The thirty who responded were from seven universities: Cambridge, Lancaster, Open University, Strathclyde, Swinburne (Australia), West of Scotland and York St John—a mix of mostly pre- and a few post-1992 universities. There was a relatively broad spectrum of disciplines—Arts, Business, Education, Humanities, Politics, Science and Social Work—and career stages—12 early-career (0–5 years), 16 mid-career (5–10 years) and 2 late-career (10+ years). They worked in a range of academic positions (17), and 13 were in academic posts, studying for part-time doctorates: 12 students, 17 academic/research staff and 1 other. Doctoral students accounted for the majority: 25 were doing a PhD or EdD when they started using micro-groups. These respondents were, therefore, relatively representative of UK doctoral students, except for an imbalance in gender—24 females, 6 males—although this is the norm for writing retreats. Respondents' characteristics are set out in Table 7.1. In the following sections, numbers after quotations denote the individual respondents listed in the table.

Table 7.1 Micro-group respondents' characteristics

Respondent	Gender	Discipline	Career stage	Job, PhD/EdD
1	Male	Business	Mid	Lecturer, PhD
2	Female	Science	Mid	Lecturer, PhD
3	Female	Business	Early	PhD
4	Female	Education	Mid	Lecturer, PhD
5	Female	Arts	Mid	PhD
6	Female	Social Sciences	Early	Tutor, PhD
7	Female	Science	Early	PhD
8	Female	Business	Mid	Senior Lecturer
9	Male	Business	Mid	Lecturer, PhD
10	Male	Education	Late	Professor
11	Female	Business	Mid	Lecturer, PhD
12	Female	Education	Mid	Lecturer, PhD
13	Female	Business	Mid	Lecturer, PhD
14	Male	Social Sciences	Mid	Lecturer
15	Female	Arts	Early	PhD

(Continued)

Table 7.1 (Continued)

Respondent	Gender	Discipline	Career stage	Job, PhD/EdD
16	Female	Business	Early	PhD
17	Female	Business	Early	PhD
18	Male	Education	Early	PhD
19	Female	Education	Late	Senior Lecturer
20	Female	Education	Early	PhD
21	Female	Business	Mid	PhD
22	Female	Social Sciences	Mid	Lecturer, PhD
23	Female	Business	Mid	Lecturer, PhD
24	Female	Education	Mid	Lecturer, PhD
25	Female	Business	Early	PhD
26	Male	Business	Early	PhD
27	Female	Education	Mid	—
28	Female	Arts	Early	PhD
29	Female	Social Sciences	Early	Lecturer, PhD
30	Female	Science	Early	PhD

What do micro-groups do?

There is no one answer to this question. There was no one mode that all micro-groups used. The following response from one participant shows the range of writing times and spaces across this group:

> I have written in groups in a range of settings: I have attended formal writing retreats of between 8 and 14 people writing for 10 hours across 2 days with a preparation evening beforehand. Writing groups in my academic department, meeting occasionally on a pre-planned basis to write for a half- or full day. Writing days at colleagues' houses, again writing for around 5 hours. Paired-writing sessions for pre-determined times, writing in a room in a colleague's department. Coffee shop sessions meeting for 60–90 minutes at the beginning of a day. (1)

These time periods were spent writing: 'Two of us meet regularly (fortnightly if we can) for 3 hours (ideally we do two slots of writing—first we set out our objectives and then we write)' (21).

In addition to these accounts of different micro-group sessions, there were accounts of how these were combined to produce a thesis:

> I used the organized writer's retreats to write up my entire doctoral thesis. During a period of 18 months I attended nine of these 2 and ½ day retreats. These took place at locations commutable from Glasgow, however far enough away to prevent any distractions from home. The groups of students who attended these retreats were very varied, with none of them coming from the same background as myself … Off the back of these writer's retreats I got to know other writers who were keen to continue the retreat structure back home. I met up with 1 other writer on approximately 4 occasions outside the organised retreats to do more structured writing. On one occasion we met in a coffee shop. We kept to the retreat timetable. (7)

All the micro-groups used the same approach of pre-determining a timeslot, defining writing goals for that time and spending most of the time writing. Most micro-groups wrote at different times and in different places, while a minority used the same time: 'Meet fortnightly at the same time for a 90 minute slot' (10).

While times and places varied, membership remained constant. With one exception, they always wrote with the same people: '[I am] better focused with fewer distractions. I seem to be able to sustain writing far better, even with only one other person' (10). The presence of even one other person who is writing and who has signed up to this approach is therefore part of the micro-group effect.

By contrast, such detailed, regular discussions of writing were not occurring in their academic and professional settings:

> No one else in my department talks about writing practices. They all present themselves as over pressured and far too busy to write … this can't be the case as they are all publishing. But writing practice is denied and not shared. (8)

Denial of the act of writing has featured in many discussions among retreat participants over the years. This was why I asked participants about how they described writing in micro-groups to others who did not write in this way. A typical answer was, 'I pretty much don't. It's like a secret activity' (8).

This is not new. There are accounts of academics and professionals feeling they have to 'sneak writing in' to their workplaces or 'not advertise the fact that [they were] writing' (Murray & Newton 2008: 31). Absurd as this may seem—that writing is not discussed in universities—it does seem to be the norm. The implications for doctoral students' writing are worth considering.

Analysis

In my initial reading of the responses I noticed that respondents had strong feelings of community, as was to be expected, in micro-group writing, so this was the starting point for my analysis. However, while recent analyses of structured writing retreats focused on communities of practice and containment theories, in this analysis I wanted to represent the diversity of practices being used. Yes, respondents were all using a version of the structured retreat program, but they were doing so in different ways. Yes, they were all happily sitting writing in silence, but they were finding ways to sustain this practice for themselves, a practice that was not generally supported by their departments or disciplines. In some instances, the practice was challenged, or, equally powerfully, there was an expectation of challenge, criticism or scepticism about writing in this way.

As I began to analyse what respondents said about micro-groups and their benefits, it seemed to me that there was something more profound going on. Micro-groups brought continuity to writing:

> In my institution I found that writing groups were an extension of the practices from writing retreat. This helped me to continue with writing all year round so I did not see retreats as isolated events ... writing groups bring continuity and discipline ... so you keep going with the writing even when you can't see the light at the end of the tunnel. (4)

I began to focus on this idea of 'continuity' in terms of coherence and connectedness, key concepts in current public health debates that have relevance for the development of research communities and activity (Greater Glasgow Centre for Population Health 2011; Murray 2012). Public health literature argues that connectedness is a key component of health and wellbeing, and there are potential links to doctoral students' experiences of micro-groups.

Having seen the importance respondents attached to community and connectedness, I decided to focus on the concept of coherence. In order to explore this further, I broke it down into three components—behavioural coherence, cognitive coherence and social coherence—and used these for further thematic analysis. The next three sections explore these themes.

Behavioural coherence

The framework of fixed timeslots that micro-groups use was identified as a key factor in developing writing capacity. They described it as organized and even 'regimented' (20), with intended associations of predictability (rather than of following orders). This structure was one of the features respondents liked most. It created dedicated writing time, collective energy, focus and discipline, as long as everyone agreed to be 'held' by the structure. What they liked least were distractions from others who had not fully bought into the model, who spent more time talking about writing than doing it, and that writing in this way could be exhausting.

The impact of fixed timeslots was expressed in terms of specific writing behaviours: 'Formalized starts and finishes are really important' (1); 'the holding of the boundaries ... (i.e. not stopping to procrastinate, stopping to take a proper break, etc.)' (22); 'Normally we start at 9.30 and write for 1 hour and half then break of 30 mins and then another hour and half' (25). This could be seen as a kind of conditioning—in the sense of writers learning to behave in particular ways—as they write regularly in these ways. Micro-group members defined their own writing goals and monitored their own writing achievements—no one did this for them. Although they did some of this work in discussions with others who were writing, there was no surveillance of practices or outputs. In this way, they learned to set goals for real-time periods. This is how they began to develop self-regulation in their writing.

Privileging the act of writing in this way established and sustained a kind of behavioural coherence:

> The structure of the group acts as a physical barrier to distractions. Sticking with the writing process, not being distracted, not checking emails, not looking up references on the internet are all part of the process of writing in a group. As a result, because the threats of disengagement with writing are largely removed, the writer is only left with their writing, and even though it is sometimes difficult, by sticking with and staying with the writing process, epistemological clarity does emerge. (14)

Micro-groups may therefore create behavioural coherence, not in the sense of modelling behaviours, but by providing continuity in writing moments. They provide a 'framework of guided activity sessions' (5), with different increments of time, rather than a uniform timeslot for each session:

> I used retreats to freewrite chapters of my thesis and found I could get to a first draft at retreat which I'd then amend and edit over 3 or 4 group writing days and I used this model for 4 of my thesis chapters. (23)

These behaviours became rituals for some: 'I also like to observe certain rituals when writing (same seat, same music [on headphones]) and having the same colleagues allows these to be supported' (1). These rituals seem to have developed over a series of structured writing retreats and micro-group meetings. In this way, writing can become 'habitual … [with] rules … discipline' (1), with the word 'discipline' appearing in many responses. The micro-groups, wherever they were, whenever they met, created a 'writing environment … dedicated time' (2). They were 'organized and directed … a structure around something that … has been a little difficult to get started' (3).

For some, this also provided a framework for solitary writing: 'Sometimes after our weekly writing meeting I book a room on another day and write on my own' (25); 'It also strengthens the capacity to write at an individual level (when alone)' (11); 'I regularly use [these] techniques when writing at home and set an alarm to go off after an hour' (5).

Many stressed the importance of having, or making 'protected space to write' (22). When this was available, it changed the experience of writing: 'generating the flow state ... mindfulness ... intoxicating sense of group energy which normally arises in the room' (9); 'a writing disposition' (4); 'collective discipline ... necessary, but not oppressive, degree of pressure on me' (10); 'focus and persistence, pushing on with the writing' (12).

References to the impact of the many distractions from writing in academic and professional workplaces and home environments are standard in the literature on writing (Mayrath 2008), but micro-groups provided a way quickly and regularly to 'unplug' from distractions. Not only were distractions removed, but also 'the threats' of distractions and 'disengagement with writing' (14) were avoided. Moreover, in this mode, it was possible to achieve the 'epistemological clarity' (14) needed for writing. This is not to say that writing was unproblematic: 'it is still sometimes difficult' (14).

There was, therefore, a group effect here, as is to be expected, but it was not achieved through much in the way of discussion or sharing of writing—since these were given little or no time in micro-groups—but through the act of communal writing.

Writing with others in these micro-groups supported the process of goal setting for writing. There were many references to goal setting, making writing incremental, legitimizing it, experiencing incremental productivity, reinforcing motivation to write and to create dedicated writing time: 'it is not just writing in a group or with others that is important to me, but the commitment to keep to dedicated writing without distractions' (7). This suggests that the model may be as important, or, for some, more important, than the group effect, although it is the group effect that sustains the model.

Micro-groups can bring behavioural coherence to writing in the sense that they make the act of writing consistent. Writers can create this coherence for themselves. This not only replicates the effect of structured retreat, but also extends it to the spaces they construct and maintain.

Cognitive coherence

Cognitive coherence is a term I am using to capture many respondents' accounts of how micro-groups affected not only their writing, but also their thinking—by which I mean both their thinking about writing and their thinking about the subjects of their writing, their doctoral research projects and theses.

Micro-group writing was described as intense, focused and enjoyable: 'I feel more concentrated' (29). Their confidence was boosted—'Confidence gained from discussions with others about writing and PhD issues' (16)—but that was less about giving and/or receiving feedback on writing (as in other doctoral writing groups) than about generating text. Privileging writing over other tasks meant that they did not have to think about giving and receiving critiques, valuable as they have been shown to be for doctoral students (Caffarella & Barnett 2000). In addition to concentration, focus, intensity and energy, there were 'unexpected spin-offs in my own thinking' (12), 'focusing the brain towards writing as a regular task' (15).

There was also cognitive coherence in the sense that micro-groups gave meaning to writing: 'you feel as though you and those around you are engaged in the same endeavour. This makes it a bit easier to feel as though what you are doing has meaning and is mutually beneficial' (18). Writing in a micro-group added meaning to the group itself: 'the sense that this is the right thing to be doing at this time in the company of these particular people. The shared practice gives it a kind of legitimacy' (19).

This was associated with positive emotions: 'Writing in a group removes the associated self-pity I often experience, which in itself acts as a writer's block. It changes my emotions associated with the task from being negative to more positive ones' (7); '[Writing] seems easier and more enjoyable' (11). While we know that structured writing retreats can reduce writing-related anxiety (MacLeod *et al.* 2012), these accounts of micro-groups suggest that not only can this retreat effect be transferred to other settings—which previous studies suggested was unlikely (Murray & Cunningham 2011)—but it may also bring cognitive coherence during periods when students are not writing in that it 'stops you spending unproductive time worrying about not writing' (1), which may have a positive effect on students' wellbeing.

Micro-groups, therefore, seem to have worked on cognitive coherence for these students by making writing meaningful—the act of writing was meaningful in these groups. They were free of review and critique, though aware that these were to come. This is not to say that these writers were naïve; they were fully aware of the many reviews and revisions that would follow their micro-group writing.

Social coherence

> People arriving late or leaving early can really break up your concentration and the cohesiveness of the group. (1)

Micro-groups created social coherence in the sense that they provided people with colleagues who accepted the behavioural and cognitive framework; indeed, social coherence may be the most important component of the framework.

The concept of social cohesion originates in the observation that, for all the variation in writing spaces and times across all these micro-groups, there was almost no variation in the composition of the groups: all but one said they always worked in micro-groups with the same people. Most had five or six colleagues with whom they wrote in different groupings, at different times and in different places, and some worked in pairs, always with the same person.

The practice of social coherence began for these respondents with their shared experiences of structured writing retreats. This meant that they did not have to look very far to find others to write with, nor did they, with a few exceptions and after some abortive attempts to include others, have to worry about whether new members would adopt or reject the framework. This cleared mental space for focusing on writing. If that seems too fixed or exclusive—as it surely will to some—it should be noted that respondents were aware of the pros and cons of the fixed composition of their groups. Furthermore, they were aware that writing in spaces outside their departments could be risky, particularly if writing groups and retreats were not valued in their departments, or if discussions of writing were marginalized—in any sense—in their departments.

Respondents' experiences of social coherence can be seen in their many comments about empathy, support, sense of shared responsibility, accountability, companionship, being invested in or committed to the group, the 'collective' (2), respect, trust, 'common experience' (4), like-mindedness (17), camaraderie (23, 24), 'writing relationship' (25), 'positive pressure … positive competition' (25) and fellowship (28). These terms suggest that they developed positive relationships around doctoral writing. Not only were they writing with the same people, but also they were developing a sense that this way of working was coherent and effective.

That this is a very different way of working from the 'norm', for most, was expressed again and again, although many said they still found it difficult to explain to others why using fixed timeslots, and writing with the same people, was so different from writing in other ways. Nevertheless, many felt that they did not need to explain it if they knew it worked for them and if there was visible progress in their writing. This could be seen as, in a sense, creating new norms:

> this isn't just sharing a space together (sharing an office or the like) it needs to be that both are engaged in the group writing ethos—because you create tacit rules and obligations—to show up, to keep to time, to make good use of the time, to be supportive. These norms are powerful and need to be enforced by the group leader or in established groups by the group itself. These keep it as a special time and form of writing. You can't let too much chat creep in or it becomes another time thief. (23)

Some will find these observations obvious—of course you have to have rules and obligations, such as deadlines, for writing; of course we have to make good use of our time and, where we can, be mutually supportive of each other's writing; of course writing, like other professional and academic tasks, must be done in defined and delimited periods of time; of course we should not be chatting when we should be writing—why, then, have other people in the room with you when you write at all? Given that we can all accept every one of these common sense points, why on earth does writing need a 'special' time? Why does it need a 'special' form or a new norm?

The answer to this last question is that micro-groups were, indeed, seen as having a special form, a new norm. Specifically, respondents valued 'the silence and the dynamics' (26), the 'atmosphere of busy productivity' (28) and having a way to make writing continuous rather than episodic or *ad hoc*: 'The thing about talking always with the same person is the feeling of continuity' (26). This, in turn, boosted intrinsic motivation to write:

a positive reinforcing and supportive writing environment and during breaks the opportunity to speak and discuss issues, successes or problems with others is intrinsically motivating for me and helps the writing process. (2)

Social coherence operated as a form of constructive peer pressure in the writing process:

> peer group pressure in the nicest sense that can kick us into action … There's nothing quite like seeing somebody in the room across from you working away to push you into keeping up. (3)

> looking up and seeing other people writing was like doing some team-work, although everyone was working on their own project … I felt 'pulled in' [by others who had been to retreats before and knew how to make best use of them]. (17)

This is not to say that everyone's writing was on view; paradoxically, writing microgroups could be experienced as combining accountability and anonymity—people shared their writing goals, but not their writing: 'in some ways individuals can still remain anonymous in terms of their work/progress' (2).

Exceptionally, one respondent said that the micro-group writing was 'Not always with the same people' (4). Although this person also talked about the value of continuity in writing through participating in micro-groups, that continuity did not seem to come from writing with the same people, unlike all the others who responded to my enquiry. It is not clear how we should account for this exception, but it could be related to this person's recent change in job.

The social coherence of micro-groups was not seen as a constant. People move on:

> Interesting 'cos [others] are into their fourth year. So when they leave I will have to find someone else. And I know from experience this is not always easy. People say they will do it but they can't or don't. Some are prepared to try but find it hard to stick with a whole day of silent writing. (8)

This suggests that there was social coherence around writing in ways that were not completely, for everyone, transferable to departments and disciplines. Microgroups provided 'neutral ground', outside of departments (15) and away from the writer's disciplines: 'Sometimes talking about your work with someone who knows nothing/very little about your topic helps you to see things in a different light' (24). This 'different light' was not so much about discussing other research approaches, for example, or other interpretations of data (since most of these groups did not discuss these topics on a regular basis), but about focusing on the writing component of thinking and researching, which was what all of them focused on in their brief discussions. This was not seen as, and was never likely to become, normal practice in academic departments. Nor did micro-group practice spill over into departmental settings.

There is another sense in which these micro-groups sat outside departments. They also operated outside regulatory processes: they were 'focussed but non-surveillanced (Is there such a word?)' (24). Given the lack of discussion of writing, and the criticism that those who write attract, or the expectation of critique for the act of writing, it is not surprising that those who want to write find other spaces to do so. Each writer will have his or her own take on the extent to which the act of writing is acknowledged and supported in the workplace. Each doctoral student will discover how much or how little their supervisors are willing to talk about the entire thesis writing process. Where writing is not regularly discussed, those who want to write can create these other spaces to discuss writing and other spaces to do their writing.

The components of social coherence are, therefore, relationships (which reinforce and are reinforced by the structured framework), intrinsic motivation (bringing meaning to the act of writing) and the performance of writing in different spaces with the same people. The success of this model, for these respondents, suggests that we should consider the development of the capacity to do academic writing in a range of times and spaces—with other people—as a component of doctoral pedagogy, not only to support thesis writing, but also to develop practices that support work-life balance:

> I make quite a lot of use of social writing. In fact, it is probably the most important component of my academic life, as it enables me to balance a challenging job and busy home life. (1)

It has been argued that most of the literature on developing writing for postgraduates focuses on the 'appropriation of disciplinary discourse conventions' (Rose & McClafferty 2001:27), although others argue that academic writing should create new conventions, new genres and be inclusive of new voices (Kamler & Thomson 2008: 513). Most doctoral courses include some instruction on writing, and often include giving and/or receiving feedback on text, with some focus on 'substance, organization and style' (Klinger *et al.* 2005:14). However, most do not privilege the act of writing over everything else, as happens at structured writing retreats and in writing micro-groups. These micro-groups show that researchers and postgraduates can create and sustain a 'social, situated practice' for their writing (Aitchison & Lee 2006) through 'social writing' experiences at structured writing retreats.

Unlike other doctoral writing groups, there was no one pattern to the work of micro-groups. Unlike some other groups, there was no critiquing of each other's writing (Aitchison 2009). While the micro-groups share some qualities with other groups—community, structure, accountability—they are different from previous models in privileging the act of writing.

These micro-groups could become mechanistic and narrow, or even narrowing. As participants routinize their writing practices, they may fail to extend their range. As they continue to do the work of writing outside the work of their departments or disciplines, they may miss important connections. By working in the margins of disciplinary writing practice, they may marginalize themselves and/or their work.

The micro-groups described in this chapter were built on relationships developed at structured writing retreats. It seems that the spaces that doctoral students create for writing may be both solitary and 'social', but the micro-group model for extending the practices of structured writing retreat suggests that it is relationships between writers that create and hold these writing spaces, sustains motivation to create them and develops confidence in running them.

Conclusion

What we can take from this exploratory study is the beginnings of the evidence—which some say is lacking (Kean 2007: 387)—of the benefits of a self-directed strategy for privileging the act of writing, and that privileging the act of writing in this way can have benefits for doctoral students (and others): developing the capacity to construct a range of different spaces for writing, increasing confidence in the ability to progress and complete a thesis, leading to timely and successful doctoral completions. On the basis of this modest evidence—which gels with other studies of writers' groups—micro-groups should be part of doctoral pedagogy. They are one way for doctoral students to initiate and sustain writing and, for some, this will produce the benefits reported by respondents in this study and theorized in the chapter as coherence.

It may be that those who are comfortable with thinking and talking about specific increments of time for writing—and with planning their writing in terms of specific numbers of minutes, hours, days, weeks and months—are more likely to benefit from this approach. Were they predisposed to working in this way? This is a difficult question to answer on the basis of such a diverse sample and their diverse micro-groups, but perhaps that is what makes it work. Certainly, they all signed up to this model, they all experienced that it 'worked' for their writing and they were all motivated to extend this effect, rather than wait until the next retreat came around.

Some will argue that these respondents exhibited not so much the success of micro-groups as the neediness of doctoral writers and other academic writers who participated in this study. Perhaps doctoral writers will benefit more from this type of mutual support. Perhaps keeping their writing away from the scrutiny of the department and the disciplines is what they need in order to write regularly. Perhaps that could have a downside, for example, if students were to stop seeking feedback on their writing. However, there is some evidence that experienced writers also set up micro-groups after attending structured writing retreats: 'What we have in common is desperation! [Some] to complete their PhDs, me to manage any writing at all and to keep the publications flowing. Or at least going!' (8). This mixture of doctoral and postdoctoral writers—for many years a feature of structured writing retreats—seems to have been carried over into these micro-groups. This is not, therefore, simply a supportive culture for student writing (Clughen & Hardy 2012); it is not only a pedagogy for doctoral students. It may also be a coherent way of practising writing, in the sense that it is a practice that brings coherence to the act of writing. This experience of coherence may be related to students' wellbeing.

By no means is this intended to be the last word on writing micro-groups; this is part of an ongoing discussion with these writers and others who write in this way and in other ways. As we try to understand the 'spaces' that doctoral students create—that they find work or don't work to support their writing and that they continue to use beyond the doctorate—we should continue to explore the specifics of their practices, how they articulate them and how they feel about them. The value of micro-groups is that they are spaces where students can do this exploration for themselves (while also getting on with their writing).

References

Aitchison, C. (2009) 'Writing groups for doctoral education', *Studies in Higher Education*, 34(8): 905–16.

Aitchison, C. and Lee, A. (2006) 'Research writing: problems and pedagogies', *Teaching in Higher Education*, 11(3): 265–78.

Aitchison, C., Kamler, B. and Lee, A. (eds) (2010) *Publishing Pedagogies for the Doctorate and Beyond*, London: Routledge.

Caffarella, R. S. and Barnett, B. G. (2000) 'Teaching doctoral students to become scholarly writers: the importance of giving and receiving critiques', *Studies in Higher Education*, 25: 39–54.

Clughen, L. and Hardy, C. (eds) (2012) *Writing in the Disciplines: Building Supportive Cultures for Student Writing*, Bingley, UK: Emerald.

Greater Glasgow Centre for Population Health (2011) *Asset-based Approaches for Health Improvement: Redressing the Balance*, Glasgow, UK: Greater Glasgow Centre for Population Health.

Kamler, B. and Thomson, P. (2008) 'The failure of dissertation advice books: toward alternative pedagogies for doctoral writing', *Educational Researcher*, 37: 507–14.

Kean, A. (2007) 'Writing for publication: pressures, barriers and support strategies', *Nurse Education Today*, 27(5): 382–8.

Klinger, J. K., Scanlon, D. and Pressley, M. (2005) 'How to publish in scholarly journals', *Educational Researcher*, 34: 14–20.

Lee, A. and Boud, D. (2003) 'Writing groups, change and academic identity: research development as local practice', *Studies in Higher Education*, 28: 187–200.

MacLeod, I., Steckley L. and Murray, R. (2012) 'Time is not enough: promoting strategic engagement with writing for publication', *Studies in Higher Education*, 37(5): 641–54.

Mayrath, M. C. (2008) 'Attributions of productive authors in educational psychology journals', *Educational Psychology Review*, 20(1): 41–56.

Moore, S. (ed.) (2008) *Supporting Academic Writing Among Students and Academics*, SEDA Special 24, London: Staff and Educational Development Association.

Murray, R. (2011) *How to Write a Thesis* (3rd edn), Maidenhead: Open University Press–McGraw-Hill.
—— (2012) '"It's not a hobby": reconceptualizing the place of writing in academic work', *Higher Education*, 66: 79–91.
—— (2013) *Writing for Academic Journals* (3rd edn), Maidenhead, UK: Open University Press–McGraw-Hill.
Murray, R. and Moore, S. (2006) *The Handbook of Academic Writing: A Fresh Approach*, Maidenhead, UK: Open University Press-McGraw-Hill.
Murray, R. and Newton, M. (2008) 'Facilitating writing for publication', *Physiotherapy*, 94: 29–34.
—— (2009) 'Writing retreat as structured intervention: margin or mainstream?', *Higher Education Research and Development*, 28(5): 527–39.
Murray, R. and Cunningham, E. (2011) 'Managing researcher development: "drastic transition"?', *Studies in Higher Education*, 36(7): 831–45.
Murray, R., Steckley, L. and MacLeod, I. (2012) 'Research leadership in writing for publication: a theoretical framework', *British Educational Research Journal*, 38(5): 765–81.
Rose, M. and McClafferty, K. A. (2001) 'A call for the teaching of writing in graduate education', *Educational Researcher*, 30: 27–33.

Chapter 8

Walking the labyrinth
The holding embrace of academic writing retreats

Sally S. Knowles and Barbara Grant

Introduction

While facilitating academic writing retreats, we have sometimes encountered the delights of a labyrinth (see Figure 8.1). When this happens, individuals or groups walk the ancient course (or, in one place, the similarly age-old spiral), captivated by the focusing rhythm of a simple exercise. In this chapter, we explore residential writing retreats for doctoral students and academic staff through the metaphor of the labyrinth. Thinking about our retreats in this way illuminates their dynamics afresh. The metaphor of the labyrinth not only underscores some of the challenges inherent in academic writing, but also reveals more about the rich possibilities the retreats offer for growth and pleasure in academic, especially writerly, identities and for exercising the generosity, kindness and obligation of academic collegiality.

We have facilitated a distinctive model of writing retreats for academic staff and doctoral students, especially women, for over a decade (Grant & Knowles

Figure 8.1 Walking the labyrinth at Jarrahdale, Western Australia.

2000; Grant 2003, 2006). While the retreat model has been relatively constant, and the goal is always to produce a piece of academic writing (for example, a journal article, book or thesis chapter, conference paper, research proposal), we have conducted retreats in many different countries and venues (including institutional and non-institutional, luxury and school-camp style ones) and under different conditions (residential/non-residential, women only/mixed gender, academic staff or students only/mixed staff and students).

Our writing retreats were originally designed specifically with academic women in mind and sought to provide them with a nourishing break from their double lives as academics and domestic workers. The underpinning model was that of the spiritual retreat, which focuses on quiet time for contemplation. In practice, the retreats typically last between three and five days and, with our original goal in mind, our preferred mode is to live in at a venue some distance removed from campus. The program is weighted in favour of quiet time for writing, only broken by a daily workshop on some writing-related topic (typically for about an hour and a half after lunch) and a work-in-progress meeting (typically for an hour after dinner), in which participants take half-hour turns to present their work for discussion to a small group. As facilitators, we are also usually working writers. Our facilitation role is to organize the program and ensure it runs smoothly, to lead the workshops (although often other participants take this role too), sometimes to hold individual consultations with writers and to evaluate the retreats.[1] The group ranges in size from half a dozen up to 20 or so. Funding varies: sometimes institutions (for example, research or equity offices, departments) fund a retreat for their own staff; sometimes participants fund attendance out of their own pockets; sometimes they apply for research-related or professional development-related funds from their institutions. In the case of one long-running retreat in New Zealand, an anonymous donor funds an award to support one woman to attend each retreat.[2] Our philosophy is to run the retreats as economically as possible so that they are seen as sustainable interventions in academic culture. There is a distinctive philosophy around the retreats (explained in more detail in Grant 2003, 2008), which is captured below in the section 'Eight Walls Holding'. We understand the retreats to be somewhat transgressive in that they seek to disrupt the individualistic and competitive tendencies within academia by fostering collaborative, cooperative models of intellectual generosity. We also see them as a slow process of change rather than a quick fix, hence the need for sustainability.[3]

Not everyone experiences our writing retreats in the same way. While the model doesn't work for some (who don't come back), many find them deeply rewarding, even inspiring. For participants, they offer unique opportunities to engage in academic writing in a *visible* way, which is not how writing usually works in academic culture, as Rowena Murray (2012) points out. Retreats also offer places for enacting some virtues in academic life that, as a counterweight to the contemporary culture of exacerbated individualism and performativity, soften and enrich it: kindness (Clegg & Rowland 2010); hospitality; and open-ended, responsive obligation towards each other (Readings 1996). As well, for doctoral students, the retreats offer a place in which the sometimes painful liminality of their condition (the sense of being in transition without knowing where you are going to, or of slipping between being a student and being a scholar, between knowing and not-knowing) may be contextualised: there is *always* something liminal about writing for scholarly selves.

Labyrinth as metaphor

Evidence of labyrinths dates back to two thousand years BCE.[4] The earliest form—the Classical (see Figure 8.2)—is a simple design based on the pattern of a seed with one entry point, seven courses, and eight boundary walls. Each course is nested inside the other, and together they lead to the central arrival point (the goal) that, simply, returns the walker onto the outgoing path. This latter feature is what distinguishes a labyrinth from a maze. While a maze requires thought and problem-solving in order to find the right path, a labyrinth instead requires a kind of surrender: there is only one right path. Navigation is simple, the walker just follows the courses. For this reason, labyrinths have been long associated with meditation. Walking along the courses, with their gradual curves and repetitive turnings, the walker loses her awareness of self and the outside world and, with a quietened mind, enters a deeper feeling for the present. From medieval times, labyrinths have also been associated with pilgrimage, providing an experience of the prolonged path to enlightenment or salvation for those unable to tread the real thing.

From the Classical labyrinth and its associated practice of meditation, we have drawn four inter-related 'principles' relevant to our model of academic writing retreats that echo in the reported perceptions and experiences of doctoral student/staff participants:

Figure 8.2 The Classical labyrinth.

Principle 1: A Classical labyrinth has seven courses (circuits), bounded by *eight walls*. The walls are suggestive of the stable, predictable design of the retreat, which holds an enclosed space open to write, provides protection from the outside world and its cares.

Principle 2: Once entered, labyrinths are single paths that *lead inevitably from the opening to the centre*. This inevitability is suggestive of the fixed and non-negotiable writing goal and a necessary element of surrender to the passage of writing.

Principle 3: A Classical labyrinth is designed on the pattern of a seed, so linked to the ideas of *germination, flowering* and *fruitfulness*. This principle suggests ideas of transformation and growth in relation to academic writing and writing identities, and evokes the often-difficult liminality associated with writing and thinking.

Principle 4: Walking the labyrinth is symbolically associated with *group and individual meditation, a practice of discipline* to achieve some personal benefit: walking the courses, we lose track of direction and the outside world, and our mind is quietened into a contemplative state. This principle is suggestive of, on the one hand, the tensions that arise in finding a disciplined balance between individual needs for time and solitude to write, and community and writing needs for sociality and reciprocity. On the other hand, it suggests the benefits of acceding to that discipline for both writers and writing.

In the following pages, we enlarge on these principles with illustrative quotations from retreat participants gathered through end-of-retreat feedback forms and an online survey (that include consent for use in publications).[5]

Principle 1: eight walls holding

[There was] space to think and collaboratively interact within a contained and supported four days in [our] bush community.

[The retreat] provided a secure, focused environment for me to be productive.

To begin, we interpret the eight 'walls' of the classical labyrinth as the design fundamentals of our retreats (Grant 2008); these fundamentals express our values as retreat facilitators and seek to attend to the complex mixture of needs of individuals, an academic writing community and the writing task itself.

One: consciously fostering a pleasant environment

The environment sets up optimal conditions for doctoral students and academics to prosper as writers. In our view, these conditions are better characterized by natural beauty, peace and remoteness from daily life than luxury accommodation and over-abundant rich food:

> The location was stunning. The beautiful view from my writing window over a mass of greenery and the native birds dropping by to suck the nectar with the misty lake and small mountains in the distance were calming and helped me to focus.
>
> A great venue cannot be over-estimated. [The venue] was perfect.

Participants enjoy tending the wood fires in their chalets and writing rooms for the winter retreats and observing the wildlife and bush around them. Food prepared by others is often mentioned as an integral part of the retreat experience, contributing towards the convivial and nurturing environment so highly valued.

When asked whether the retreats should continue to be residential (which makes them more expensive and life-interrupting), most participants favour getting away to dedicate time and energy to writing alone:

> The time and collaborative research atmosphere was perfect. Research was 'the only' thing in the world at that time. It was delightful.

The confidentiality rule for personal and intellectual matters, broached in the opening session, is a crucial and cherished environmental element: it establishes a foundation for trust. Trust involves 'a willingness to be vulnerable to another based on the confidence that the other is benevolent, honest, open, reliable and competent' (Tschannen-Moran 2004: xiii); trust does not always arise particularly quickly, so our ground-rule setting in the opening session is crucial, as is the principle of reciprocity underpinning writing workshops and group exercises, in which all are required to share draft writing and receive feedback. In foregrounding trust, the retreat provides a basis for early-career scholars to form social bonds as writers, to gain confidence in their abilities through collaborative processes, and to experience the enabling and enjoyable closeness with others that is a fruit of cohabitation. Over the days, the budding level of trust enables work to be shared more easily and enjoyably, which is vital for the daily work-in-progress sessions and other moments of encounter over writing.

Practically speaking, the ideal retreat venue is one that can provide a mix of spaces to support a mix of communal activities and quiet writing, and a mix of self and provided-for catering (for example, at many retreats we make our own breakfasts). The venue owners need to understand the needs of writers—and minimize disruptions from grounds maintenance or the presence of other groups.

Two: securing a removal from the outside world

Removal from the distractions of external demands and responsibilities is generative for writing and writing identities, and can provide the space for significant shifts in thinking to occur. Participants frequently note the value of having dedicated time and space for thinking away from busy work and lives:

> At the 2011 retreat I worked out a problem in my writing. After attending, I was able to write over 100,000 words in 2012. It was literally just a tiny piece of feedback about my writing but it was a very big conceptual shift and I just knew what to do. These retreats are incredibly important and [the facilitator] does such a wonderful job of supporting, nurturing and inspiring attendees ... It is also very important that the retreats allow the space for candidates to withdraw from everyday life and really focus on their work, without everyday distractions.

> Personally, I would say [the retreat] almost harks back to another time ... where writing was valued more. We cannot be productive without setting a clear agenda and dedicating appropriate time. I have a very clear focus on a paper and I will finish it during this time.

> I cannot underestimate the value of a supported PLACE and time for writing AWAY from my in-tray/email and family needs.

A sense of liberation can be found in the revelation of the fruitfulness of blocks of undisturbed writing time:

> [The retreat] helped me realize how a bulk of writing time can positively contribute to writing progress. ... Time and freedom to write.

> Residential is essential to allow immersion in writing and to allow opportunity for new behaviours to develop.

Withdrawal from cyberspace can be a bone of contention but it is something we both fight for as facilitators (sometimes with the helpful assistance of the venue's limitations):

> Internet access would have pleased me. I'd like to keep in touch with the world, though not be dominated or distracted.

Not being seriously distracted by internet access is much more difficult than most of us admit. While such access is increasingly essential for research purposes, we prefer writers to have done that work before arriving at the retreat (just as they will have had to do library research). With access, the temptation to check email is unbearable for some, yet email acts as a rent in the painstakingly woven fabric of seclusion, allowing all sorts of unwelcome news and interruptions to enter the retreat space. Such interruptions often have consequences not only for the writer, but also for those around them who sense that something is wrong and feel obliged to assist. We have both observed this happen during retreats and so we urge participants not to engage with email and to limit internet access as much as possible (understanding that individuals will make their own decisions on such things).

Three: supporting a deliberate process of change in personal writing practices

Both during and after the retreat, participants are encouraged to make deliberate changes in how they go about their writing. Changes experienced during retreats can alleviate anxiety about the quality of the work or the fear that it won't get done in the allocated time:

> I am very grateful with the opportunity that [Faculty] granted me with the writing retreat experience. It has changed my writing habits forever! It grounds me in the sense to be more realistic when I am setting my writing goals.
>
> I honed my writing from tips that [the facilitator] gave. From the first day, I threw away my opening preamble to my thesis and started again, and had completed chapter one to my and my supervisors' satisfaction by the end of the retreat. It gave me a different perspective and the time and space and quiet to write and achieve.
>
> The title of my thesis was for the last time revised by colleagues from the English literature and Creative writing department during the Writing Retreat, and this never changed again. Also, the Retreat helped me to begin to pay more attention to expressing my thoughts in simple, concise and shorter/brief words, when I write.

On the final day, we invite proposals for deliberate changes to sustain writing momentum back in everyday life; these proposals often entail intentions to repeat the kinds of practices and environments experienced during the retreat:

> I appreciated the need for a quiet, specific time to write and have endeavoured to apply this since the retreat.
>
> [By attending the retreat] I learnt to discipline myself to sit down for longer writing periods, which helped improve my productivity.
>
> [I have experienced] positive changes in writing habits (more consistent routines), increased motivation and output in the weeks after the retreat. Several of the editing practices ... have become part of my 'kitbag', and in fact I am about to employ this strategy with my current editing. I also benefited from the group critique time. I had initially been unsure of this as I was not with anyone from my specific area; however, the insight from other group members was very helpful, as they each focused on different aspects of the writing.

Many mention introducing goal-setting, which is modelled in the pre-retreat questionnaire and revisited in the opening and closing sessions of the retreat:

> The writing retreat provided me with skills that facilitated better writing practices. These skills helped me to overcome writing blocks, which had prevented me from undertaking efficient and effective writing. I am still using the skills obtained such as time allocation, goal setting etc., to achieve real advancement in my writing output.

Changes in practices, in particular establishing continuity in writing, appear to be linked to shifts in identity, which are crucial for doctoral students but also relevant to academics, whose identities are already multiple (teacher, researcher, servant) and who often struggle to find a place for the 'writer' (Grant & Knowles 2000; Murray 2012):

> I 'feel like' a researcher now, and my output will continue with my new writing practice. ... I needed a more balanced approach to the different categories of my work, and I think I've achieved that. Now I need to keep it up for the long haul ...

Four: exploring ways to find pleasure in writing

The retreat model engenders generous nurturing of the academic self as well as others through collaboration and collegiality. And it makes a place for experimenting with the fun of writing—writing in different voices, 'playing with' texts such as titles and first sentences. With a changed mindset and sense of renewal, writing productivity can be enhanced:

> My time at the retreat reignited my enjoyment of writing and this has continued to influence my state of mind when I write such that it is an enjoyable process.

> Yes, not only did I complete a first draft, I also renewed my pleasure in writing, which has been buried for years.

What we borrow from the religious retreat tradition is a focused fidelity to the difficult thing being undertaken in a nurturing and restorative setting. The benefits are often felt after the fact as well as in the moment:

> Writing support is very important for staff and postgraduate students on an ongoing basis. Writing is lonely and hard work, so being able to talk about obstacles and share strategies one has developed could greatly assist people to move forward with the writing. For me, the writers' retreat has helped me to build and maintain my momentum as a writer.

Five: making space for writing together

The disfiguring kind of loneliness experienced by many doctoral and other academic writers is offset during the retreats by collegial aspects engendering a sense of camaraderie. As much as possible, we provide communal writing spaces, where participants not only know others are writing at the same time but they also get to see them doing so. Exposure of this kind is strangely comforting and helps break down the myth that others always write more easily than we do:

> [It's] nice to know you are not the only one struggling to write a piece.

> [The retreat] gave me a broad range of benefits—mainly being in the company of other writers and realizing they all have similar challenges. The sharing of work and support was invaluable.

Workshops often include actual writing activities, individually, in pairs or small groups. Over time we have learned that these kinds of workshops are the most valued. The desire to form writing groups after the retreat expressed (and enacted) by many participants endorses the benefits derived from connecting over shared writing activities:

> I feel very strongly that these workshops should become part of an ongoing series in order to build our expertise as writers. Facilitating us as a group to continue meeting would be helpful. I plan to form a small group to keep writing together.

Six: enabling collegial professional development

The collegial atmosphere in which participants learn from each other actively disrupts the isolated model of writing that many academic writers follow. A core element to the retreats is the daily work-in-progress meeting (in which participants take turns, within a sub-group of four to six people, to present their current writing) and topic-based workshops. Both modes feature planned elements of reciprocity. Much can be learned about the art of academic writing through showing our work to each other and inviting feedback, as well as sharing useful writing strategies:

> [The communal activities] made me more aware of the best conditions for my own writing and exposed me to some of the fantastic techniques/strategies that other colleagues use.

> The ability to bounce the drafts off colleagues greatly assisted the writing process.

> The workshops were specific, useful and stimulating. Peer discussion was very beneficial, sharing ideas and collaborating about successful writing strategies.

Such processes can lead to a validation of identity, as writer and/or academic, a validation that is most powerfully achieved by the recognition of others:

> Through the collegiality of the retreats, I learnt so much about structuring and planning writing, publishing, and also giving and receiving feedback. It also allowed me to see my place in the academic community.

Seven: establishing a balance between communal and solitary time

As retreat designers and facilitators, we walk a fine line in the labyrinth of the retreat. We want to protect as much time as possible for the demanding work of writing because we don't want the retreats to become yet another space to talk about writing without actually doing any! At the same time, we share the view of other writers that writing is a social practice (see, for example, Creme & McKenna 2010; Lee & Aitchison 2009), so time must be made for communal activities that directly engage with writing strategies and, perhaps more importantly, individuals' actual writing.

Many participants recognize the balancing act that is going on and remark that it works for them:

> To have a personal space and dedicated time to writing was invaluable. Plus the input/editing from [the facilitator] and colleagues about my writing resulted in work being completed in a timely manner.

Many affirm the value of the after-lunch workshops for maintaining a productive rhythm and contributing to the processes used during personal writing time:

> The workshops helped to focus attention on improving writing practice, clear the mind and break up the day.

> I thought the workshops in the afternoon were great after a morning's work—it was like a pleasant break from writing and you could talk about what you were doing with the other participants.

However, for some the interruption to either writing flow or solitude is inconvenient, and they—and we—have to live with the slight tensions this may create during the retreat:

> [P]erhaps allow for some more [writing] 'space' [as] sometimes it takes a few hours to get into the right frame of mind to write, only to have to attend a workshop or presentation. I think that these are 'optional' to attend but as there aren't many people attending I did feel a sense of obligation to attend the [communal] sessions.

Eight: ensuring retreats change organically over time

Our practice as retreat designers is to ensure the retreats change organically over time in response to participants' input. This is achieved through the end-of-retreat discussion where suggestions are actively sought for changes to the model (and, if there is enough agreement, acted upon). Other ways that changes leak into the retreat design include conversations in cars on the way to and from retreats, as well as reading the growing literature on academic and non-academic writing exercises, groups and retreats. Also, from time to time, we invite feedback through formal processes—for example, the survey reported in Grant (2006) and the recent Edith Cowan University Qualtrics Survey, data from which are reported here.

Our data suggests that it is not only retreats that are changing in this way: in some cases, attendance at retreats is producing changes to institutional cultures:

> I think regular retreats like this are really, really important. For me, it is the annual regularity to reinforce improvements and create new research-related habits that is important. The faculty culture collaboratively changes to reinforce new cultural practices and commitments too.

We are aware of many spin-off writing groups and retreats initiated by retreat participants.

Principle 2: a single path to walk

> A labyrinth, after all, need not always be threatening; for its tortuous windings offer privacy and darkness, values to be retained as long as they are balanced by social communion and the light promised in the completion of one's journey to its center and safe exit again.
>
> (Faulkenburg 1993: 5)
>
> The structure of the retreat helped me develop good routines in terms of consistent writing times.

The labyrinth's erratic windings with no end in clear sight are suggestive of the emotional, intellectual, psychological disorientation many writers experience in the liminal space of producing new writing and a new self who thinks differently from the old. As the writer negotiates the twisting paths that take them to the heart of their writing, s/he may experience a 'dark night of the soul'. Writing often invites us to venture beyond familiar territory and into what we do not know, have not yet thought. During and beyond doctoral education, this experience can induce feelings of fear and self-doubt, a precariousness of identity. The singleness of the path and its goal supports the writer in making their way (and emerging safely) despite those fears. The holding framework supports a kind of surrender to the process that, paradoxically, can be one of the writer's most powerful defences.

Getting into the rhythm of walking the path takes time (although those of us who have attended many retreats notice how much faster this happens with practice and familiarity):

> It takes time to connect to the process, at least a day and a half—the continuity of residence is required otherwise the connection is severed.

> Yes, [residential retreats are important] as you to tend to only get into the zone after some time.

The value of prior goal setting is often noted, despite the pressure it exerts:

> Normally it would take me two weeks of solid work to complete a first draft of a short story, so setting a goal to complete a first draft within the five-day period of the retreat was a stretch in every way. I managed it—just—thanks to the luxury of having uninterrupted time, a quiet tranquil setting and good collegial support.

This practice requires care to give the best outcome, as setting unrealistic goals can lead to writers feeling disappointed afterwards. We want participants to leave the retreats feeling inspired about their writing practice so that they will keep going.

Doctoral and early-career researchers gain much from walking on the path with more senior academics who can act as powerfully encouraging role models:

> I benefitted from meeting and speaking with women who are more senior than me, and who have maintained an active academic career and had a rich family life too. This is incredibly inspiring for me and has changed my attitude and outlook towards my own career.

For this reason, retreats with vertical membership—for example including doctoral students and/or early-career academics as well as more senior academics—offer some distinctive benefits. Any attendance by supervisor–student pairs, however, must be carefully negotiated so that both have space to pursue their writing and thinking outside the supervision dynamic. In our model, *everyone* is there to write!

Principle 3: from seed to fruit

Germinating from a seed into a fruit evokes the often difficult liminality associated with writing and thinking. The process of producing ideas and the language with which to express them clearly requires properly fertile conditions. A pre-retreat questionnaire, with Robert Brown's (1994/5) embedded questions, asks participants to dig over the soil in their minds in advance of attending the retreat. The questionnaire enquires about writing goals; it also provides a focusing exercise that imagines audience, canvasses the central question and proposed answer, and requires the writer to think about the *significance* (the 'so what?') of the piece to help them into a state of writing readiness.

Many participants describe how retreats produce the fruits of writing outputs (theses, articles, chapters, proposals), as well as providing the right conditions for strategic decision-making to flourish:

> The writing retreats are the primary reason I am in a position to submit my thesis in a few weeks. They took months off my writing time.
>
> Sometimes, good planning isn't quite enough, though, and staff need to secure real research time. I found I produced two different articles in 2012 in response to particular publishing opportunities, and the retreat helped me to make such decisions, so has led to publications.

Relationships that develop during the retreats—and sometimes continue afterwards—are another kind of fruit:

> On both retreats, my PhD students have been present, as have my staff. Being away together has added a new dimension to our relationships. Networking opportunities with staff and students outside my school have been beneficial.
>
> The value of this retreat extends far beyond my writing outputs. I now feel a part of the [university] community and far less intimidated by academics further up the hierarchy. I have met women who will become mentors—at least momentarily, as they have agreed to be guests at the social breakfasts I organize for women at work. All in all, the retreat has lifted my motivation for my work and I really value that.

For some, the seed sown is that of increased self-assertion, confidence, or the ambition to stretch themselves:

> [I now have] a focus on not being afraid to try for an international or 'major' journal.
>
> [I feel more] confidence [in my] identity as writer, [and from the] knowledge that others face similar obstacles, especially the 'imposter syndrome'!

Validation is a condition that promotes growth as a writer. Shared discussion about the writer's struggles for time, the difficulties of writing well and the challenges of publishing implies that these struggles are not the product of personal inadequacy but are part and parcel of the work:

> ... it was good to know everyone has good days and bad, just like me. It was a pleasure to be in the company of people with such broad interests—some fascinating conversations emerged.

> ... regardless of discipline area, everyone shares similar issues with writing and publishing, and it was great to get feedback with others outside the disciplinary area.

The rewards gained from these discussions include intellectual stimulation and cross disciplinary fertilization. Feedback—either from each other through work-in-progress or during individual consultations with the facilitator—is another condition that provides such rewards, stimulating growth from seed to the fruit of more accomplished writing:

> I hadn't thought of picking up the metaphor/example used in introduction and referring to it again in conclusion [until I had the consultation with the facilitator].

Principle 4: submitting to individual and group discipline

> I thought the [retreat] structure well balanced. At times I thought I'd rather keep working but instead found I enjoyed the company and content after all!

> I was reluctant to share/talk about my work but now see how useful it is in making progress.

There is something inherently disciplining about the retreats—both for an individual writer with an obligation to pursue the writing goal they have set, and for a group that is writing together. Discipline entails tensions and compromises between what works best for an individual and for the collective. For example, timetabling writing and workshop times raises just these kinds of issues. Most people write best in the mornings but some do not: making mornings the main writing time supports the majority in their writing rhythms but not the minority. Likewise, timetabling the workshops after lunch supports the majority who find the post-lunch period unproductive for writing but not those who do. As well, in the program there are some activities that are *required*, such as work-in-progress meetings and presentations: conforming to this discipline also creates tensions for some participants. In submitting to the retreat program, however, other kinds of 'freedom' follow: the freedom that comes from knowing one is contributing to a common good, or the freedom to explore pedagogical dynamics that might not otherwise be experienced. These partial freedoms are built on an ethics that foregrounds kindness, generosity, reciprocity, as well as obligation.

A particular kind of discipline that emerges as a result of group discussions is that entailed in good communication:

> The collaborative work helped me to visualize the paper and the chapter as a whole but at the same time showed me that every single sentence counts in the objective of getting the message across. As a result I am writing with great care; it means avoiding too many words and selecting accurate and precise words.

> [The cross-disciplinary group work] made the focus on expressing yourself clearly and powerfully to appeal to the educated general reader—not just people in my own field.

Group discussions are unpredictable: despite the careful framing of protocols (i.e., disciplining of process) for feedback in particular, writers will sometimes feel challenged as others disagree with their work, or do not understand it—or even sometimes legislate disciplinary expectations from other quarters:

> I find some of the collaboration difficult. I had a member of my [work-in-progress] group dismiss qualitative data collection for mathematics education journals. I found this difficult.

> If I am honest, I think I found the group setting a bit intimidating. I have had people at conferences respond very positively to my work and did not really find this in my group.

At best, such challenges can help to strengthen a writer's position:

> I felt I needed to justify my qualitative approach to the scientists I was constantly meeting with—and this strengthened my own resolve (as just a few years ago I too thought the scientific approach the 'only right way').

Critical challenges are important for writing and thinking clearly: a crucial factor in their reception is how they are offered. In our introduction to feedback, we frame it as a gift that allows the writer to see her work through other's eyes and then think about how she might address that view constructively (and she may choose to put it aside). In that spirit, such challenges are best given gingerly. However, in the heat of the discussion, feedback does not always play out in this way—there is much about our academic training that works against care in such matters (Knowles 1999, 2007).

The benefits of submitting to group processes are reiterated in participants' feedback. They regularly express pleasure and gratitude at the opportunity to talk about their research and writing to others; they describe the benefits furnished by access to a new audience:

> [The group work] was perhaps the most outstanding aspect [of the retreat]. To develop communication and open dialogue with those unfamiliar with my work was a powerful gift.

> [The benefits for me include] having to explain my own work simply, learning what other disciplines think about writing, realizing how much I do know about writing, so feeling more confident about my own role in working in a group.

> I tend to write very concisely and sometimes everything ends up too tightly knotted. The perspective of those outside my field helped me think about teasing things out more, give points more space and more discussion.

The holding embrace of writing retreats

> [The retreats] are the most valuable thing I have encountered in my entire PhD candidacy.

> As part of building a supportive framework and ethos for staff and HDR students to write, the retreats are invaluable and inspiring. I sincerely hope [our university] can continue to facilitate their existence.

In this chapter, we have explored the experience of participating in writing retreats through the ancient figure of the labyrinth in order to illuminate some of the productive rhythms and tensions that occur there for doctoral (and other academic) writers. For most, academic writing is not easy: it can produce intense feelings ranging from elation (even an inability to sit still) right through to paralysing depression (and the condition known as writer's block). Retreat participants often describe a yearning for vibrant writing communities that are largely absent from the normal course of academic life. Writers' retreats, as we describe them, are not a panacea for all the ills of writing, but their embrace has much to offer by way of comfort, pleasure and stimulation, as we learn about ourselves as academic writers and about the shared craft we practise. The carefully prepared confines of the retreat-as-labyrinth hold writers for a little while in place and time as they journey together through the liminal processes of producing good academic writing and becoming more accomplished academic writers:

> I had contact with lots of people and each person added something to polish my writing or build my confidence. The solitude and beauty of the surroundings mattered a lot to me. The retreat was very well structured, researched and prepared. The fact that it seemed to 'just happen' reflects the immense underlying thought and work that has gone into it over many years. [The facilitator's] genuine enthusiasm and excellent scholarship added a great deal. Thanks also to [the institutional contact] for actively creating this opportunity and to [university] for supporting us in doing this.

Evidence gathered over the years suggests the effectiveness of the writing retreats arises from a highly innovative ethos and practice, explicitly applied and sustained over a series of days, and where repeat engagement is encouraged and valued. The repeat engagement lays down a foundation of comfort and predictability that is supportive for the rigours of writing. Crucially, as the metaphor of the labyrinth evokes, we are committed to sustaining a balance between the, sometimes difficult, disciplines of structure and community and the equally testing provocations of freedom and solitude. The establishment of a collegial atmosphere that enshrines continuities of practice, relationships and scholarly approaches across disciplines is one of the most distinctive benefits of these retreats.

To usefully extend our metaphor, we can think of academic writing itself as labyrinthine. Entering the courses of composing an original piece of scholarly writing inevitably takes the writer to strange, sometimes dark, places, where we can feel there is no way out and we lose heart for the writing at hand. To survive such experiences, we suggest that writers flourish best in environments with aspects of the labyrinth about them, as we have described in this chapter. In particular, finding a fecund balance between technique and flow, between community and solitude, between structure and freedom, between disciplinary allegiance and risky disruptions, between doing the writing and talking about it, between repetition and revision, is a demanding process. Writing retreats, spiritedly conceived and facilitated, provide a holding embrace that allows writing to happen in the face of the unstable but productive tensions that lie at the heart of producing original academic work.

Acknowledgements

We wish to acknowledge the many colleagues over the years who have shared writing retreats with us and generously offered ideas and energy to make those events lively, instructive and fun. We thank those, too, who offered the written feedback featured in this chapter. We are very grateful to Dr Susan Hill (Research Development Officer at Edith Cowan University) for kindly assisting with the survey design and analysis and her ongoing interest. Photograph (Figure 8.1) taken by Anomie at the Faculty of Education and Arts Writing Retreat, 14 December 2012.

Notes

1 For a detailed account of how the retreat model works, see Grant (2008).
2 *Women Writing Away (WA)* awarded an inaugural bursary to a doctoral candidate from Edith Cowan University in Western Australia in September 2012 for its 32nd retreat.
3 In Australia and Aotearoa/New Zealand (NZ), we are both involved in pan-university writing retreats that have convened about 30 times in the past decade or more (see Grant 2006). We have also done retreats for groups from our own universities and, by invitation, for other institutions in Australia, Canada and NZ.

4 A source of comprehensive information about labyrinths and Figure 8.2 is the Labyrinthos website http://www.labyrinthos.net/typolab02.html, accessed 3 February 2013.
5 Most of the comments included here were written immediately after retreats held between 2001 and 2012 by participants (doctoral students and academic staff); some were gathered as part of formal surveys (e.g., Grant 2006; Knowles in progress).

References

Brown, R. (1994/5) 'Write right first time', *Literati Newsline*, Special Issue, 1–8. Available online: http://web.archive.org/web/19971014014626/http://www.mcb.co.uk/literati/write.htm (accessed 23 August 2013).

Clegg, S. and Rowland, S. (2010) 'Kindness in pedagogical practice and academic life', *British Journal of Sociology of Education*, 31(6): 719–35.

Creme, P. and McKenna, C. (2010) 'Developing writer identity through a multidisciplinary programme', *Arts & Humanities in Higher Education*, 9(2): 149–67.

Faulkenburg, M. T. (1993) *Church, City, and Labyrinth in Brontë, Dickens, Hardy, and Butor*, New York: Peter Lang.

Grant, B. (2003) 'Professional development in retreat', in H. Edwards, D. Baume and G. Webb (eds), *Staff and Educational Development: Case Studies, Experience and Practice from Higher Education*, London: Kogan Page.

—— (2006) 'Writing in the company of other women: exceeding the boundaries', *Studies in Higher Education*, 31(4): 483–95.

—— (2008) *Academic Writing Retreats: A Facilitator's Guide*, Milperra, NSW: HERDSA.

Grant, B. and Knowles, S. (2000) 'Flights of imagination: academic women be(com)ing writers', *International Journal for Academic Development*, 5(1): 6–19.

Knowles, S. (1999) 'Feedback in writing in postgraduate supervision: echoes in responses—context, continuity and resonance', in A. Holbrook and S. Johnston (eds) *Supervision of Postgraduate Research in Education*, Victoria: Australian Association for Research in Education.

—— (2007) 'Getting up close and textual: an interpretive study of feedback practice and social relations in doctoral supervision', unpublished PhD thesis, Murdoch University.

—— (in progress) 'Scholarly writing community project: review of academic writing retreats 2009–2012', Office of Research and Innovation, Edith Cowan University, WA: Unpublished Report.

Lee, A., and Aitchison, C. (2009) 'Writing for the doctorate and beyond', in D. Boud and A. Lee (eds) *Changing Practices of Doctoral Education*, London: Routledge.

Murray, R. (2012) '"It's not a hobby": reconceptualizing the place of writing in academic work', *Higher Education*, 66(1): 79–91.

Readings, B. (1996) *The University in Ruins*, Cambridge, MA: Harvard University Press (see in particular, Ch. 10, *The scene of pedagogy*).

Tschannen-Moran, M. (2004) *Trust Matters: Leadership for Successful Schools*, San Francisco, CA: Jossey-Bass.

Chapter 9

The gift of writing groups
Critique, community and confidence

Cally Guerin

Introduction

Much of the literature on doctoral writing groups indicates that a key benefit of participation in such groups results in members becoming more confident and developing a sense of belonging to a scholarly community (see, for example, Ferguson 2009; Guerin *et al.* 2013; Maher *et al.* 2008; Mullen 2003). This is especially evident in the type of writing group in which members critique each other's work. The consistency of this finding is intriguing, given that the participants in these groups have already shown themselves to be capable, clever, organized individuals who are actively undertaking research at a relatively high level. At first glance it might be surprising that so many of them are not confident about their work when they have clearly been sufficiently successful to have been accepted into doctoral programs. One explanation might lie in the highly competitive research climate of universities—where individuals compete for scholarships, grants, jobs and promotions—despite the active promulgation of discourses of scholarly collaboration and communities of practice. Flying in the face of this competitive attitude, doctoral writing groups can create a space which privileges collaborative practices and peer learning as members provide each other with reciprocal feedback on their writing.

This chapter argues that reading the experience of doctoral writing groups through the lens of gift exchange theory (Mauss 1950/1969) offers a means of understanding the powerful effect of those groups in building participants' confidence. The chapter considers the significance not only of offering gifts, but also the mutual obligation that ensues from accepting gifts. Thus, if we interpret the giving and receiving of feedback on writing as gift exchange, we can see how membership in a writing group develops important ties of mutual responsibility, reciprocity and trust, all of which contribute to members' sense of belonging to the academic community, and consequently build confidence. In these ways, then, feedback in writing groups takes on different meanings from that provided more formally by supervisors.

In what follows, I propose that gift exchange theory can offer one way of understanding why many PhD students report having very positive experiences in doctoral writing groups that allow them to feel more connected to their scholarly communities and build confidence in their academic and researcher identities as a result.

My context

The reflections in this chapter arise from my experiences working with doctoral students in writing groups with four to fifteen members, usually in loosely related disciplines. I attend the first five sessions in my role as an academic developer and then leave the group to continue critiquing each member's writing in turn. Overall, the majority of students are women and English as Second Language (ESL) speakers, but this varies according to disciplinary grouping. The participant quotations provided in the discussion below are from a series of focus group discussions undertaken with members of doctoral writing groups I had established according to the model described above. Four different groups provided information, one each from Public Health, Health Sciences, Humanities and Social Sciences, and Bioscience. The focus groups were conducted during normal meeting times and members were asked to reflect on their experiences in the writing group. In this way, I came into their space and could observe their usual interactions with each other.

Gift exchange

Theories about gift exchange have provided a powerful explanatory framework for understanding certain aspects of the bonds between individuals and groups. From the original work of Marcel Mauss (1950/1969) and Mary Douglas' (1990) commentary on his work, the symbolic meanings attached to the giving and receiving of gifts have been explored in cultural anthropology in relation to the mutual benefits and responsibilities attendant on such gift exchange.

Mauss explores the social and economic implications in traditional societies of the obligations to give, to receive, and to repay gifts: 'although the prestations and counter-prestations take place under a voluntary guise they are in essence strictly obligatory' (Mauss 1950/1969: 3). Here, 'prestations' are symbolic offerings of hospitality, goods or property; these offerings carry with them powerful contractual obligations of acceptance and consequent indebtedness. As Douglas points out, there is no 'free gift' (Douglas 1990). Thus, the offering of a gift is an invitation to enter into a relationship. The response to this offering is not simply a matter of free choice, however. Accepting the gift/prestation establishes an ongoing alliance; the receiver must repay this gift with a counter-gift (of hospitality, services or goods), and guarantees willingness to do so. Refusing a gift, on the other hand, indicates hostility towards the giver. Equally, failure to offer gifts can also constitute an act of aggression.

That is, gift exchange marks the beginnings of a reciprocal relationship of trust and mutual obligation: to refuse a gift is to refuse a cooperative relationship. There is, then, an element of self-interest in the giving of gifts in order to draw others into reciprocal alliances, an exchange that might be characterized as utilitarian and strategic (Antal & Richebé 2009). Mauss reminds us, though, that freedom and obligation, generosity and self-interest are not mutually exclusive, but 'a kind of hybrid' (Mauss 1950/1969: 70); gifts can be used 'to maintain a profitable alliance' and often operate as 'pledges' that bind individuals and groups together (Mauss 1950/1969: 71). Thus, the exchange of gifts is central to social relations and to building communities, the effects of which can be seen in contemporary society: by entering into acts of gift exchange, we demonstrate our willingness to participate in relationships of mutual obligation, reciprocity and trust.

These core ideas from gift exchange theory have been used by anthropologists and organizational psychologists to interpret human relationships in various contexts, including within the academy. As has been suggested, much of contemporary academic life is competitive, but alongside this is also a strong tradition of gift exchange in terms of the sharing of knowledge and expertise. For example, undertaking tasks of peer review for academic conferences and journals does not attract monetary reward in most disciplines. The progress of science is dependent upon the sharing of information (Haeussler 2011), as is the development of thinking about complex ideas in other areas. Indeed, this sharing of knowledge—and of one's passion for the field—is a driving force for many scholars in their teaching, writing and reviewing activities (Antal & Richebé 2009), just as it can be for classroom teachers in schools (Game & Metcalfe 2012). Knowledge sharing is also a powerful force in developing collective group identities, and can be instrumental in creating a cohesive community out of diversity in university settings (Lauring & Selmer 2011).

In considering how gift exchange operates between academics, Antal and Richebé (2009) provide some particularly useful insights regarding the relationships that develop between individuals in writing groups. They argue that effective gift exchange creates a personal connection between participants. Importantly, though, such gift exchanges are necessarily characterized as disinterested and without expectation of reciprocity: these exchanges must be treated as simply gift giving with no strings attached. In reality, however, this might be somewhat disingenuous. Antal and Richebé's (2009) research uncovers just how necessary it is that knowledge sharing appears as a simple, one-way gift in the academic context; however, it is expected that such generosity will later be balanced by a reciprocal favour. Importantly, this takes place over time, so that the giver does not have an expectation of precisely when their gift giving might be repaid. Indeed, since this generally occurs in a collective context, the repayment may not be directly offered by the same individual; rather, it becomes a normalized behaviour between members of the wider scholarly community. Further, they also point out that the impulse to share in this way appears to spring from personal liking and a desire to develop an ongoing working relationship with another scholar. Hence, the complex relationships of mutual reciprocity set up through knowledge exchange and sharing contribute to the strong sense of belonging to a scholarly community.

In the following discussion, I consider the implications of thinking about the feedback that participants give and receive in writing groups as a kind of 'gift'. What insights can this lead to in terms of how and why some writing groups seem to work so well, and in particular, what can it tell us about the learning that occurs in doctoral writing groups? Why does the feedback from peers seem to have different effects from that provided by supervisors?

Feedback as gift

Considering the feedback offered in doctoral writing groups as a type of gift publicly offered between peers has the potential to inform us about how this activity binds individuals into a community. I bring this theory of gift exchange to my observations of writing groups in order to theorize how some doctoral writing groups act as a powerful mechanism for integrating individuals into the scholarly community and also for building students' confidence in their emerging scholarly identities. Gift exchange theory offers new possibilities for interpreting the activities of writing group members and understanding the effectiveness of these groups; it also potentially helps us to appreciate why feedback received in doctoral writing groups might produce different outcomes from that given by supervisors.

Feedback from writing group peers: reciprocal gift giving

In doctoral writing groups the reciprocal gift-giving of feedback between peers draws members into the academic community as they learn from each other about the practices, norms and expectations of the research world. There is a substantial literature on peer learning and the related concepts of communities of practice and situated learning (Lave & Wenger 1991), distributed and horizontalized learning (Boud *et al.* 2001; Boud & Lee 2005) and constructivist, collaborative, social learning (Bruffee 1999; Gere & Abbott 1985). Boud and Lee (2005: 510–11) argue that peer learning has particular resonance for researchers:

> The peer is a defining figure in research practice. The institution of peer review, for example, is both indexical and productive of what comes to be accepted as good research among licensed members of scholarly communities. A discourse of peer learning which attends to the specificity of learning in relation to research allows us to attend to the complex dynamics of peer relations in the research environment itself, then to the relationships and the learning that obtain to developing these specific kinds of peer relationship.

The peer learning that occurs for doctoral candidates in writing groups plays a valuable role in promoting confidence in their own capacity to legitimately participate in their disciplinary communities; the giving and receiving of gifts of feedback provide one mechanism by which this is achieved.

The following discussion during a focus group interview directly links the receiving of peer critique to confidence building for the emerging scholar:

Deb: But there's no point coming along and saying that's great, that's great, if you think it's not, because then that's just a waste of everybody's time … we want to hear what's wrong …

Vera: Or for you then to send it off to a journal and have it …

John: And at the end of the day, I would rather hear it from these people than from the supervisors swearing at you saying, why did I hire you? Or from a journal reviewer.

Deb: That's right, you build more confidence […] Once we've discussed it in the group you feel like, well okay, you know, I've got comments that weren't too scathing, so it might be okay.

These students articulate their desire to engage in serious critique of each other's work—empty praise is seen as time wasting. Rather, the writing group is a place where peers can provide real learning opportunities for each other. Receiving insightful feedback from their peers is regarded as a valuable opportunity for developing writing skills. Further, receiving these feedback gifts reassures these doctoral students they are working at an appropriate level; the process of gift exchange affirms their emerging researcher identities in the safe environment of sympathetic peers. Instead of feeling that they are 'bottom of the ladder in the group' or 'very small' in the academic hierarchy (in the words of the participants), they can receive affirmation of their work that leads to increasing confidence in their own capacities. Of course, it is perfectly possible to feel utterly discouraged by rigorous critique, but peer feedback presented appropriately is more often well received. Importantly, this opportunity to learn the conventions and expectations of academic life in a generally supportive environment provides a valuable training ground for developing the skills of robust academic debate.

In another writing group, participants speak directly about the satisfaction of being able to offer useful gifts of feedback and how this too helps build a confident scholarly identity in having those gifts accepted by others, further confirming their place within the community. These gifts are not presented with the overt expectation of being immediately repaid, but can be understood as a demonstration of a scholarly comportment which appreciates that the collegial sharing of knowledge is a traditional characteristic of belonging to an academic community (Antal & Richebé 2009):

Joy: There's a lot to be said for doing something for another colleague =Exactly! Yes!= and that's what the collegiality of the university is all about. The spin-off that we've all enjoyed is a bonus in a sense. It's helping somebody else

Alice: through a stumbling block or over a hurdle with their work, or helping them find a venue to discuss it, that's part of this […]
And sometimes you can help when you think you can't. Like when I first read [Joy's] work I thought, 'Oh my God! What is she talking about?' [laughter all round] It was so scholarly and such dense writing, and I didn't think I would be able to help you. But somehow it worked, because … It's good to have difficult work to look at—not that your work is difficult—but you know what I mean. A completely new field.

This excerpt from the transcript indicates the participants' willingness to engage with each other intellectually and on a personal level, again articulating their awareness of learning about scholarly behaviours and developing academic identities along the way. They affirmed each other's comments with verbal cues; they often spoke directly to each other in discussing how they benefited from the group rather than addressing comments to the interviewer; and they laughed together frequently. Together they had created a group dynamic that was marked by a spirit of generosity in finding satisfaction by helping each other over stumbling blocks and hurdles. Gift exchange in terms of giving each other carefully considered feedback on their writing is central to this small community.

Being part of a community is clearly a stimulating learning experience that is about much more than just getting the writing right. Seeing what other students produce breaks down the intensely individualized, isolated experience of doctoral candidature and draws attention to writing as a social practice, not only in the practical doing of writing, but also in the dissemination of that writing. This interaction also actively demonstrates to participants that their skills are valued by others, that they can indeed contribute to each other's development (McAlpine & Asghar 2010), even when the initial response is that this writing is too scholarly and dense. Successful negotiation of these experiences clearly increases confidence in individuals' own ability to operate effectively in the world of research and academia. Research has demonstrated that students learn more about writing when giving feedback than when they receive feedback (Aitchison 2009; Caffarella & Barnett 2000; Lundstrom & Baker 2009); the transcripts above demonstrate that the two-way process is also a valuable ingredient in developing confident researcher identities and binding collaborative communities of scholars together.

Food gifts and community

Some of the groups interviewed provided food for the participants during the writing group sessions, and another referred to the fact that they go out together for coffee after the business part of their meeting is completed. Mauss's early work on gift exchange theory explored the importance of offering and receiving food as 'potlatch'. In the societies investigated by Mauss,

> gifts are always accepted and praised. You must speak your appreciation of the food prepared for you. But you accept a challenge at the same time. You receive a gift 'on the back'. You accept the food and you do so because you mean to take up the challenge and prove that you are not unworthy.
>
> (Mauss 1950/1969: 40)

Similarly, the hospitality offered and accepted in a writing group might be interpreted as a sign of ongoing commitment to engaging with this particular community. It would be rash to make too much of this, of course (students are notorious for their eagerness to accept free food!), but this sharing of food could add to the binding power of a community engaged in gift exchange. In one group that enjoyed freshly baked cakes each session, the cook explained: 'I just kept doing it every time ... this is my stress control'. In another group where food featured, one member encapsulated the relationships between group members thus: 'I'd invite them to my birthday party!' While all of the groups were serious about critiquing the writing proffered by members each session, the added dimension of food seems to be an affirmation that this is a community bound together by reciprocal personal ties of friendship as well as a workplace for learning about research writing.

Feedback from supervisors: unequal gift exchange

Supervisors are a major source of feedback on thesis drafts, of course, so what might gift exchange theory tell us about feedback from supervisors and how it works to draw doctoral students into the academic community? It would seem that supervisor feedback is rarely perceived as a 'gift' that requires reciprocal giving, perhaps partly because of the institutional relationship (part of the supervisor's paid job includes supervision responsibilities), but perhaps also because of the asymmetry of the relationship:

> Status influences the balance that is considered appropriate in gift exchange, such that it is acceptable to receive more than one gives when engaging with someone of higher status, but one is expected to give as much as one receives from an equal, and a senior is expected to give more to partners of lower status. Each exchange therefore contributes to demarcating (and sometimes changing) the boundaries of status in the community.
>
> (Antal & Richebé 2009: 89)

When it comes to feedback on doctoral writing, supervisors are mostly giving, while the student is mostly receiving that feedback, rather than being in a position to reciprocate directly. Indeed, that supervisors give more could be interpreted as a means of establishing their authority over the student, as a demarcation of their status in the hierarchy. Thus, the status of supervisors in this exchange relationship means that the feedback is received by students as qualitatively different from that offered by their peers. Perhaps it follows then that a different kind of reciprocity is expected in return?

If gift exchange indicates a willingness to establish a relationship of trust and mutual obligation, how does this play out between students and supervisors? Presumably students on the whole trust that supervisor feedback is genuinely helpful, and demonstrate this trust by attempting to act on that feedback; reciprocating here is seen as responding in a scholarly manner, rather than offering feedback in return. Hence, 'repayment' in this situation could take the form of being obliged to try to use the feedback respectfully and effectively—which might also include demonstrating a capacity to critically evaluate that feedback and ultimately reject elements of the advice/gift. Clearly, this is further complicated if students receive conflicting feedback from different members of their supervisory team, and must therefore carefully negotiate their acceptance of some feedback gifts and not others (Guerin & Green 2013). Handled badly, rejection of feedback gifts potentially contributes to the breakdown of the relationship, rather than working to build a sense of belonging to the scholarly community.

Sometimes students do not know how to respond to the feedback received from supervisors, despite their willingness to engage with it. Again, such gifts may not work immediately to draw students into the scholarly community represented by the supervisors (Green 2005). In these situations, writing groups can play an active role in averting damage to the relationship with the supervisor. One student in the focus groups explained:

> When you send your manuscript to your supervisors, you don't always get an explanation for why it's bad, there's just a big line through it saying this is bad. Whereas here [in the writing group] it's like, 'This is bad because …' or 'This needs reworking …' I don't think I've actually heard the term bad or crap, or anything used. [general laughter] It's 'This doesn't make sense'. It's explanatory, it's not just 'Rework this', because sometimes you'll get that back [from the supervisor] and what do I do?

Another explained that she submits her work to the writing group in order to

> get constructive feedback on it. And it's on little things that your supervisor will not be, like, 'I'm unhappy with the way this sentence is constructed'. They [supervisors] don't have the time or inclination to do that [i.e., provide specific solutions] … and you don't feel like you are being judged by your supervisor. They're not going to be like 'Oh my goodness, look how bad this work is!' I can bring it here, make it better, and then give it to him.

That is, writing groups can play an important intermediary role for students who are learning to negotiate their place in an academic community. Writing groups make space for detailed discussion of each member's writing, allowing sufficient time to explain reasons for making particular choices and recommendations, so that a variety of opinions can be explored around word choice, grammar questions, etc. But these discussions about writing also overlap with other more general concerns about expectations and conventions in the world of research. In this sense, they create a safe space to trial the behaviours and practices that are part of scholarly identities. The gift on offer in writing groups, then, is more than a gift of time devoted to detailed discussion and attention to the students' concerns about writing; these gifts are also influencing and forming the scholarly identities that are developing during the doctoral program. Considering this complex web of gift exchanges between peers and between students and their supervisors highlights the different versions of reciprocal obligation that build towards a sense of belonging to the scholarly community.

The dark side of the gift

Of course, it is not all rosy in the world of gift exchange, nor in all writing groups. There is a 'dark side' (Marcoux 2009) when it comes to gift giving that can disrupt the bonds between individuals, and those proffering gifts do need to recognize that they are taking risks in how those gifts might be perceived by the receiver. If gifts are regarded as negative, inappropriate or are actually rejected, ties between members of a writing group risk being damaged. In the context of doctoral writing groups, the dark side of the gift resonates in particular ways.

A 'negative gift' is one which demonstrates an imbalance of power between the parties involved, and which results in the receiver being indebted to the giver because they feel they are entering into an ongoing, asymmetrical 'perpetual obligation' (Marcoux 2009: 673). This is perhaps one reason why writing groups, with their focus on turn-taking between colleagues, create a very different dynamic between participants from situations in which one asks a friend to read and provide feedback on writing. The possibility of the negative gift provides a strong reason to set up writing groups in the workplace, where a professional, scholarly attitude can be expected, and perhaps also points to the essential difference between 'peers' and 'friends' in such exchanges: individuals may often be more willing to accept criticism in a setting where academic debate is the norm, whereas in the context of friendship the same feedback might risk damaging the relationship. The negative gift also sounds a cautionary note to remind us that, if we want doctoral writing groups to build students' confidence in their own capacities as autonomous researchers, we need to establish clear expectations of reciprocity and equality between members. The purpose of such groups is for all members to participate equally in actively giving and receiving feedback. Another variation on the negative gift is the individual who is keen to present their own work for discussion, but then claims to be 'too busy' to read and critique in return, hence not repaying the debt. It can be useful to point out to writing group participants that it is in both giving and receiving feedback gifts that community can be built and confidence nourished.

Another risk attached to gift giving is the possibility that the gift be regarded as inappropriate or even rejected. Choosing a wrong or inappropriate gift can actually disrupt relationships rather than strengthening them, as well as draw attention to asymmetries in the relationships (Davies *et al.* 2010). In the context of writing groups, this might be evidenced in a sense of hierarchy developing between members of the group, if individuals appear to be asserting some kind of superior knowledge or seniority over the others instead of working according to principles of reciprocity. Alternatively, if the advice on writing is regarded as wrong or ill-informed, this too can disrupt relations (whether or not the advice is in fact perfectly sound). Rejecting the feedback gifts in deciding not to act on that advice can further break down the relationships on offer.

The public nature of giving feedback during writing group discussions can further complicate the gift exchange, possibly influencing the kind of feedback participants are willing to offer. Rather than risk an inappropriate gift, there may sometimes be a temptation to provide only encouraging or positive comments on the writing. However, as we have seen earlier, this potentially leads to the failure of the writing group; it is perceived as 'just a waste of everybody's time' if no critical engagement with the material occurs.

Concerns about taking risks in such public gift exchange might also provide insight into the face-saving behaviour evidenced by Confucian-heritage students who are sometimes characterized as reluctant to participate in seminar discussions in ways that demonstrate critical thinking (Li & Vandermensbrugghe 2011; Wang & Li 2008). These students might remain relatively silent and apparently passive in writing groups. While this is often attributed to a desire not to embarrass the scholar whose work is being exhibited, anxieties about the risk of the feedback gift being rejected might also play into this response.

International students in writing groups—rejected gifts?

It is common for international doctoral students, particularly those using ESL, to join writing groups to improve their language skills. This poses some interesting variations on the relationships between writing group participants, and a reminder that gifts of feedback can be received differently in different contexts. There is some evidence to suggest that peer learning can be problematic in situations where the students may not have strong language skills. Studies have found that students in English language classrooms can distrust feedback on their writing from peers, preferring feedback from teachers. Reluctance to trust the feedback from other ESL students does not appear to have been a problem in the writing groups reported by Li and Vandermensbrugghe (2011), perhaps because they continued to be led by the academic developers endowed with institutional authority. Nevertheless, Li and Vandermensbrugghe do report an initial reluctance on the part of students to critique each other's work, and the need to actively teach participants effective and appropriate methods of offering constructive feedback.

Nevertheless, gifts of feedback from ESL doctoral students can sometimes be regarded with suspicion in writing groups, occasionally even resulting in rejection of the feedback. Chinese students in one of the focus groups confided their mistrust of feedback from other international students who had similar levels of English competence to their own. The interviewer took up this concern by asking about a previous writing group composed entirely of ESL speakers that dispersed as soon as the facilitator had completed the initial series of workshops:

Dan:	'Cause, I mean, international students, are of a like, similar level =Sam: No, no= *Most* of them, I mean, I mean, the *true* international, you guys [who did undergraduate studies in Australia] are not. =[three or four talking at once clarifying]: Yeah I get that/ No I came= So when we get some, like, comments we think, I think, it's not that [hesitantly] ... authentic! [lots of laughter around the table]
Interviewer:	Maybe not completely valid, that they might not know what they're talking about?
Dan:	Yeah.
Steven [originally Hong Kong]:	It's interesting though, I always thought, um, Chinese from from China have really good grammars =Dan: Yeah, yeah, yeah, sure!= because you guys were taught really well how to structure grammar and stuff. So if you tell me something I did wrong, I'll believe more as well, so I don't understand where the mentality came from of not trusting other international students.
Dan:	Well trust because, I think, like the first PhD student [in a previous writing group] are similar level, they can't be really helpful like my own ...
Interviewer:	But you know that your suggestions to this group are good?
Dan:	But something is weird because of—you know, [Sam] also speaks Chinese and some his mistakes I know very ... very conscious about his mistake because common mistake from people only speak Chinese! [awkward laughter from speaker]
Others:	Yeah, yeah, yeah!
Dan:	But if people are all from like same culture ... I think, you have to mix like local students with international students [...] I didn't only learn the writing, but also the listening. The conversations between them are quite like, sounds, sounds very 'native' [loud laughter from group]
Interviewer:	Not the same as the textbooks?
Dan:	No, no, no, no. Is some difference between the conversation amongst international students.

Dan struggles to articulate his meaning in this exchange. There is palpable uneasiness in the room while the group strains to understand his point about what might prove to be a taboo subject (the failings of international students, criticism based on cultural differences); that uneasiness is relieved by outbursts of laughter as group members recognize shared interpretations of what happens in their meetings. Dan's insights into first language interference in comments about the 'weird' recognition of Chinese speakers' mistakes could in fact be harnessed in situations where international students share the same language background because students are alert to particular writing issues they are likely to face. Rather than being a problem, this could benefit the group (Guerin *et al.* 2013). More importantly, perhaps, there can be advantages to having access to the grammar knowledge of ESL students who have learnt English formally and often have ready access to a vocabulary for talking about grammar and writing.

Conclusion

The discussion above leads to a number of useful insights when it comes to establishing doctoral writing groups. If we think about the feedback activities in writing groups as gift exchange, the focus shifts towards the central importance of reciprocity. The reciprocal offerings in doctoral writing groups draw on the benefits of peer learning to strengthen ties between students, drawing individuals into scholarly communities and building their confidence as autonomous researchers. By taking the extended time required to engage with the particulars of each other's writing and to provide detailed feedback, writing group participants indicate their willingness to take each other seriously as scholars.

Considering feedback in doctoral writing groups as gift exchange also highlights the potential risks in these situations. It is necessary for groups to start from a basis of mutual respect so that feedback gifts have a positive rather than disruptive effect on relationships between group members, regardless of language background or place in the academic hierarchy. Articulating the importance of the reciprocity of both giving and receiving feedback is critical here. For students to get maximum benefit from participation in the groups, it is useful to draw their attention to the importance of listening to (that is, receiving) the feedback being offered, instead of leaping to defend their writing before considering the value of the critique: accepting the gift is just as important for binding communities together as is offering the feedback gift.

We know that writing groups are very useful in building collaborative communities (Guerin *et al.* 2013; Stracke 2010), and for developing confidence in doctoral students (Ferguson 2009; Maher *et al.* 2008; Mullen 2003). By considering writing groups through the lens of gift exchange theory, we can understand that the reciprocity of both giving and receiving is key to this effect, and thus explain at least some of how doctoral writing groups provide an important space for developing confident, autonomous researchers ready to thrive in collaborative scholarly communities.

References

Aitchison, C. (2009) 'Writing groups for doctoral education', *Studies in Higher Education*, 34: 8, 905–16.
Antal, B. and Richebé, N. (2009) 'A passion for giving, a passion for sharing: understanding knowledge sharing as gift exchange in academia', *Journal of Management Inquiry*, 18(1): 78–95.
Boud, D. and Lee, A. (2005) '"Peer learning" as pedagogic discourse for research education', *Studies in Higher Education*, 30(5): 501–16.
Boud, D., Cohen R., and Sampson, J. (eds) (2001) *Peer Learning in Higher Education: Learning From and With Each Other*, London: Kogan Page.
Bruffee, K. A. (1999) *Collaborative Learning: Higher Education, Interdependence, and the Authority of Knowledge* (2nd edn), Baltimore, MD: Johns Hopkins University Press.
Caffarella, R. S. and Barnett, B. G. (2000) 'Teaching doctoral students to become scholarly writers: the importance of giving and receiving critiques', *Studies in Higher Education*, 25(1): 39–52.
Davies, G., Whelan, S., Foley A. and Walsh, M. (2010) 'Gifts and gifting', *International Journal of Management Reviews*, 12: 413–34.
Douglas, M. (1990) 'Foreword', in M. Mauss, *The Gift: The Form and Reason for Exchange in Archaic Societies* (trans. W. D. Halls), New York: Norton.
Ferguson, T. (2009) 'The "write" skills and more: a thesis writing group for doctoral students', *Journal of Geography in Higher Education*, 33(2): 285–97.
Game, A. and Metcalfe, A. (2010) 'Presence of the gift', *Cultural Studies Review*, 16(1): 189–211.
Gere, A. R. and Abbott, R. D. (1985) 'Talking about writing: the language of writing groups', *Research in the Teaching of English*, 19(4): 362–85.
Green, B. (2005) 'Unfinished business: subjectivity and supervision', *Higher Education Research and Development*, 24(2): 151–63.
Guerin, C. and Green, I. (2013) '"They're the bosses": feedback in team supervision', *Journal of Further and Higher Education*, DOI:10.1080/0309877X.2013.831039.
Guerin, C., Xafis, V., Doda, D. V., Gillam, M., Larg, A., Luckner, H., Jahan, N., Widayati, A. and Xu, C. (2013) 'Diversity in collaborative research communities: a multicultural, multidisciplinary thesis writing group in Public Health', *Studies in Continuing Education*, 35(1): 65–81.
Haeussler, C. (2011) 'Information-sharing in academia and the industry: a comparative study', *Research Policy*, 40: 105–22.
Lauring, J. and Selmer, J. (2011) 'Social climate in diverse university departments: the role of internal knowledge sharing', *Educational Research*, 53(3): 347–62.
Lave, J. and Wenger, E. (1991) *Situated Learning: Legitimate Peripheral Participation*, Cambridge: Cambridge University Press.
Li, L. Y. and Vandermensbrugghe, J. (2011) 'Supporting the thesis writing process of international research students through an ongoing writing group', *Innovations in Education and Teaching International*, 48(2), 195–205.
Lundstrom, K. and Baker, W. (2009) 'To give is better than to receive: the benefits of peer review to the reviewer's own writing', *Journal of Second Language Writing*, 18: 30–43.

McAlpine, L. and Asghar, A. (2010) 'Enhancing academic climate: doctoral students as their own developers', *International Journal for Academic Development*, 15(2): 167–78.

Maher, D., Seaton, L., McMullen, C., Fitzgerald, T., Otsuji, E. and Lee, A. (2008) '"Becoming and being writers": the experiences of doctoral students in writing groups', *Studies in Continuing Education*, 30(3): 263–75.

Marcoux, J-S. (2009) 'Escaping the gift economy', *Journal of Consumer Research*, 36: 671–85.

Mauss, M. (1950/1969) *The Gift: Forms and Functions of Exchange in Archaic Societies* (trans. I. Cunningham), London: Cohen & West.

Mullen, C. A. (2003) 'The WIT cohort: a case study of informal doctoral mentoring', *Journal of Further and Higher Education*, 27(4): 411–26.

Stracke, E. (2010) 'Undertaking the journey together: peer learning for a successful and enjoyable PhD experience', *Journal of University Teaching & Learning Practice*, 7(1): 1–10.

Wang, T., and Li, Y. L. (2008) 'Understanding international research students' challenges and pedagogical needs in thesis writing', *International Journal of Pedagogies and Learning*, 4(3): 88–96.

Part III

Pedagogy in practice

Chapter 10

Scaffolding the thesis writing process

An ongoing writing group for international research students

Linda Li

Introduction

Writing a thesis in English often poses tremendous academic and linguistic demands on international research students using English as a Second Language (ESL).1 Research has revealed a wide range of challenges multilingual and ESL research students encounter in their thesis writing process (Bitchener & Basturkmen 2006; Cadman 1997, 2000; Cotterall 2011; Ryan & Zuber-Skerritt 1999; Tang 2012; Wang & Li 2008). Coming from diverse linguistic, educational and cultural backgrounds, ESL research students encounter academic writing conventions in western universities that are different from those in their prior educational systems (Paltridge 1997). Such differences may intensify their struggle to come to terms with the writing requirements during research candidature.

ESL research students are required to write with clarity and confidence in English despite often lacking confidence, especially for expressing complex ideas using formal academic language in English (Wang & Li 2008). Supervisors of ESL research students can also find language and writing-related problems present challenges in their supervisory practice (Robinson-Pant 2010). ESL research students' sense of inadequacy in English may influence their academic performance, slow their research and writing progress, affect their interaction with supervisors and peers, and discourage them from taking up available resources and seeking support (Sung 2000; Deem & Brehony 2000). Besides, social isolation can be more of an issue for these students than for their native-speaking peers (Dong 1998; Trice 2004). All these add to ESL students' struggle in completing a lengthy and complex thesis in English over a sustained period of time. To assist such students, it is imperative to provide writing support that can both address the students' pedagogical needs in thesis writing and connect them with peers in a supportive learning environment.

This chapter discusses an ongoing writing group as a viable approach to writing support for multilingual international students at an Australian university. The chapter draws on literature from the process approach to writing, the rhetorical genre perspective on second language writing, and research on cultural impacts on second language writing, with reference to my own observations and reflections on the writing group pedagogies and the students' perspectives and voices. Information from the students was gathered through surveys, interviews, focus groups and student written work-in-progress as part of the writing group processes. I begin the chapter with a brief description of the unique features of a writing group for multilingual international research students, highlighting linguistic and cultural diversity as the most challenging aspect. I then discuss five main themes from my pedagogical practice in facilitating a writing group of ESL research students. I conclude by suggesting an empathetic and culturally sensitive approach for facilitating writing groups of research students from diverse linguistic and cultural backgrounds.

The challenges of facilitating a writing group for multilingual research students

In response to the needs of international research students for additional practical writing support, I set up a writing group in 2005 to complement the existing program of thesis writing workshops for all research students. Since then, the writing group has been a regular feature of our provisions available across all faculties.

This writing group is characterized by the diversity of its participants, which presents challenges to both the participants and the facilitator. It is multidisciplinary, involving ESL research students at varying stages of candidature. Attendance at writing group meetings is voluntary, depending on students' interest, needs and availability. The idea is to run the group meeting weekly at a regular time and place, making it available as a space for ongoing writing support. Because group membership is not constant and participants can change from semester to semester, and even from week to week, it poses great challenges to participants and the facilitator for managing and maintaining the group dynamics. As pointed out by Aitchison (2010), the facilitator needs to attend to scheduling and organization details in order to keep the group running smoothly. Students intending to come to the writing group in a particular week respond to an email reminder from the facilitator with a short piece of writing of no more than five pages. They receive a compiled copy of all the papers and are expected to read the papers before the meeting. The number of pieces of writing the group work with depends on the number of participants, which varies from week to week, with an average of five or six at any one time. An email list is created which is updated regularly as a channel of communication for the group.

The most challenging aspect of the writing group is the linguistic and cultural diversity of the participants and how this affects writing group processes and pedagogies. The participants come from countries in Asia, the Middle East, South America, Africa and Europe, bringing diverse prior educational experiences, different conceptions of learning and research, and different learning styles. They also have varying levels of competence in academic English and different prior experiences with academic writing in their first language and in English. They often also have different expectations of the writing group and different understandings of its purpose and function, which influence their participation. These students' education and cultural traditions also influence interpersonal relationships and interactions with the facilitator and peers in the writing group. Such factors present challenges necessitating appropriate pedagogical responses on the part of the facilitator and mutual understandings and cooperation from the participants. A good understanding of the particular challenges of ESL student writers, as well as a genuine appreciation of their linguistic and cultural diversity, forms the basis of the writing group pedagogies presented in this chapter.

Attending to the thesis writing process

Writing skills and abilities are developed over time. For second language writers, it requires even more time and greater constant effort. As Paltridge and Starfield (2007) point out, research students need to see writing as an integral part of the research process, and this is especially vital for ESL students 'as the skills of writing are acquired developmentally over time and language continues to develop incrementally' (45). To assist ESL students to develop competence and confidence to tackle the challenge of thesis writing, it is important to attend to and scaffold their thesis writing process through its stages.

For this group, I draw on the 'process approach' to writing, which emphasizes the processes of writing (White & Arndt 1991), and the rhetorical genre perspective on second language writing, which highlights the use of language within social contexts (Tardy 2012). Attending to writing processes emphasizes writing as a cycle of revision consisting of drafting, revising and editing at different stages of the writing process, as well as the importance of feedback in developing writing skills and competence (Badger & White 2000). The ongoing writing group creates a learning space for ESL research students to experience process writing with regular feedback and discussion of their work-in-progress from peers who face similar writing challenges. Shared texts include the research proposal, draft thesis chapters, and other writing related to the thesis, such as the ethics application and conference papers. Students do not necessarily have to present a completed piece of work to the group. The student writer gets feedback from the writing group, revises the writing, and brings in another excerpt the following week. Sometimes the revised text is looked at again and further feedback offered for another round of revision. The drafting, revising and redrafting cycle thus goes on throughout the writing process. ESL students who attend the group meetings regularly over the span of their candidature gain sustained support from the early stage of research proposal writing, to the final stage of finishing up the thesis. One student who participated in the writing group regularly for two years commented:

> I got a lot from the writing group in the past two years. I started to join when I was writing my research proposal, now I have finished four chapters ... the most motivating one is my writing is progressed, it makes me feel good when I see one more piece of my writing is produced ... Feedback from the writing

group is very helpful, it helps me to improve the quality of my writing bit by bit ... If I say my supervisors guide my thesis writing, the writing group gives good assistance throughout the writing process.

The writing group focuses its discussion on using language effectively to make meaning clear. It involves 'hands-on' close reading and critique of the text. To facilitate collaborative revision on the text, I project a piece of writing onto a screen using a computer and a data projector. I then guide the group to look at the text closely, make comments and suggestions, and use Microsoft Word's *Track Changes* facility to revise the text collaboratively. The *Comment* option is often used for recording questions and comments. As there is limited time for each text, only a selected section, which is often chosen by the student writer, will be projected. The following excerpt shows both the draft and the revised version, providing an example of how collaborative group effort improves the clarity and quality of the writing. Unclear or problematic language usage is highlighted in italics, and the questions and comments are in brackets. The sentences are numbered for the sake of analysis here.

Draft version with questions and comments from the group

[1] Whenever new technologies *invented*, debates about whether the new technology can foster the citizen participation or not in the policy making process *rose*
[The structure of this sentence is not so balanced; the verb 'rose' is put at the end of the sentence. Maybe change the sentence structure?]

[2] The debates about the internet's potential for engaging the citizen participation have been *distinguished as ever*.
[Not clear what you mean with the word 'distinguished'. Do you mean a lot of debates about the issue?]

[3] The *internet's strength*, such as freedom of speech and non-limitation in the space and time, provide *more chance* to involve the citizen participation in the policy making process than any other technologies.
[This sentence can be restructured too.]

[4] Especially, the internet's effect of democracy is no longer the theoretical domain of utopian dreams but it is increasing embedded in the real of politics.
[It is not easy to understand what you mean here. Do you want to compare theory and practice?]

[5] *On the one hand*, E-democracy conjures up the new arguments around the political participation, sovereignty and direct democracy.

[6] *One the other*, e-democracy can *make* more accessibility and higher citizen participation in public decision-making process.
[Is this the correct use of 'on one hand, on the other hand'?]

> **Revised version with questions and comments for further revision**
>
> [1] Whenever a new technology is introduced, it brings about debates about whether the new technology can foster citizen participation in the policy making process.
> [2] The debates about the internet's potential for engaging citizen participation have been the most controversial so far.
> *[Why? You can provide a brief explanation in 2–3 sentences here]*
> [3] The internet provides more chances to involve citizen participation in the policy making process than any other technologies because it has no limitations of space and time, and it provides more opportunities for freedom of speech from anyone.
> [4] In particular, the internet's impact on democracy is no longer in the theoretical domain of utopian dreams; it is increasingly embedded in the reality of politics.
> *[What does this mean? Maybe you can explain it a bit.]*
> [5] While e-democracy conjures up new arguments around political participation, sovereignty and direct democracy, it provides citizens more accesses to public decision-making processes.

The draft version with questions and comments summarizes several writing issues identified by the group and their collaborative effort to improve the clarity of meaning-making here. In sentences [1] and [3], the sentence structure is improved so the message is more clearly delivered; in sentences [2] and [4], ambiguous words are replaced; sentences [5] and [6] are combined to make a more coherent statement about e-democracy. It is important to point out that the revised text is not yet a finished product, as the group left questions and comments for the writer to further develop and revise the writing.

Receiving regular feedback on writing increases awareness of the reader, allowing authors to focus on making writing clear and readable, an important aspect when it comes to doctoral thesis examination (Carter 2008). One participant reflected:

> It is a good opportunity to check whether others can understand what I'm trying to explain. In other words, people in the same area of interests may understand and follow my writing while others may find difficulty in understanding ... so I have to think of the reader when I write, will my writing make people understand?

In offering comments and suggestions for revision, participants are reminded to place the text in context. This focus is in line with the rhetorical genre approach which emphasizes that writing varies with the social context in which it is produced (Tardy 2012). In thesis writing, the disciplinary practices and conventions are an important part of the social context (Hyland 2000). Participants from different disciplines have the opportunity to compare and contrast disciplinary differences in thesis writing, for example, the structural elements of varied research designs, and the writing conventions and distinctive styles of particular disciplinary discourses. The use of language is viewed with regard to the social and cultural contexts of writing, with particular assumptions about knowledge and inquiry, shared values and reader expectations (Hyland 2000). When immediate answers cannot be found to address discipline-related language issues, I advise the students to pick up the clues from the literature in their own field of study. Thus, the specific questions raised in the writing group become the starting point of learning that further engages the research students beyond the writing group, and within the disciplinary context of their research. They not only develop self-awareness of linguistic forms, but also critical awareness of disciplinary discourses and rhetorical genre knowledge related to their field of study.

Risk-taking with language use in a threat-free peer learning environment

Writing a lengthy and complex thesis over a sustained period of time can be a highly emotional process (Aitchison *et al.* 2012). There is a range of psycho-affective issues that may affect the student writers' ability to write and the writing process (Wellington 2010). For ESL students, the emotional stakes are sometimes even higher. Research reveals that international students' lack of confidence about writing 'up to the standard' in English is a common cause of writing anxiety, which can become paralysing (Paltridge & Starfield 2007). Murray (2002) points out that the student's fear of judgement from the supervisor may even lead to avoidance behaviour, which can hinder the development of the student writer. ESL student writers might need particular support to build writing confidence.

A writing group that consists of ESL research students provides a safe and threat-free space for participants to share their written work-in-progress with peers who experience similar writing difficulties, and who, like themselves, are struggling to express complex ideas in English. As one participant put it:

> English is not our first language so it's not easy for us to write well in English. I usually took my writing to the writing group, then I showed it to my supervisor ... This is a threat-free place to test my writing. Other students help to correct my mistakes. I find it's not easy work for everyone. Sometimes I find they are making the same mistakes like the tense, sentence structure so I know I'm not the only one having problems in writing.

The peer readers in the writing group empathize with the kind of mistakes the writer makes in developing advanced level writing skills in English. As second language writers themselves, they too make similar mistakes and experience similar frustrations. The empathy from the participants as first readers of work-in-progress is emotionally helpful. The student writers are not intimidated by the feeling of their unfinished writing being judged by the authority or experts in an either 'accept' or 'reject' situation; they are reassured that they are not alone in their struggles and blunders. Such emotional and psychological support from the writing group helps to reduce writing anxiety and enhance the intangible result of building confidence. One student commented:

> We got many benefits from this writing group, we can share our ideas and we help each other. Everyone in the group seems to understand what we are doing and give comments and ideas. This is very helpful, I feel supported … I'm not so worried about making mistakes now, I can see improvement in my writing … the confidence we gain from this group, what we did and what we wrote is not too bad.

The writing group also contributes to lowering the writer's anxiety through collaborative group efforts to revise and improve written work-in-progress. Second language writers often grapple with getting 'the right words to say the right things'. They often have to check words in the dictionary and are not certain about the appropriateness of certain linguistic choices. To maximize the opportunity for peer learning and peer support in the writing group, I often turn to participants for suggestions about revision on ideas and, more importantly, on using language to express ideas. In the close reading of an excerpt, we stop at certain sentences or words and look for alternative expressions. This happens when someone raises a question about the meaning of certain sentences or words. I ask the group: 'Is this clear to everyone?', and then ask the student writer: 'What do you mean here?'. Comments and discussions then follow, focusing on restructuring the sentence or rewording to make meaning clearer.

Sometimes the process is straightforward as the group agrees on suggested changes without further questions, yet at other times the process is more involved and reiterative as the group try different alternatives in restructuring a sentence or rewording a phrase. Learning happens when students are collaboratively playing around, testing and deciding on the best ways to use words to make meaning clearer. At such learning points, participants would often turn to me as the language expert. Instead of giving the answers, I seize the opportunity to guide the group to explore risk-taking with language use. The group try different words, or different ordering of words in a sentence, then look at the change, read aloud the text to hear how it sounds, and ask the writer whether this is what is meant; if not, the group try out more alternatives. If needed, the dictionary or thesaurus is used. The end product is more than just a changed or better sentence or word; students have also learnt how a more effective sentence structure or a more specific word can be used to make a clearer and stronger statement. Experimenting with the use of language to enhance meaning-making helps ESL student writers realize the power of words in accurately expressing meaning, reflecting the writer's attitude, and representing the writer's voice. As one participant commented:

> I think my language is better and when I write, I know how to use words, what word is suitable, what word is proper, what word is more academic, what word will make the misunderstanding for the reader.

To extend the learning for ESL students from the writing group, we take collective quick notes from the discussion; I then organize and circulate the notes to participants after each meeting. The following is an example of the summary notes from a meeting during which four papers were discussed:

Notes from a writing group meeting

For Paper 1 – excerpt from the Results chapter of a Masters' thesis in Tourism Management

- Be selective in explaining the figures, highlight the most significant ones
- Tense – use past tense when reporting findings, present tense when referring to tables and graphs, comparing results
- Use consistent terms – e.g. participants/respondents, 30%/thirty percent, online/on-line, web-site/website
- Prepositions – for, of, in

For Paper 2 – excerpt from the Introduction chapter of a PhD thesis in Public Administration

- Avoid assuming the reader will know – give clear information about the background of your topic
- Break up some long sentences, state the main point first, give the explanation in another sentence
- Ways to provide references, avoid always starting with xxx states/claims
- Use of pronouns – must be clear what nouns they refer to, or repeat the nouns
- Use of article 'the' and 'a' – be careful when to use them and when not to use them

For Paper 3 – excerpt from the Literature Review chapter of a PhD thesis in Education

- Need to conclude this section, relate it to the relevance of your topic, i.e. the relevance of Piaget's developmental theory to child language learning and teaching

- Work on sentence variety, use different ways to start a sentence, combine short sentences
- Consistency of terms, e.g. second language/L2, students/pupils
- Paragraph level – need to have a topic sentence, use some linking sentences between paragraphs

For Paper 4 – excerpt from an Honours' thesis in Literary Analysis

- You have used a lot of quotes. Can you paraphrase them? Separate long quotes from your sentences
- Be consistent in your use of quotes, sometimes they are in quotation marks, sometimes they are in italics
- Confusing use of punctuation, e.g. colon, pay attention to the use of commas when using 'therefore', 'however'
- Be careful with the correct use of linking words, e.g. however, on the one hand, on the other hand
- Sentence structure – don't over use 'but' and 'and' to link sentences

These notes not only document the learning that takes place, but also point to further learning the student writers can take up to expand their linguistic and rhetorical repertoire. The sharing of notes that summarize a variety of writing issues common in second language writing also provides pointers for ESL student writers to enhance their self-awareness of language use in thesis writing. As a result, they are able to take more control of their own use of language, leading to enhanced confidence in writing in English as a second language.

Learning to incorporate feedback to improve written work-in-progress

The opportunity to revise written work based on feedback is considered key to the development of scholar writers (Knowles 1999). The benefits of giving and receiving feedback as a means of learning and writing development have been well documented (e.g., Aitchison 2010; Caffarella & Barnett 2000). Research on feedback highlights the importance of international research students learning how to receive and act upon feedback by incorporating useful elements of it in their writing (Wang & Li 2011).

The critiquing process of the writing group creates a number of opportunities for ESL student writers to learn how to respond to and act upon feedback on their writing in a supportive peer learning environment. In this process, students develop the skills to respond to questions and the ability to articulate their agreement or disagreement with feedback on their writing. There is constant negotiation of meaning between the writer and readers. Participants often seek clarification of meaning; the writer has the opportunity to explain, restate, rephrase or reword. There are extended discussions about the appropriate choice of words, or the reasons for re-organizing or re-structuring sentences, and how the changes would make meaning clearer to the reader. The process is iterative, involving turn-taking to question and answer, inquire and clarify, agree and disagree, and probe and confirm ideas. Such a feedback process helps to establish the student writer's self-confidence and enhance the sense of ownership of one's own words in writing. One student commented:

> The feedback is very useful because when you get questions and suggestions from others and that make you think, you have to look at your writing again and again and decide how to change the way you say things so people understand what you are saying … Most times I found the suggestions very useful, sometimes I had to explain more, why I use that word and why I wrote like that.

ESL research students also learn to develop a positive attitude towards receiving critical feedback through the writing group critiquing process. The process of receiving feedback, particularly critical comments on one's writing, may involve anxiety, fear or doubt about one's ability to write (Caffarella & Barnett 2000). Critical feedback is particularly sensitive in a writing group of ESL research students as some participants may come from cultures where open and direct critique is not encouraged (Li & Vandermensbrugghe 2011). As Aitchison (2010) points out, the crucial role of the facilitator in modelling, monitoring and providing explicit instruction for critiquing makes a difference to peer interaction in the writing group. To scaffold and guide the critiquing process, I use specific questions, prompts and explicit instructions. I invite participants to make comments, starting with a positive prompt: 'What I like about this piece of writing is …'; I ask questions such as 'As a reader, do you feel you've got any questions to ask the writer?', 'What else do you want to know about this method/concept?'. This is another way of saying 'Is there anything unclear to you?'. Guiding the critiquing process with questions which prompt the writers to rethink the clarity and logic of their writing is a less direct way of challenging the ESL student writers than negative comments. Such a technique can also be applied to scrutinize the use of language. Participants learn from asking and answering questions that direct their attention to look closely at specific linguistic forms that relate the use of language to meaning-making. When participants understand the purpose of feedback and the value of learning from each other's feedback, they can appreciate and learn more from what they receive. One participant commented:

> I learnt a lot from the feedback from other students. At first I was nervous when other students pointed out my writing mistakes, I got the grammar wrong, or I got a wrong word, like there were a lot of mistakes in my writing. But I made

the corrections, and I looked at my writing again, and it got better ... It's actually very helpful to have those questions and get suggestions how to correct the mistakes, it improved my writing.

The writing group provides a regular time and space for multilingual student writers to experience writing and rewriting through learning to incorporate feedback from peers, which leads to improved clarity in writing, and increased confidence about writing.

Exploring the cultural impacts on second language writing

Apart from the linguistic challenge of struggling to express complex ideas in a second language, multilingual research students are also confronted by a western academic culture where the conventions and expectations of academic writing may be quite different (Ha & Baurain 2011; Wang & Li 2008). A culturally diverse writing group creates a space for participants to explore cultural impacts and develop critical awareness of their personal approach to academic writing in English.

One common topic for discussion is the 'different ways of thinking' in academic writing, which influence the way second language writers organize and structure their writing. Even with an essential writing skill such as paragraphing, there are obvious differences in how the text is expected to be constructed in different languages. In English academic writing, it is conventional to state the main idea at the beginning of a paragraph, then elaborate with evidence and logical reasoning. However, this approach may be quite unfamiliar to some writers, as is evidenced from these student comments:

> I think we have different thinking ways, because I am from China and most Chinese people will put the most important sentence at last. But in Western style they put the most important sentence at the beginning ... If I change my thinking ways, it's difficult for me. And sometimes this is the great challenge.

> As an Arab we have a different writing. We give direction first and at the end you will find like the conclusion or the things you want to say. I find in English it is not that way, it is mostly you find the important things in the top and down is the explanation ... so in my thinking, I have to switch from this idea to the English idea.

Being aware of such differences helps multilingual student writers develop a critical awareness of the rhetorical conventions of academic writing in English. When the group looks at a piece of writing and a question about the order or the organization of ideas is raised, I seize the opportunity to invite participants to share and reflect on writing in their first language. A comparing and contrasting approach is useful in this case. It is interesting for participants to share how the same thing is done in writing in different languages, and what cultural considerations are important in understanding why writing is done in a particular way.

Differences in academic writing conventions in different languages and cultures may also impact on second language writing. For example, while precise referencing to sources of ideas is an integral feature of academic writing in English, it is not practised in some academic traditions (Ballard & Clanchy 1997). Students coming from such traditions need to develop a different understanding of academic integrity and practise referencing conventions. In the writing group, the writer may be asked: 'Is this your own writing, or somebody else's?' Such questions heighten the writer's sense of the need to acknowledge sources and the writing of others in English academic writing. In facilitating the exploration of cultural impacts on writing, I draw on relevant principles from research in contrastive rhetoric. Derived from Kaplan's (1966) original work, research in this area has identified important differences in the ways academic texts are written across different languages and cultures (Connor 1996). Although I am aware of the criticism of the reductionism and oversimplification in contrastive rhetoric research, and the stereotyped view of the writing of students from certain cultures (Leki 1997), it has proved useful to help students understand important aspects of their writing.

While guiding multilingual student writers to explore the cultural impacts on their academic writing in English, I have found it is useful to encourage them to examine their personal and individual writing style, focusing on their own distinctive patterns of language use. A participant reflected:

> I found I wrote very long sentences, sometimes other students can't understand, I have to make my sentence short ... I used long quotations like paragraphs. My supervisor told me to write more in my own words. I did my Masters thesis in Chinese, it's okay to use a lot of quotations, I think we should quote the experts.

This student's comment reflects how cultural beliefs and values influence the approach of second language writers to academic writing in English. In Asian countries of Confucian heritage cultures, for example, there is a tradition of demonstrating respect for scholarship through verbatim repetition of the sayings of the great thinkers and the words of leading scholars (Ballard & Clanchy 1997). Such belief in respecting the 'words of wisdom' may result in what is regarded as excessive use of quotations in English, where writers are expected to adopt a critical approach to scholarship and establish their own writer's voice; they are expected to write in their own words rather than repeating the words of the experts. A critical awareness of how cultural beliefs and values impact on their writing in English helps multilingual student writers develop understanding of the expectations of the academic reader in English, and the ability to adopt appropriate writing practices within the social context of research writing in their own field of study.

Capitalizing on linguistic and cultural diversity

International research students in western universities bring with them rich linguistic and cultural resources from their previous educational and professional experiences. They may hold academic or professional positions in their home country; they can be well-established academics or professionals with substantial experience, knowledge and skills in their field of study or profession; they may enjoy high status and shoulder enormous responsibility in their previous positions. Some of them speak multiple languages other than English. These students' prior educational, professional and cultural knowledge and experience should be acknowledged, validated and capitalized on. A PhD student in computer science stated:

> I used to work in the military in the computer department for eighteen years. My past experience is useful for my PhD research because I got a lot of ideas, I have a lot of technical skills ... I'm trying to develop a new model, trying to create a new relationship between human and the computer so they cooperate in problem solving.

In facilitating the writing group, I encourage students to make full use of their linguistic and cultural resources that are relevant both to their mother tongue and the English language. One advantage multilingual students have is their linguistic knowledge of English learned through formal instruction. Often they are taught English grammar in their early language learning years, thus they have the linguistic knowledge and metalanguage to critique the use of language in their peers' academic writing. In examining the use of language in writing, I guide students to draw on their linguistic and grammatical knowledge of both their first language and English. For example, a Thai student compared the differences between Thai and English in terms of word order and tense:

> One example is like adjectives and nouns, we place differently. In Thai we put noun first and we put adjective. In English, we put adjective and then noun ... there is no tense in Thai, we have one word for all the time, it's very different from English. This is one example I know that can affect my writing in English. So I always pay more attention to tense.

As illustrated in the comment above, being aware of some salient linguistic differences in one's mother tongue and English enables multilingual students to turn the differences from sources of difficulty to resources useful for developing writing skills in a new language. Some students in the writing group have more metalanguage for the linguistic system of English, for example, one member is a PhD student writing a thesis on teaching English as a second language, who was a university English lecturer before enrolling in her doctoral study. At times, I step back and let this student take the role of the teacher to explain to peers particular language usage problems. Entrusting students with the role of sharing and passing on knowledge about how English works boosts their confidence in their ability to control the language. It makes them notice their particular strengths as writers of English as a second language, in contrast with the deficit model of international students that focuses only on their problems with the English language (Robinson-Pant 2010).

It is empowering for multilingual research students to realize that their second language learning experience can actually give them the advantage of writing in English with a good knowledge of its formal linguistic properties and grammatical rules. Such knowledge enables them to talk about writing by focusing on specific linguistic forms that must be clarified for meaning-making. This makes the kind of discussion in the writing group of multilingual research students different from writing groups consisting of mainly native speakers of English, where the conversations do not often deal with specific linguistic forms (e.g., Aitchison & Lee 2010). It is important to point out that the group discussion does not focus exclusively on linguistic and grammatical matters. Often the discussion goes beyond the sentence level to the discourse level of the text, looking at the links between ideas, the logic in developing an argument, and group members offer responses as interested readers.

Multilingual students' knowledge and experience of writing in their first language can also be utilized to expand their rhetorical genre knowledge of academic writing in English. By reflecting on their first language writing experiences, students can draw on their personal strengths in writing while they develop writing skills in a new language, as the following comment illustrates:

> In my home country I have won the gold medal in education from our King. I was a good student there … In Arabic I wrote to the newspapers, I wrote a lot. I had to know what the newspaper, who read the newspaper, and I used a way to convince others, yeah in my opinion this by itself is an art … for me writing is like programming language for knowledge. This is how I see writing. If you don't have the knowledge you can't do a computer program … I have to know more about English writing so I can appeal to the people like in Arabic.

Conclusion

The writing group creates a supported space to motivate multilingual/ESL research students to engage in regular production of writing through a productive cycle of drafting, giving and receiving feedback, revising and redrafting. ESL research students are scaffolded and guided through the thesis writing process with regular sharing and discussion of their work-in-progress with peers in the writing group. Supported throughout the thesis writing process, students set specific writing goals following the pace of the writing group, break the lengthy thesis into more manageable bite-sized texts, and make gradual and incremental progress in their thesis writing journey. Understanding and empathy from peers who face similar writing challenges help to reduce writing anxiety and enhance confidence about writing. Non-English speaking background research students learn how to incorporate feedback into their revision through the interactive critiquing process by responding to and addressing questions about their written drafts and acting upon suggestions and comments from peers. A positive learning attitude towards critical comments enhances the benefits of learning from peer feedback.

In facilitating a writing group for doctoral students from diverse linguistic and cultural backgrounds, it is important to bear in mind that international research students are not a homogenous group; rather, they represent a variety of backgrounds and needs. Those working with international research students should show a genuine interest in understanding the challenges and struggles faced by students coming to terms with the academic and linguistic demands of writing a thesis in English as a second language. Instead of seeing international students as problems, we should take a more positive and encouraging approach to international students that respects the cultural resources and the varying strengths students bring to academic research and writing. While helping these research students to explore the cultural impacts on their academic writing in English, we should also encourage them to draw on their knowledge and experience of their first language as linguistic and cultural capital for developing advanced academic writing skills in English. An empathetic and culturally sensitive approach is suggested for facilitators of writing groups for working with students from diverse linguistic and cultural backgrounds.

Note

1 There is considerable discussion regarding the most appropriate terminology to use when referring to the linguistic background of international students. In this article, I have elected to use 'English as a Second Language' (ESL) as this term has currency in the literature and in language teaching. Given the fact that many international students speak more than two languages, I have referred to 'multilingual' students wherever ESL fails to communicate the cultural and linguistic richness of these students.

References

Aitchison, C. (2010) 'Learning together to publish: writing group pedagogies for doctoral publishing', in C. Aitchison, B. Kamler and A. Lee (eds) *Publishing Pedagogies for the Doctorate and Beyond*, London: Routledge.

Aitchison, C. and Lee, A. (2010) 'Writing in, writing out: doctoral writing as peer work', in M. Walker and P. Thomson (eds) *The Routledge Doctoral Supervisor's Companion*, London: Routledge.

Aitchison, C., Catterall, J. Ross, P. and Burgin, S. (2012) '"Tough love and tears": learning doctoral writing in the sciences', *Higher Education Research and Development*, 31(4): 435–47.

Badger, R. and White, G. (2000) 'A process genre approach to teaching writing', *ELT Journal*, 54(2): 153–60.

Ballard, B. and Clanchy, J. (1997) *Teaching International Students: A Brief Guide for Lecturers and Supervisors*, Deakin, ACT: IDP Education Australia.

Bitchener, J. and Basturkmen, H. (2006) 'Perceptions of the difficulties of postgraduate L2 thesis students writing the discussion section', *English for Specific Purposes*, 5: 4–18.

Cadman, K. (1997) 'Thesis writing for international students: A question of identity?', *English for Specific Purposes*, 16(1): 3–14.

—— (2000) '"Voices in the air": evaluations of the learning experiences of international postgraduates and their supervisors', *Teaching in Higher Education*, 5(4): 475–91.

Caffarella, R. S. and Barnett, B. G. (2000) 'Teaching doctoral students to become scholarly writers: the importance of giving and receiving critiques', *Studies in Higher Education*, 25(1): 39–52.

Carter, S. (2008) 'Examining the doctoral thesis: a discussion', *Innovations in Education and Teaching International*, 45(4): 365–74.

Connor, U. (1996) *Contrastive Rhetoric: Cross-Cultural Aspects of Second-Language Writing*, Cambridge: Cambridge University Press.

Cotterall, S. (2011) 'Doctoral students writing: where's the pedagogy?', *Teaching in Higher Education*, 16(4): 413–25.

Deem, R. and Brehony, K. J. (2000) 'Doctoral students' access to research culture – are some more unequal than others?', *Studies in Higher Education*, 25: 149–65.

Dong, Y. R. (1998) 'Non-native speaker graduate students' thesis/dissertation writing in science: self-reports by students and their advisors from two U.S. institutions', *English for Specific Purpose*, 17: 369–90.

Ha, P. L. and Baurain, B. (2011) (eds) *Voices, Identities, Negotiation and Conflicts: Writing Academic English Across Cultures*, Bingley, UK: Emerald.

Hyland, K. (2000) *Disciplinary Discourses: Social Interaction in Academic Writing*, London: Longman.

Kaplan, R. B. (1966) 'Cultural thought patterns in intercultural education', *Language Learning*, 16: 1–20.

Knowles, S. (1999) 'Feedback on writing in postgraduate supervision: echoes in response—context, continuity and resonance', in A. Holbrook and S. Johnson (eds) *Supervision of Postgraduate Research Education*, Coldstream, VIC: Australian Association for Research in Education.

Leki, I. (1997) 'Cross-talk: ESL issues and contrastive rhetoric', in C. Severino, J. C. Guerra and S. E. Butler (eds), *Writing in the Multicultural Settings*, New York: Modern Language Association of America.

Li, L. Y. and Vandermensbrugghe, J. (2011) 'Supporting the thesis writing process of international research students through an ongoing writing group', *Innovations in Education and Teaching International*, 48(2): 195–205.

Murray, R. (2002) *How to Write a Thesis*, Buckingham, UK: Open University Press.

Paltridge, B. (1997) 'Thesis and dissertation: preparing ESL students for research', *English for Specific Purposes*, 16(1): 61–70.

Paltridge, B. and Starfield, S. (2007) *Thesis and Dissertation Writing in a Second Language*, London: Routledge.

Robinson-Pant, A. (2010) 'Internationalising of higher education: challenges for the doctoral supervisor', in M. Walker and P. Thomson (eds) *The Routledge Doctoral Supervisor's Companion*, London: Routledge, 147–57.

Ryan, J. and Zuber-Skerritt, O. (1999) *Supervising Postgraduates from Non-English Speaking Backgrounds*, Buckingham: The Society for Research into Higher Education and Open University Press.

Sung, C-I. (2000) 'Investigating rounded academic success: the influence of English language proficiency, academic performance, and socio-academic interaction for Taiwanese doctoral students in the United States', unpublished PhD dissertation, University of Michigan.

Tang, R. (ed.) (2012) *Academic Writing in a Second or Foreign Language: Issues and Challenges Facing ESL/EFL Academic Writers in Higher Education Contexts*, London: Continuum International Publishing Group.

Tardy, C. M. (2012) 'A rhetorical genre theory perspective on L2 writing development', in R. M. Manchón (ed.) *L2 Writing Development: Multiple Perspectives*, Boston: Walter de Gruyter.

Trice, A. G. (2004) 'Mixing it up: international graduate students' social interactions with American students', *Journal of College Student Development*, 45(6): 671–87.

Wang, T. and Li, Y. L. (2008) 'Understanding international research students' challenges and pedagogical needs in thesis writing', *International Journal of Pedagogies and Learning*, 4(3): 88–96.

—— (2011) '"Tell me what to do" vs. "guide me through it": feedback experiences of international doctoral students', *Active Learning in Higher Education*, 12(2): 101–12.

Wellington, J. (2010) 'More than a matter of cognition: an exploration of affective writing problems for postgraduate students and their possible solutions', *Teaching in Higher Education*, 15: 135–50.

White, R. and Arndt, V. (1991) *Process Writing*, Harlow: Longman.

Chapter 11

'If they're not laughing, watch out!'
Emotion and risk in postgraduate writers' circles

Lucia Thesen

The comment 'If they're not laughing, watch out!' in the title of this chapter is from a recorded discussion in which facilitators reflected on the emerging practices in multidisciplinary writers' circles and attempted to identify pointers for colleagues who might want to initiate similar circles. We noted several tensions in the fine line that facilitators walk in leading these circles. One of the most significant is the line between the need to offer a space where an 'august' rational and serious postgraduate writer identity is acknowledged while at the same time a range of emotions such as anger, envy and particularly parodic laughter, is regarded as legitimate and productive. We interviewed a member of our group, Clement Chihota, a colleague who was central to developing writers' circles in our Writing Centre. The recorded discussion shows our preoccupation with laughter. In the recording, I recall how when I first started running circles, they were much too earnest: I envied Clement's circles, which were jokingly referred to as 'laughing circles'. Some colleagues even complained about the noise. Clement reflects that 'Laughter is an index of how well it's worked, and how likely people are to come back. If they're not laughing, watch out!'. This chapter tries to understand the place of laughter in the emerging pedagogy of the writers' groups that we have offered at a university in South Africa.

The chapter begins with a brief location of our approach in the field of postgraduate writing pedagogy, which emphasizes the importance of low stakes peer writing spaces. This is followed by a description of one of the forms—the weekly multidisciplinary circle—that writers' circles have taken at my university. I focus on who comes and what we do. Then some moments of laughter are reconstructed, before establishing a link between emotion, specifically laughter, and writing. I do this via an exploration of risk, not in the 'cold' sense of risk management that McWilliam (2009) regrets, but in a warm and productive sense, in which emotion is central. I hope to suggest some productive links between writing, risk and laughter. We need to put the full complexity of the writing experience back into research writing and pedagogy, to unite laughter and seriousness as envisaged by Bakhtin, 'to offer a chance of a new outlook on the world' (Bakhtin 1968: 34).

In the years since we started writers' circles, interesting work has begun to emerge about the writing group and its place in postgraduate pedagogy, and we are now able to relate practices in writers' circles to similar scholarly work elsewhere. The principle of peer-based writing pedagogy is well established in undergraduate writing scholarship, particularly in the process-writing movement (Murray 1978; Elbow 1998), but it is relatively recent in the postgraduate sphere. Boud and Lee (2005) argue for a shift in the discourse from seeing research as training to seeing research as education. The training discourse is saturated with an emphasis on vertical 'provisionism', with strategies for more effective supervision and funding to improve graduation throughput. The shift that Boud and Lee argue for seeks a more horizontal, distributed notion of peer learning. For them, the notion of the peer group is useful in the research-writing field as it is already present at the centre of the research identity: the researcher works collaboratively, 'at the centre of a constellation of others' (Cullen *et al.* cited in Boud & Lee, 2005: 21). The interest in writing pedagogy, and particularly in writing groups, signals a desire for a more nuanced understanding of the challenges of research completion, and the need for a wider range of responses to support postgraduates in their writing. This need is enhanced by the changing context in which geographical and conceptual mobility are rapidly becoming the norm. Thus, Cuthbert *et al.* (2009) emphasize the role of multidisciplinary groups in enhancing the likelihood of getting published, Parker (2009) evaluates the possibilities for community-learning approaches in 'scholarly writing groups', and Aitchison (2009) analyzes how the pedagogy of writing groups for doctoral researchers actually works, noting an unintended but crucial shift in disposition: a growing confidence in the value of critique. Collectively these articles attempt to share the practice and possibilities of this emerging pedagogy.

Those who argue for a role for peer-based writing groups (and their possibilities for dispersed authority) caution against any easy claim that peer pedagogy is a 'good thing'. Boud and Lee (2005) warn that 'questions of power and difference are conceptualized only in terms of a reduction in top-down imposition of pedagogic authority' (514). They note that 'There is a general need to surface assumptions of the "good" in pedagogical discourses such as peer learning and to be vigilant in relation to the dangers of idealizing which accompany horizontalizing moves in pedagogy' (515). They call for situated and nuanced approaches that do not romanticize peer relationships. This chapter is written partly in response to their call, as it seeks to make links between laughter, risk and postgraduate writing. The paradox of laughing while at the same time engaging the seriousness of postgraduate writing is invited in the flatter spaces offered by writers' circles. I believe that these practices have a place, but only as one of many responses to the complexities of the postgraduate experience. There is no single pedagogy that can hold all that is going on. Perhaps the greatest strength of writers' circles is that they can open up our understanding of the predicament of being a postgraduate. They can offer a multifaceted lens for what is going on in a time of intense institutional change in internationalizing universities.

The thursday multidisciplinary writers' circle

Several different forms of writers' circles have evolved since they were first introduced at the University of Cape Town under the umbrella of the cross-faculty postgraduate writing development project I work in. There are cohort-specific circles such as the one offered for scholarship students in their Honours year, or 'tailor-made' circles for groups of students where there is a need, such as a conference to prepare for. These tend to be tightly structured and sequenced. For this chapter and its focus on laughter, the most interesting circle is the weekly multidisciplinary Thursday circle, which has been running for six years. While the students in this group come and go, continuity has been provided by the facilitators, initially Clement, and then me, once I had developed the confidence to take over. Both of us have backgrounds in applied linguistics and writing pedagogy. In general, the students who come to this circle are in search of community. They have typically not come through the University's undergraduate and Honours programs and so don't know the institutional ropes. They reflect the changing demographics of the globalizing university with its drivers of internationalization and widening participation. Many are international students, usually from sub-Saharan Africa; they are typically older, often women, have careers in service professions and are returning to university after an absence. Many are between disciplines, or find themselves in disciplines that are changing rapidly or look different in the form they have taken at this university. Most who attend are in the social sciences and humanities, where the cohesion of the research lab is absent. Some have only recently adopted English as the primary language of learning, and welcome the opportunity to speak English in a low-stakes environment. There are a few students who are also staff members who attend, perhaps because they find it easier to risk vulnerability outside of their departmental settings.

The practices in this lightly held circle are described more fully in Chihota and Thesen (in press). We conceptualize these circles as rehearsal spaces where writers may try out their attachments to ideas and styles. A key feature is that membership of this group is very fluid. People move in and out as it suits them. Sometimes students come once or twice and then move on. Others won't attend for months due to clashing commitments, then reappear to report on progress, or get a hearing for a poster they are about to present at a conference. A loose presence is maintained through the university's internal online learning interface, known as Vula, which enables us to keep in touch through a virtual presence. The circles are held together by weekly messages that I send to the whole group. We use these messages to make announcements and share resources. The focus of the circle is usually two pages of writing offered by one of the members. There is a second element to the organization of the circles—a focus on some aspect of skill or theory that has a bearing on writing. The facilitator, or one of the members, chooses a skills focus that ideally complements the piece offered for review that day. The skills focus may be on an aspect of writing, for example, voice in the literature review, or something else on the edges of the writing process—blogging as a parallel practice, or managing your supervisor, a discussion of what Bourdieu's habitus means for us as writers. The idea is that peer review is done in the group, so there is no homework, although members often make their own plans for peer reading outside of the circle.

It must be said that the circle sometimes feels very fragile, and the flattened hierarchy of the group does not solve all problems. When students leave the circle, I am often not sure of the reasons. Some leave because they have graduated. The 'acknowledgments' in their theses often attest to the role that these peer circles have played in their lives. Others leave because a need has been met, and they are ready to move on, having enjoyed the structure that a weekly forum offers. Or sometimes a need has *not* been met. I have not followed up on those who do not attend for more than a few sessions. Perhaps they were frustrated by the lack of uptake for their research; or perhaps they found the gender balance in the group unsettling.

Laughing and writing

I now reconstruct some moments in the circles where laughter was the defining experience in the group, before trying to theorize this emotional modality. Later I will look more closely at the quality of this laughter, and how it is never laughter directed at the individual, but always involving the group, as if pointing to some deeper shared aspect of postgraduate identity. The laughter seems to index community, spontaneity and a critical commentary on the prevailing image of the cerebral, isolated, gendered postgraduate student.

'You need to have a crush on your theorist'

In this circle, I had read the group a page from Geoff Dyer's book *Out of Sheer Rage: Wrestling with D.H. Lawrence* in the skills part of our circle. Dyer poignantly describes extended writer's block while working on his study of Lawrence (1998). This led to a discussion in the circle about points where circle participants felt blocked. Devi said that, for her, the hardest part was moving from reading others' theories to committing your thoughts to paper in the literature review. She said that she prolonged the reading, and delayed the writing: 'I think you need to have a crush on your theorist, enough of a crush to keep you going through the thesis'. This caused much laughter, reflections on what theorists were really like, their looks, politics, foibles, and what made ideas 'sexy'. We also explored the difference between flirting (i.e., on the internet) and developing a crush. The laughter in this circle seemed to play with and deflate the disembodied, cerebral, male image of the researcher and of theory itself, bending it to a different image—intense, personal, consequential.

'Are we actually enjoying this?' Drawing the feeling

The second moment I have chosen is also from the skills part of the circle. Someone in the circle suggested that we explore some creative ways of doing our skills activities, so I asked everyone to draw where they see themselves at this point. Most of the drawings had strong emotional content: there were beasts, crocodiles, fraught journeys, supervisors about to pounce. Ellen's drawing stays in my mind. It shows a desk with papers piled high: books on the right, and printouts of drafts on the left. In the centre is a small terrified pop-eyed cartoon face peering over the back of a chair, at an animated open laptop, with sharp teeth defining its edges. A heavily drawn cord links it to a plug, which has come adrift from its safe socket in the wall, and rears up, snake-like. We laughed when we saw her drawing, but also reflected on why the negativity in all our drawings. When we remembered this moment later, Ellen recalls the laughter, but says: 'We're having fun and laughing, but this makes me depressed. Are we actually enjoying this?' Here it is the drawing activity that opened up the suppressed territory of the emotions, as an alternative to the written word. Writing and printing have been tools of colonialism and the Enlightenment (Hofmeyr 1993; Delmas 2011). Ellen's changing emotions over time are interesting: her drawing, which turned struggle into the pleasure and release of laughter, enabling her to move beyond a moment of being 'stuck', is later questioned and seen as 'depressing' in its indulgence in the negative.

'Laughter unites us'

The final illustration is from a particularly challenging circle. Jo brought some of her data from her study of death and dying in Intensive Care Units (ICUs). She brought a drawing of a dying patient done by one of the participants in her study, a young male nurse, and read us an extract of her interview with him. Some members of the group gently challenged her for saying that the participants' words are 'a bit incoherent' as 'English isn't his first language'. The comments gradually moved away from the charged reality of the image, and Jo's interpretation, to safer ground where we could reflect on the difficulties of doing qualitative research. Towards the end of this intense and draining session, Elizabeth, a clinical psychologist, mimicked our different responses to Jo's introduction of her data. She went round the room, facing us one by one, acting our disbelief, sorrow, relief, scepticism and scholarly concern. Laughter united us, as she mirrored our different responses. What strikes me about the laughter here is the contrast to the seriousness of the subject of Jo's research on death and dying, as well as to the seriousness of the ensuing conversation in the group. By translating our stances into an embodied form recognizable through the emotions, Elizabeth did the emotional work to close the circle, helping us find common ground and repair the difficult session. In this sense it releases the tension.

These vignettes capture different facets of the writing experience that are brought to these rehearsal spaces. They index desire and fear, rationality and emotion, caught up in the same moment. They are in the wings, not at centre stage—that would be the completed thesis, the supervisory relationship. They are tangential, but strongly present, and ask us to expand our notion of research writing to include the centrality of emotion, that is not often afforded us in the cool and objective tones of the research register. They also suggest that different modes and genres brought alongside scholarly writing may open up new kinds of insight. I believe that our postcolonial context shapes these emotional experiences of writing in fundamental ways.

Writing in the contact zone: shadows and dilemmas

The 'contact zone' is Marie Louise Pratt's term, but it has strong echoes with Bakhtin's similar concept in which different social languages meet and refract. For Pratt (1999), the contact zone is 'social spaces where cultures meet, clash and grapple with each other, often in contexts of highly asymmetrical relations of power, such as colonialism, slavery and their aftermaths' (2) that people have to negotiate in educational settings. For Bakhtin (1981), the contact zone refers to the space where 'authoritative discourses' that come to us fused with patriarchal power meet 'internally persuasive' discourses which are more open to critical re-accentuation. The metaphor of the contact zone foregrounds the postcolonial context in which we are writing and the high stakes attached to writing.

The materiality of writing is one of the aspects of these high stakes that requires attention in a postcolonial setting. The etymology of the word 'write' indexes the technologies of writing. The roots of 'write' are in Old English *writan*, meaning to cut, tear or scratch. This connects us with the early history of writing as a form of record on clay, bark or papyrus. Writing has always been double sided, associated with the affordance of relative permanence. It can travel, holding its form across time and place—but not its meaning, as Blommaert (2005) reminds us. The shadow of this materiality is that, while speech is a universal human capacity, writing is not. Rather, it is seen as an accomplishment of elites. Its materiality gave it the power to function as a tool in colonialism. As Delmas (2011) puts it, 'writing was the medium by which Europe discovered the world' (xxviii), in this process taking on many 'top down' functions—technical, administrative, religious, scientific, educational. However, colonised people have always appropriated the written word as a tool for resistance, as accounts such as Hofmeyr's (1993) description of orality and literacy show. She documents the colonial imposition of bureaucratic and religious written text on communities in rural northern Transvaal (now Limpopo). In exploring the orality–literacy interface she shows how, in the early stage of this encounter, it was orality that transformed literacy rather than the other way round. In contact zones, particularly those in the global south, there is always a gap between the written forms handed down, and the functions of historically disenfranchised writers who are new arrivals as full participants in writing practices.

For research genres in English, Cadman (2003) calls these inherited forms into which new writers of research need to make their mark 'divine discourse'. This term signals the constraints on what counts as a relevant area of study, the criteria by which a thesis is assessed and the embedding of acceptable forms in a worldview that 'does not recognise, and therefore cannot know, the limitations of its own taken for granted, almost sacred understanding of what constitutes knowledge and its expression in the English language' (2003: 1). In the world of research, writing is the material expression of this rational modern world, yet many of us do not see ourselves as belonging. In the words of a first year first generation student at this university, 'With writing I can never come from my home' (quoted in Nomdo 2006).

When my colleague and I started offering writers' circles to postgraduates at the University of Cape Town, we tried to capture the complexity and paradox of the experience of writing a thesis. We knew that we couldn't focus on writing without acknowledging the research activity in which writing is embedded, and Clement coined the term 'the postgraduate condition': a pervasive state in which the individual tussles with the structural over time. Like the human condition, it is a predicament, full of paradox—we are original, yet tied to the old voices, anglicized but not English, independent yet in need of supervision, assertive yet humble. These tensions are felt strongly in postcolonial contexts—we are always catching up, or pretending, or resisting. In South Africa, categories that are elsewhere seen as distinct often cannot be separated, instead present paradoxical puzzles to be solved and lived with eyes wide open. As Soudien (2012) observes it is 'simultaneously about integration and segregation, tradition and modernity, being safe and unsafe, being well and unwell' (5) that makes South Africa a space that needs to be understood.

Writing as a 'risk object'

In these rehearsal spaces, one is often a witness to weighing up, to giving up, and tuned to loss and risk: what was set aside, silenced, asserted and strongly felt yet not always witnessed. Herman cites Nettles and Millet's memorable observation that doctoral students are 'silent leavers ... they leave without saying goodbye' (Herman 2008). In reflecting on the emerging pedagogic practice in these rehearsal spaces, we started to use the word risk. The circles provided a space where students could weigh up their options. They debated *what* they wanted to say: 'Should I mention this difficult interview I had with one of my participants? I really want to use this theoretical resource, but I'm not sure if it's OK.' They weighed up *how* they wanted to say it: 'Is it OK to use a picture on the first page of my thesis? Do I sound too dry here?' They juggled who it was they were writing for: 'I know my supervisor wouldn't like that! I've no idea who my external examiner is going to be. What if she doesn't understand the African context? How much do I need to explain?' Although the students didn't use the word risk very often, their supervisors did: 'Careful—you run the risk of showing you don't really understand the methodology/sound too subjective.' I know from my own experience as a gatekeeper and supervisor that I use this kind of language. As we get closer to the hand-in, I will do a risk analysis of where the student could be misunderstood.

Initially we used the term 'risk' intuitively. But as we began to theorize more deeply, we realized that it was a term we could not use innocently and that it is being used more frequently in other contexts. Zinn (2010) shows a rise in the risk semantic across disciplines from medicine to media studies, as well as in the public media. The meaning of the term has changed. It no longer has connotations of an adventure-ordeal (Bernstein 1998). The dominant meaning of the term is in the context of risk *management* where the techno-scientific disciplines such as economics and statistics provide numbers to help institutions manage their profits, their reputations and their legal skirmishes. The word is occupied, particularly if you talk to academic colleagues in the UK and Australia. McWilliam (2009), for instance, writes persuasively about the prevailing audit culture in universities in Australia and regrets the 'cold' meaning that now haunts the word. Insights from the social sciences and humanities help us understand more about how risk functions socio-culturally. In sociology, Giddens (1991) in the UK, as well as Luhmann (1991/2002) and Beck (1992) in Germany, writing at the same historical juncture but initially without reference to one another, explore how the rise of what they call 'the risk society' accompanies a loss of faith in the enlightenment goals of objective, rational scientific knowledge that could be harnessed to tame uncertainty, fate and chaos. Anthropologist Douglas (1992) helps us to see how risk functions to create an 'other', how group identity is invoked to construct insider/outsider binaries, in the name of a perceived danger.

For the purposes of this focus on emotion, there are interesting insights to be taken from this literature and applied to the lived world of novice writers of research making their way through the postgraduate condition. It is clear that risk talk is discursively sensitive, that it varies with time and place. It communicates as well as constitutes and manages perceived threats and dangers.

Risk implies its other—a danger or hazard. Luhmann (1991/2002) notes that the notion of risk 'protects a precarious normality' (xxvii) and we need to pay attention to how it creates a symbolic industry: if a demand is created, resources need to be put to reducing the risk: 'demands are created by varying the definition of risk' (56).

We need to be alert to how our universities construct risk objects. It is interesting to track the use of the concept of the 'at risk student' across time and place. It is my impression that it is a recent arrival in higher education, and has gained currency with the 'widening participation' agenda. In South Africa the term first appeared in the mid-1980s when historically white, English-speaking liberal universities such as mine began to admit historically excluded students—typically black, working class, speakers of English as an additional language. In other parts of the world, and times and places, a different category of student would be considered 'at risk': older women, working-class 'home' students, religious groupings and castes.

Elsewhere (Thesen & Cooper in press) we make the argument that writing is becoming a risk object in globalizing universities where the notion of the 'knowledge economy', with its emphasis on research as a commodity, is growing. The challenge is that novice researchers are entering the university from increasingly diverse lifeworlds, and these will show in their writing, as writing can never be entirely separated from identity. We always carry traces of the 'autobiographical self' (Ivanic 1998) in our writing. But gatekeepers often deem it too risky to allow texts to travel with their marks of context. Hence the surge in the 'self-help' literature on how to write a thesis (Kamler & Thomson 2008). These generic 'paint by numbers' approaches to writing research genres can never fill the gap between what writers bring and what may be required of them in the often alien forms that research genres present.

Another insight is that the gap is growing wider between those who define risk to manage institutions and those who move through institutions in less expert positions. Those who define use numbers, those who are defined as 'at risk' do not have access to these 'expensive' symbolic resources. Often they do not have the confidence or experience to articulate where the risk lies. That is left to the gate-keepers. This data from Cooper's (in press) study illustrates the losses that students often experience in the writing of a thesis. Cooper interviewed Masters students she had supervised, long after they had successfully completed their theses, to get a better understanding of the process of thesis writing: her ex-student Jerry reflects back on a moment in the process: 'I was so annoyed. I prepared that whole section where I had learners' photographs and all. ... yes Linda, you cut all that out [...] I lost everything, the gravy'. Interestingly, for whatever reason, he could not express this in the supervisory relationship at the time, although his supervisor is known to be a generous and empathic person.

That lay people are often seen to respond to risk 'unscientifically' is underlined in this quotation:

> Warm-blooded, passionate, inherently social beings though we think we are, humans are presented [...] as hedonic calculators calmly seeking to pursue private interests. We are said to be risk-aversive, but, alas, so inefficient in handling information that we are unintentional risk-takers; basically, we are fools.
>
> (Douglas in Lupton 1999: 22)

Against this dominant reductive notion of risk which is informed by the modernist 'myth of calculability' (Reddy in Lupton 1999: 7), it is important to assert a 'warm' and productive vision of risk from below, as it plays out in the lives of postgraduate researchers. The first meaning attempts to manage, calibrate and fix risk; the second is interested in emergent meaning, and in what is realized as well as what is lost or deleted in postgraduate writing.

This warm concept of risk is an analytical space for bringing into focus the tilting point between self and other, where 'other' refers to beliefs, ideas, places, relationships, audiences and forms. Risk lies on the cusp, unstable and volatile, between production and reception. It is rooted in Bakhtinian understandings of the utterance as dialogic, always oriented towards competing heteroglot others. The act of writing involves decisions about which representations of the research world will prevail, which meanings will be invested and find semiotic form capable of carrying meanings across contexts. It is also interested in what is deleted, suppressed, crossed out—those meanings that do not see the light of day. Decisions about what will or will not be included will always be emotionally invested.

Writing and emotion

There is a surge of interest in emotion in education (Zembylas 2005, 2007). The focus is not so much on what emotion is, but on what it does as discursive work in social practices. Thus, like risk, it is socially produced and validated or subjugated. The procedural, bureaucratic 'provisionism' that Boud and Lee (2005) speak of, which increasingly shapes much of our activity and institutional strategy in the postgraduate research terrain, drives a wedge between the sacred and the profane and, in the process, raises the emotional stakes. Hargreaves (2001, 2004) writes of the 'emotional geographies' of teaching and learning, showing how an economy of emotions functions in educational institutions. As we move through the schooling process from primary school to a PhD, emotions are increasingly set aside as rationality officially takes over. The increased emphasis on throughput and accountability measures in higher education has the potential to heighten difficult emotions for both students and their teachers. Douglas's (1992) work on purity and danger shows how the interplay between emotions of disgust and distinction work in establishing failure for school students who are 'other'. These emotions also play a strong role in shaping how risk is experienced and made sense of. As Steinberg (2008) shows, in her analysis of emotions around assessment practices in schools, there is a contradiction between the informal, lived emotional experience in the private sphere and what is signalled in public. This contradiction is strongly evident in the postgraduate sphere too. There is an outpouring of research which either explicitly or implicitly touches on emotions in postgraduate pedagogy and practice. Writing features in many of these as an emotional 'object' (Cotterall 2013), expression of gendered emotional labour (Aitchison & Mowbray 2013), or as a complex translation of different aspects of the research journey, including dealing with the emotions of research participants themselves (Herman 2008). Burford (2013) in an engaging online post explores shame and writing—the shame of not being able to do justice to your research topic. He sees shame as productive, as an indicator of our commitments and politics—something to mobilize. It requires intense emotional work to retrieve positive emotions that enable postgraduates to find agency in their research journeys.

An important thread in much of the literature that refers to emotion is a post-Enlightenment critique of the way modes of knowing related to lived experience, feeling and embodiment have been pushed underground by the dualisms of modernity. The earthy poles of these dualisms don't go away. They are lived as contradictions, and these contradictions are powerfully experienced in the contact zones of the postcolonial university. Johnson, Lee and Green (2000) have written about the persistence of the image of the 'always–already' autonomous, independent self, who arrives ready to undertake a PhD as if prepared by years of socio-cultural priming. This image, forged in the Enlightenment, persists in spite of the profound changes in the classed, raced and gendered identities of the students entering postgraduate studies. In moving on to laughter, I draw mainly on Bakhtin because he grasps how and why the meaning of laughter has changed over the centuries.

Bakhtin on laughter: 'to liberate from the prevailing point of view of the world'

Bakhtin's (1968) critical re-appraisal of Rabelais is an opportunity to write a history of laughter, to show how it was discursively channelled and suppressed, through the middle ages to the twentieth century. For Bakhtin laughter is a universal, a human accomplishment. He cites Aristotle's popular saying 'of all living creatures only man is endowed with laughter' (1968: 68). In its pure form, laughter 'does not deny seriousness but purifies and completes it' (1968: 122–3). It 'does not permit seriousness to atrophy and to be torn away from the one being, forever incomplete' (123). He sees the Enlightenment attitude to laughter as an expression of its weaker points, the lack of sense of history, an 'abstract and rationalist utopianism, a mechanistic conception of matter, a tendency to abstract generalization and typification on the one hand, and to documentation on the other' (1968: 116). This splitting of head from body exacts a heavy toll on knowledge. The writers' circles, I argue, provide a more open space, in which the fully lived research life can be held and enjoyed.

The medieval co-existence of the serious and the laughing aspects is illustrated in illuminated manuscripts of the thirteenth and fourteenth centuries in which handwritten illustrations of the lives of the saints combined pious images with 'free designs' combining different elements—'fantastic forms, masquerade figures, and parodical scenes' (Bahktin 1968: 96). These images show the interplay between the official and the carnival, the serious and the laughing, interwoven in one consciousness. The writers' circles seem to permit this weaving into one whole and integrated consciousness.

Discussing 'peoples' ambivalent laughter', Bakhtin shows how laughter distrusts seriousness and turns prevailing fear on its head: it 'liberates from the fear that developed in man during thousands of years: fears of the sacred, of prohibitions, of the past, of power' (1968: 94). We see this inversion in all of the moments of laughter described earlier in this paper. They deflate the seriousness of the image of the rational scholar, head severed from heart. Laughter is always ambivalent, argues Bakhtin, 'it asserts and denies; it buries and revives' (1968: 12). Unlike satire, a private response which is directed at others, the peoples' ambivalent laughter is also always directed at itself, as it includes the whole world. Again, we see this ambivalence in all three moments of laughter. The laughter is always directed inwards to oneself as well as outwards. In her sketch Ellen parodies herself, while at the same time drawing attention to the limits of language and writing to express the full range of human experience. The ambivalence captured in 'asserts and denies; it buries and revives' is also evident in all three stories, but most noticeably in the last moment, in which Elizabeth rescues us from the seriousness of death where words fail us, the prickliness of the discussion about language and research, and also possibly my failure as facilitator to draw the circle to a satisfactory close. Bakhtin shows us how laughter works to

> consecrate inventive freedom, to permit the combination of a variety of elements and their rapprochement, to liberate from the prevailing point of view of the world, from conventions and established truths, from clichés [...] offers the chance to have a new outlook on the world.
>
> (Bakhtin 1968: 34)

In the final part of this chapter, I explore some thoughts provoked by the last few words in this quotation—'the chance to have a new outlook on the world'.

Final comments: 'a new outlook on the world'

This brief exploration of writing, risk and laughter has recreated some moments from the Thursday writers' circle in which a group of people from very different lifeworlds come together to share their writing. They are also there to refract the dominant image of the postgraduate student, and make it in their own collective image—embodied and whole as they explore how we can be together in this post-apartheid contact zone. I argue that laughter in the ambivalent sense allowed us by Bakhtin plays an important part in allowing this re-making to happen. This laughter explores the boundaries of the edges that involve different kinds of risk. There is the risk defined by the managerial discourses of the university, in which writing is becoming central as a risk object. There is also the risk of doing difficult kinds of research—about death and dying, about loss—and there is the risk of how we can be together, in this moment.

To return to my colleague's advice, 'If they're not laughing, watch out!', I have tried to explain why this observation, which seems to have a paradox built into it, might be the case: that laughing/writing circles that work best are the ones where writers can take risks and reconcile sacred and profane, desire and fear, and where the profane can actually elaborate the official. Writing groups have a central role to play in how the dilemmas and contradictions that haunt the writing of research may be more fully lived. The closer these groups become to 'mainstream' practices of writing and supervision, the more likely they are to be spaces in which new images of the postgraduate writer may emerge. There is also the possibility of exploring new forms. This is the part that interests me most: that laughing *with* writing enables writers to escape cliché and empty pro forma moulds to allow the possibility of a 'new outlook on the world'. Isn't this what research, at its best, is about?

References

Aitchison, C. (2009) 'Writing groups for doctoral education', *Studies in Higher Education*, 34(8): 905–16.

Aitchison, C. and Mowbray, S. (2013) 'Doctoral women: managing emotions, managing doctoral studies', *Teaching in Higher Education*, 18(8): 859–70.

Bakhtin, M. (1968) *Rabelais and His World*, Cambridge, MA: MIT Press.

—— (1981) *The Dialogic Imagination: Four Essays*, Austin: University of Texas.

Beck, U. (1992) *Risk Society: Towards a New Modernity*, London: Sage.

Bernstein, P. L. (1998) *Against the Gods: The Remarkable Story of Risk*, New York: John Wiley.

Blommaert, J. (2005) *Discourse: A Critical Introduction*, Cambridge: Cambridge University Press.

Boud, D. and Lee, A. (2005) '"Peer learning" as pedagogic discourse for research education', *Studies in Higher Education*, 30(5): 501–16.

Burford, J. (2013) Emotions and doctoral writing: Shame. Available online: http://doctoralwriting.wordpress.com/2013/08/02/emotions-and-doctoral-writing-shame/ (accessed 5 August 2013).

Cadman, K. (2003) 'Divine discourse: plagiarism, hybridity and epistemological racism', in S. May, M. Franken & R. Barnard (eds) *Refereed Proceedings of the 1st International Conference on Language, Education and Diversity*. On CD available from http://www.waikato.ac.nz/wmier/publications/books/led2003.

Chihota, M. C. and Thesen, L. (in press) 'Rehearsing "the postgraduate condition" on writers' circles', in L. Thesen and L. Cooper (eds) *Risk in Academic Writing: Postgraduate Students, Their Teachers and the Making of Knowledge*, Bristol: Multilingual Matters.

Cooper, L. (in press) '"Does my experience count?" The role of experiential knowledge in the research writing of postgraduate adult learners', in L. Thesen and L. Cooper (eds) *Risk in Academic Writing: Postgraduate Students, Their Teachers and the Making of Knowledge*, Bristol: Multilingual Matters.

Cotterall, S. (2013) '"More than just a brain": emotions and the doctoral experience', *Higher Education Research and Development*, 32(2): 174–87.

Cuthbert, D., Spark, C. and Burke, E. (2009) 'Disciplining writing: the case for multi-disciplinary writing groups to support writing for publication by higher degree by research candidates in the humanities, arts and social sciences', *Higher Education Research and Development*, 28(2): 137–49.

Delmas, A. (2011) 'Introduction: the written word and the world', in A. Delmas and N. Penn (eds) *Written Culture in a Colonial Context: Africa and the Americas 1500–1900*, Cape Town: UCT Press.

Douglas, M. (1992) *Purity and Danger: An Analysis of the Concepts of Pollution and Taboo*, London: Routledge.

Dyer, G. (1998) *Out of Sheer Rage: Wrestling With D.H Lawrence*, New York: North Point Press.

Elbow, P. (1998) *Writing With Power: Techniques for Mastering the Writing Process*, London: Oxford University Press.

Giddens, A. (1991) *Modernity and Self-identity: Self and Society in the Late Modern Age*, Cambridge: Polity.

Hargreaves, A. (2001) 'Emotional geographies of teaching', *Teacher's College Record*, 103(6): 1056–80.

—— (2004) 'Distinction and disgust: the emotional politics of school failure', *International Journal of Leadership in Education*, 7(1): 27–41.

Herman, C. (2008) 'Negotiating the emotions of change: research, restructuring and the doctoral student', *South African Journal of Higher Education*, 22 (1): 100–15.

Hofmeyr, I. (1993) '*We spend our lives as a tale that is told': Oral Historical Narrative in a South African Chiefdom*, Portsmouth NH: Heinemann.

Ivanic, R. (1998) *Writing and Identity: The Discoursal Construction of Identity in Academic Writing*, Amsterdam: John Benjamins.

Johnson, L., Lee, A. and Green, B. (2000) 'The PhD and the autonomous self: gender, rationality and postgraduate pedagogy', *Studies in Higher Education*, 25 (2): 135–47.

Kamler, B. and Thomson, P. (2008) 'The failure of dissertation advice books: toward alternative pedagogies for doctoral writing', *Educational Researcher*, 37(8): 507–14.

Luhmann, N. (1991/2002) *Risk: A Sociological Theory* (trans. R. Barratt), New Jersey: Aldine Transaction.

Lupton, D. (1999) *Risk*, London: Routledge.

McWilliam, E. (2009) 'Doctoral education in risky times', in D. Boud and A. Lee (eds) *Changing Practices of Doctoral Education*, Abingdon, Oxon: Routledge.

Murray, D. (1978) 'Write before writing', *College Composition and Communication*, 29(4): 375–81.

Nomdo, G. (2006) 'Identity, power and discourse: the socio-political self-representations of successful black students at UCT', in L. Thesen and E. van Pletzen (eds) *Academic Literacy and Languages of Change*, New York: Continuum.

Parker, R. (2009) 'A learning community approach to doctoral education in the social sciences', *Teaching in Higher Education*, 14(1): 43–54.

Pratt, M. L. (1999) 'Arts of the contact zone', in D. Bartholomae and A. Petrosky (eds) *Ways of Reading: An Anthology for Writers* (5th edn), New York: Bedford/ St Martins.

Soudien, C. (2012) *Realising the Dream*, Cape Town: HSRC Press.

Steinberg, C. (2008) 'Assessment as an "emotional practice"', *English Teaching: Practice and Critique*, 7(3): 42–64.

Thesen, L. and Cooper, L. (eds) (in press) *Risk in Academic Writing: Postgraduate Students, Their Teachers and the Making of Knowledge*, Bristol: Multilingual Matters.

Zembylas, M. (2005) *Teaching with Emotion: A Postmodern Enactment*, Greenwich, CN: Information Age Publishing.
—— (2007) 'Theory and methodology in researching emotions in education', *International Journal of Research & Method*, 30(1): 57–72.
Zinn, J. O. (2010) 'Risk as discourse: interdisciplinary perspectives', *Critical Analysis of Discourse Across Disciplines*, 42(2): 106–24.

Chapter 12

A weekly dose of applause!
Connectedness and playfulness in the 'Thesis Marathon'

Judith Wolfsberger

Writing often is a lonely endeavour. Unfortunately in the central European university tradition this is sometimes even seen as a necessity, expressed as 'No pain—no gain'. Having practised Anglo American writing pedagogy in my private writing institute the 'Writers Studio' in Vienna, Austria, for more than ten years, I—in contrast—firmly believe that students, indeed, all writers, become more productive through community, where there is acknowledgement, sharing and feedback. At best, writers thrive with a weekly dose of applause.

Community also helps build momentum in writing. Every writing project, be it a dissertation, a non-fiction book or a novel, must pick up speed at some point. There is value in a writing project starting slowly, to give ideas time to form, to research and read and write bits and pieces for a while. But if the text is large, it cannot be written in the last days before the deadline, and long-term strategies must be found. At some point we need momentum. At some point the writing project needs to become first priority, with regular hours and a fast rhythm. At some point perfectionism and postponing must stop, otherwise the greatest ideas will become dull or bigger writing projects will never be finished. The aim of the 'Thesis Marathon' was to provide an infrastructure for building such momentum.

Following the concept of NaNoWriMo (an online community for writing a quick draft of a short novel within one month), in 2006 a group of teachers from the small private enterprise, Writers' Studio in Vienna, developed the idea of a Thesis Marathon incorporating applause for Masters and doctoral students. The aim of this external-to-university writing group that playfully enacts the metaphor of a marathon is to build connectedness and productivity outcomes for thesis writers. The idea of 'connectedness' and 'applause' for writers derives from the American feminist writing therapist and former director of the Writers Centre at Harvard, Joan Bolker.

For this paper I sent out an informal questionnaire to 52 participants from eight rounds of the marathon. The answers surprised me and gave me the chance to rethink the value of this academic writing marathon. In this chapter I will try to answer the following questions: How can connectedness and playfulness support doctoral writing? How does the enacted metaphor of a marathon work to improve writer productivity? How do the structures and settings of a writing marathon enforce connectedness and playfulness? And, what are the results for the students and their writing projects?

The central European university context

This unusual writing group must be understood in the European academic writing context. At Austrian universities, writers of dissertations and Masters theses (and even shorter papers) don't usually receive deadlines from their professors and advisors. A related problem is that, in general, writing processes are rarely taught or discussed. Writing classes, writers' centres and counselling on writing problems are brand new innovations. In general, the central European mass universities have high dropout rates, even of students in the final stages of their studies. There are many cases of 'all but dissertation/thesis dropouts'.[1]

In this climate, the Writers' Studio, a private business where students can attend privately paid workshops on writing strategies, could thrive. The workshop program 'Written Freely: Writing your Masters thesis with power and strategy' has been running successfully for ten years, and provides the basis of my book of the same title. As a follow up to this workshop, the Writers' Studio offers various writing groups (feedback and group counselling), writing dates (set group appointments for writing next to each other) and this Writing Marathon.

Thesis marathon: the background

Joan Bolker (1997) wrote in her inspiring essay 'A room of one's own is not enough' that academic writing 'threatens connectedness' and at the same time 'is an act that hopes for connection' (188). In particular, women students feel they must choose between their need to be socially connected and their wish to succeed academically through their writing. Bolker urges us to make it possible for female doctoral students to write 'not alone, but within structures and settings that support their efforts and applaud their industry and their success, and allow them to strengthen connections' (1997: 198). This has become the credo of the Writers' Studio and my own work as a writing teacher. For many years before we invented the marathon, I offered a writing group for doctoral and Masters students, in which three to five students met fortnightly for feedback. This 'Work-in-progress' group became my personal favourite and most successful workshop. The students gained a lot through sharing their freshly written pages about interesting topics in different academic fields. They talked regularly about the writing process and strategies, they enjoyed being together and shared genuine interest across disciplines for texts, research and arguments. I felt that that Bolker's proposition had become true in my Work-in-progress group: it offered structures and settings that supported students' efforts, applauded their industry and their success, and allowed them to strengthen connections. I was in awe of how much better they wrote and how much they enjoyed their work through this group.

This group—as in most other workshops—consisted mainly of female students and I began to reread Bolker's essay about internal and external barriers for women in the academy. The Central European university system seems to enhance these difficulties. One could say, when it comes to writing, that all students in our universities, male or female, at times feel there is little respect for their work, and that the limited direct support makes it difficult for them to express their authentic voices within a very abstract and narrow academic discourse. At the Writers' Studio we see many students who are struggling within a system where they feel their work and their writing is unsupported—and, in addition, many students struggle financially to undertake further study. No wonder writing frequently doesn't go well.

The Work-in-progress group which I ran over many years with changing participants, was not only a supportive playground for my students, but it also facilitated an environment to try new teaching methods. Over time the biweekly meetings became fun events with playful, even child-like materials and strategies. On a chart we marked every page that each participant planned to write. At the start of the meeting they announced what they had written and got great applause no matter how many or little pages they had managed. As a reward we put kiddies' stickers next to the page mark on the chart. Some of the students also put stickers onto their printouts. Most participants came with new pages every second week; some finished their papers within months, for others it was a joyful but long journey—sometimes too long.

Thesis marathon: scoping the field

In 2005 I participated in the 'National Novel Writing Month' (NaNoWriMo, website NaNoWriMo.com), an online community for writing a quick draft of a short novel within one month. Chris Baty, the founder, started this writing event with a group of friends in San Francisco who each set out to write 50,000 words of books they otherwise would have postponed endlessly. Aiming to write a 'shitty first draft' (Lamott 1995: 21) within a ridiculously short time was their antidote to too much respect for literary writing and to writers' block. NaNoWriMo grew quickly into a US-wide and then an international online event, with over 250,000 participants from all over the world in 2012. Baty's (2004) book, *No Plot, No Problem*, with its mix of irreverence, humour and practical advice, became a great resource for me for working with writers of academic papers of all levels. In my Work-in-progress group I had experienced how students enter into the flow when they lose fear and how they lose fear when they play and laugh. Their texts and research were, and remained, serious enough; the topics they wrote about were often 'not fun', happy, resolved or easy. Such work needs comic relief for balance. (See also Chapter 11 in this book about laughter in writing groups by Lucia Thesen.)

Through NaNoWriMo I had managed to write 50,000 words of a mystery novel; I had met up with strangers in San Francisco and Vienna, I had exchanged my writing questions and anxieties online, I recorded my word count daily and

I enjoyed every part of the rush. That's what I wanted for my students too: a happy rush, the joy and satisfaction of getting a big chunk of writing done. So I proposed to a group of trainees, two who were on their way to becoming writing teachers, that we undertake this project to design and run an academic writing marathon for our students.

The following fun features of Chris Baty's (2004) book and the website NaNoWriMo.com were helpful for designing our academic writing marathon:

- 'A good deadline is hard to find' (28): It is good to have a high, but attainable, goal for a set time in order to make that activity a top priority and forget about perfectionism.
- Baty offers a 'time finder' (41) to record how one usually spends the days and to identify and halt certain time-consuming habits for the writing phase.
- Intense writing times need multiple supports from others: form a team of supporters. Ask friends and family to take over certain tasks of daily life for a while.
- Share your goal and your path with others; don't write alone just for yourself. Be in daily contact with other writers, for example, check in on the phone, meet for writing dates or via social media.
- Visualize your success. Baty offered various ways to chart every written page: from paper charts with golden star stickers for every written page to an online graph that plots daily and cumulative progress.
- Don't reread and don't revise during the writing month.
- Ups and downs are normal, so don't let yourself be discouraged: 'Hope for the Best, Plan for the Worst' (46).
- Intense writing times should be the best times: so pamper yourself with food, drinks and other goodies.
- Use playful writing exercises and conversations with friends about your story to regain energy.

Thesis marathon: the preparation

One thing was clear, we couldn't simply copy the novel writing marathon for academic writing. *No Plot, No Problem* is not just the title of the founder's book, but also the core slogan of this novel writing month. It is probably disturbing enough for some in the literary world to allow the writing momentum to develop a story rather than planning it; writing a longer academic work without a plot/plan/focus was just what we usually did *not* want students to do!

Our marathon started with a one-month preparation time, where participants showed work on their table of contents, research question and literature review. Each participant received a one-hour counselling session and we encouraged them to meet with their official advisors beforehand, in order to gain approval. You cannot start if the road is not clear. So our project was in this respect like a real running marathon, where the route is set and public. At a marathon you don't run just anywhere in the city, and so too, in a thesis you need to follow a set route. In our first marathon there were several students who unfortunately had not managed to get their advisors' approval for their outline and thesis argument, and they couldn't use the writing momentum properly. They were constantly sidetracked by questions like: What is it about? What is the next chapter? Which literature shall I use? In the following years we emphasized the need of a 'plot'.

Also, we quickly realized, one month wouldn't be sufficient time to write a Masters dissertation, even if the reading and research process was mostly completed. The NaNoWriMo word target was greater than that required for Masters dissertation. We needed more time for fewer pages. Borrowing from 'Around the world in 80 days', we adopted the fun slogan '80 pages in 8 weeks'. Ten pages a week or two pages a day seemed a possible goal, considering that students also had to consult or read while writing. And many also had other commitments during the time of the marathon. The aim was 80 pages of a very first draft. We encouraged the students not to reread the previous days' work, not to edit, not to share work, but to get on with it as much as possible.

We were inspired by the NaNoWriMo recommendation for writing dates in cafés, libraries, homes, and a buddy system where pairs of students were in daily contact. In the preparation month we discussed how each participant could reorganize daily life to gain time for writing, how they could ask for support of friends, partners or spouses—in short, how they could integrate this writing marathon into their daily life. Baty's 'time finder' (2004: 41) was helpful here. The academic marathon was not set in a retreat situation: participants went to work, cared for their children and loved ones and had leisure time. This seemed to answer a question that Joan Bolker raises in her essay: How can we help—especially—female students to get on with their writing without fear that it threatens their social life, connections and expectations in their everyday lives? She says it is useless to scold women for caring too much for others, for not being able to cut themselves off from duties and role expectations. They should not have to choose between writing and their need for connectedness. A marathon, like other writing groups, strengthens connections: the participants care for and spur each other on; they watch each other's progress and help each other; and most of all they have fun together. And it allows the participants to stay within their everyday lives and still perform in an extraordinary way.

An important feature of our marathon is the weekly meeting, usually at the end or the beginning of the week. During these 'update workshops' we playfully enact the marathon metaphor fully. Participants get together for a couple of hours at the Writers' Studio to share their progress of the previous week and fire each other up for the next week. For this we use a track made of a long strip of paper or a textile curtain; each participant can move along a 'runner', a cardboard figure, according to the number of pages written. On the track are lines for each five pages, so it can quickly be seen how many pages each person has written, from five to 80 or often beyond. Each writer announces separately how many pages she has written in the previous week and, while the group applauds and cheers loudly, accompanied by whistles, drums and bells, she moves her runner to the appropriate point on the track. It is simply amazing how the possibility of moving a paper figure forward and receiving applause motivates a person to write a few more pages beyond what would be easy to do. In our first Thesis Marathon, I also participated as a writer and worked on my guidebook on academic writing. On the day of one update meeting I produced some extra pages, quickly, almost carelessly, just to move my figure further and hear the applause.

I believe in applause. It is a non-verbal and physical sign of success, of being seen, and of being part of something. Bolker (1997) inspired me when she explained that women writers need 'structures and settings that support their efforts and *applaud* their industry' (198, my italics). I wondered if she meant an abstract applause, such as structural or verbal praise of students' work, or if she asks us to clap our hands for ovations as in the theatre or in sports, for example, in a runners' marathon, where the streets are filled with supporters, who clap and motivate: 'You can do it!'. Structural applause can be feedback or time to discuss one's questions and progress.

The distinctiveness of our writing marathon is the physical applause of which participants get a weekly dose. The applause stays with them for a long time after it is over and they go back to writing the next day, long after the writing marathon, and possibly long after they have completed their dissertation. In the film *A Million Dollar Baby*, a female boxer rises from poverty to the highest international ranks of the sport. After an almost lethal accident during a fight she lies in hospital paralyzed and asks her coach to pull the plug. She explains that having had that kind of success, recognition and that applause was more than she ever could have hoped for in her life. She cherishes those memories, saying, 'I can still hear them chanting'. In this moment the audience remembers the scene of her last fight, in which she enters the stage in a red velvet robe with a hood like Santa Claus, followed and lifted by waves of applause. She wants to die rather than lose that memory.

In the Austrian academia, students traditionally rarely receive 'applause'—neither as sufficient feedback, nor as physical clapping and chanting. Students are also rarely encouraged or supported to form writing groups; experience and know-how to set up such groups is mostly lacking. So our writing marathon comes almost like an overdose of structure and applause, and I think that is why it works so well.

The question of whether or not the pages written in the marathon in this special rush are good enough is raised often during our marathon. The fact that the marathon urges one to write quickly, to set aside hypercritical questioning and to stop procrastinating is actually its highest value. Students must also learn that in a good writing process it isn't necessary or possible that every written page be used directly in the final draft. In the traditional European writing approaches there is, unfortunately, little understanding of writing as a process. At high school, assignments are set up to teach students that texts must be written in one sitting. This is very hard to change. So the figures on the marathon track, designed to reward nothing but forward movement to reach the endpoint, help a great deal. In a real runners' marathon it also doesn't matter how you reach the finish line—you can crawl the last metres.

Thesis marathon: the training

Positive group dynamics are essential for the success of the marathon—if one had a track for oneself alone, one wouldn't care so much how far the runner moved. But ours is a very friendly competition. Depending on the type of project, some write slower than the others, and some need to do more reading or outlining for each chapter. Others find it is all there in their heads and only needs to be written out. Like in the NaNoWriMo, every written page counts, be it preliminary thoughts, journal entries, notes on a book, etc. Writing encourages writing, so whatever they write is progress.

After the round of cheering in the update meetings, the students usually get a writing prompt, often some creative topic or a reflection on their writing process and progress. Then they set up writing dates for the next week and think about their personal writing goal, which each of them separately marks on the track with a little paper flag.

These weekly meetings of the whole group usually have a high-pitched atmosphere, and the group bonds rapidly. They chat wildly, laugh, and form friendships and writing partnerships that often continue beyond the marathon. Laughing, playing and writing together connects, and the connectedness empowers their writing.

The playfulness of the whole set up of our marathon, the craziness of the goal—to write so much in so little time—makes it even easier to connect. Also, playfulness enhances performance and learning:

> Dozens of experiments have shown that … pressure worsens performance in those who are not yet highly skilled at a task or who are just beginning to learn it. People 'just playing' at pool, or at math, or at coming up with clever rebuttals to arguments, do better than those who are trying to impress an evaluator—unless they are already highly skilled at the task'.
>
> (Gray 2012)

For the following marathons, therefore, we included additional playful elements:

- Find a new home for the inner censor/editor. In a special ritual in the preparation workshop we send the inner censor into an 'Inner Editor Kennel' (Baty 2004: 107). The participants write a letter to explain to the caregivers of the home the special habits of one's censor, what he or she likes and needs. The censor is symbolically put in an envelope and sent away for the time of the writing marathon.

- For the weekly update meetings we always provide runners' food: muesli bars, bananas, fruit drinks.
- Starting with the second writing marathon we also offered an online forum, where marathon participants could exchange experiences and ask questions and arrange real-life writers' dates. The clear focus of our marathon is to get writers to leave their lonely home and offices where most of them have already been stuck for too long, and meet in cafés, parks, homes, and in the Writers' Studio.
- There is a system of symbolic goodies, which each writer receives for written pages. On their online profile and on the paper track in the Writers' Studio they earned symbols of strawberries, ice cream and cocktails.
- We also produced Writing Marathon T-shirts for the participants that showed a figure of a runner with a pen in her hand. In the future we plan to add the slogan 'Writing connects', following Katrin Girgensohn who runs writing groups at the University of Frankfurt (Girgensohn 2007: 30).
- Final celebration. At the end of writing week 8, we always organize an award ceremony and party. We do a real run through the rooms, and have a goal line marked on the floor. Then each participant gets to stand on the winners' podium, a simple stool. While everybody applauds, making noise with drums and whistles, the 'runner' gets a handshake from the organizers and a certificate read out loud: 'xx wrote in only eight weeks an incredible xx pages first draft of her thesis/dissertation'. Afterwards we serve real cocktails, write a group poem and celebrate everyone's success.

Thesis marathon: the results

What are the results? We have now staged eight writing marathons each with four to eleven participants, 52 in total. Most writers were able to write beyond their page aim; mostly they managed 80 pages (1½-line spaced) and some opted from the beginning for a half-marathon, 40 pages. For this chapter, I sent out a brief informal questionnaire to all the participants of the marathon. Questions asked were: How do you remember the marathon? How much did you get written? Could you use those pages for your actual thesis/dissertation? How was your writing process after the marathon, including revision? Have you finished your project? What did you learn long term from the marathon? I received very long and enthusiastic answers from eight former students. Despite this low response rate, the students' responses highlight significant change in their approach to writing.

All of them remember best the joy of the project:

> The marathon was a wonderful time. Before, writing was horror for me, each word, each sentence was torture. Through the structure of the marathon, setting reachable goals together and through sending off the inner censor, a positive process was started. Now I enjoy writing! Each week was a success;

each day when I reached my writing goal was a silver lining in this very challenging time of writing my thesis next to a full-time job. The marathon was such a good experience also because of the shared joy at the weekly meetings, and being responsible to the group about certain writing goals and to be able to discuss difficulties and strategies.

I was part of the very first writing marathon (2006): It was interesting to pursue a writing project so very differently. I very much liked the whole playful setup with all the fun extras, the group was very motivating. I loved the figures of the marathon runners, which moved forward on the wall, the musical instruments for cheering, the big table around which we sat, the atmosphere of the Writers' Studio, the tea and the cookies.

So much support! I was thrilled about the joyful approach.

What surprised me in the answers to my questionnaire was that many of them replied that they could not directly use what they had written during the marathon for their thesis/dissertation. Nevertheless, the intensive and uplifting writing experience had finally broken their writers' block, or propelled them to start writing a 'zero draft' (Bolker 1998: 49), thoughts about their topic and literature. Baty (2004) points out that most participants in the novel writing month do not write a publishable novel in the first round. Many never even revise their first attempts, but the writing experience is an important building block for the next novel they start. Eventually, many do get novels published. One student of our academic marathon writes:

> Only after I had participated in the marathon was I able to overcome my inhibitions to decide on the focus and outline of my thesis. So what I wrote during the marathon was not really geared towards the final product. But it helped me immensely to get into writing flow, to lose the fear of starting to write. Through the marathon I was able to start reading and writing about literature (summaries) and get used to the specific style of the research field.

The one participant of the first marathon, who had a very hard time because her topic and structure was still in negotiation with her advisor, has very fond memories and tells me that even though she wasn't able to write her thesis in the marathon itself, it helped her immensely later on when she did write it.

In the sample of answers there are all levels of success. Some put aside completely what they had written during the marathon and started from scratch with the actual thesis, empowered and energized; some were able to use most or some of their first draft; most—but not all—of them finished their projects within the following year or two.

The most positive result in the questionnaire was that all of them continued to organize writing dates with friends of the marathon for months and even years, or started meeting with other people to write. One summarizes what she has taken from the long run of the marathon: 'If I try to cop out from a new writing project, it is always helpful to find a writing partner'.

It seems that the participants in the marathon were able to incorporate deeply a truly positive writing experience and some very useful writing strategies. Baty (2004) writes about the novel writing marathon: 'The lesson you take from your travels across novel-land this month will serve you well throughout the rest of your life. You will walk away from the four-week escapade with a mischievous sense of boldness and an increased confidence in your creative abilities' (106). I, too, believe that our marathon changes the participants' writing lives for the better. In this sense, whether they finish their thesis quickly after the marathon, or only much later, or never, seems secondary.

Future thesis marathons: lessons learned

Over the years of offering the academic writing marathon we gained experiences and insights regarding timing, group size, risks and gender:

- *Season/timing*: We have learned over the years that it's not useful to start our marathon in the European winter, because of the Christmas season. So we have settled on spring. We start with informational meetings in February, and start officially in March with a month of preparation. April and May are the writing months. The spring light and the warmth motivates participants; they also meet in outdoor cafés and parks for writing dates. Many keep up the writing speed after the marathon during the summer.
- *Size of the writing marathon group*: Over the years we also realised that the minimum number of participants is five, otherwise it's hard to achieve this special group energy and high level of adrenalin. After all, a runners' marathon includes thousands of participants and spectators. Since our marathon is paid for by the students themselves, it is not always possible to gather a big enough group to proceed. On the other hand, I think the maximum number of participants is quite open, as long as everybody gets a seat in a room and one has a wall big enough for a chart for posting the runner figures. For an online marathon all this can of course be achieved on a website, but I do think that it makes a big difference to meet in person and hear live applause. Especially those students who are struggling with academic texts can gain a lot through haptic communication and approval, rather than pure online support.
- *Gender*: Most participants of our writing marathon were women, as is the case in general for all our writing workshops, whether academic, creative or professional writing. The Writers' Studio—whose teachers are also mainly female—seems to cater to women's needs and expectations. However, it is not only that women might seek social connection more than men, as Bolker says. they might also be more open to discussing writing processes, difficulties

and strategies. (See also Agnes Bosanquet *et al.*, Chapter 14 in this book, on the gendered membership of writing groups.)
- *Follow up workshops/groups*: In some cases participants of a marathon have continued meeting regularly for writers' dates for some months after the workshop. We invited them to join our Work-in-progress groups for group tutoring and feedback. For those who used this opportunity especially to revise and rewrite their first draft, the whole endeavour was most successful.
- *Risks*: There are also risks in entering a writing marathon, which is quite a challenging project. A sound psycho-physical condition of participants is a prerequisite. We had one incident where a student had a history of burnout that we were unaware of. She had a relapse after the marathon, and later told us that she had previously been hospitalized due to burnout. Since that experience, we have regularly checked with participants regarding their health.

An additional risk arises from insufficient pre-marathon preparation. In the first marathon one person dropped out, because she had not managed to clarify her topic, research question and literature beforehand. When she eventually got an email from her advisor that her concept wasn't satisfactory, she quit. We now are especially careful to make students aware of what they need to start, go with each participant through their concept, selection of literature and research, and help them to find a place where they can start writing. Without a good selection of literature, reading notes, a functioning chapter structure, research question, and approval of the advisor, one cannot write a quick draft of an academic writing project, just as one cannot write a quick novel without some characters, a setting and a potential conflict. We tell the students, just as Baty (2004) does, that you don't need to know and understand every step of the way, but the above prerequisites are absolutely necessary.

Conclusion: why it works

Summing up, I would like to suggest there are multiple connecting strategies for why the Thesis Marathon works so well. These include: entering the marathon as a common enterprise, sharing the same goal and timeframe; the somewhat absurd, exaggerated role play; the weekly check-in meetings with weekly applause; writing dates during the week using both online and real spaces; and daily contact with one buddy (meetings, phone, e-mails, text messages).

How is playfulness enacted? The marathon metaphor is played out on many levels: an aim that is almost too high; being in a group (the marathon doesn't work for one person, even if you set up all the features!); and doing all of this in a safe and creative place outside of the academy.

I have heard of a few students, particularly one group of dissertation writers, who have organized their own little marathon in very small groups. The success of such autonomous marathons greatly depends on the self-discipline and skills to maintain a group over the weeks in a good working spirit. While I was writing this paper, news about an online Academic Writing Month, 'AcWriMo', set up in 2011 by Charlotte Frost, a doctoral student in England, reached me. It says on the website:

> AcWriMo is a month-long academic virtual write-a-thon. And it happens every November. It is inspired by the amazing NaNoWriMo (National Novel Writing Month) but caters to the specific needs of academic writers at all stages of their career (from undergraduates to the most distinguished of professors).
>
> (AcWriMo 2011)

This online project seems to suggest a growing interest in collaborative writing in academia and shows the versatility of the concept of a time-structured academic writing marathon.

Finally, I would like to discuss what seems special about our academic writing marathon in relation to the other writing groups presented in this book. These could be important points to consider if a similar academic marathon is to be staged elsewhere:

- This writing marathon takes place *outside* of academia, in a private enterprise.
- It is staged *outside* of the English-speaking world, in which writing has a much longer tradition of being thought about, discussed and fostered.
- The marathon is a project with a very strong structure and tight timeframe, but with very little attention on content and quality, following the motto 'You take care of quantity and quality will occur'. This again seems easier in a setting *outside* of academia, in which the emotional support of the writers and the process of academic writing are the focus.
- The marathon is not a writing group nor a feedback group; it is merely a *frame* for making appointments, weekly plans, that helps participants to write a lot within a rather short time. They write daily, alone or together at writers' dates with other marathon 'runners'. They are encouraged to suggest a place and time where others can join in, and the facilitators of the marathon each offer at least one open writing date per week. Usually there is at least one option per day on our online timetable of writing dates.
- This newfound connectedness seems to be especially important in European mass universities, in the Humboltian system, where students on every level (BA, MA, PhD) are rather *left to themselves*, each as individuals. The connections between students and between professors and students are traditionally loose, compared to the North American university where I have studied.
- Central European universities are not experienced as a 'home ground' or place of high personal identification and integration. In this way the Writers' Studio as a place outside of academia seems to substitute for a missing feeling of being welcome, being home (some students have called the Writers' Studio an 'oasis') and even being able to enjoy writing for once. In other university systems with better writing support, the emotional push produced

by the marathon's connectedness might either not be so necessary or work even better. It might be the case that students who have had more support in their writing all along could write more of the actual first draft of their thesis (rather than preliminary writings) during the marathon. They don't have to climb such a high mountain of disconnectedness, fear of academic writing and lack of functioning writing strategies. But any writer, academic or other, I am sure, would thrive on a weekly dose of applause.

Notes

1 Unfortunately, statistics on research student dropout rates are not readily available in relation to the students' specific stage within the study programs. However, my experience, and that of colleagues in the sector, suggests that attrition rates are of concern and many Austrian students fall into the All But Dissertation category. For further information refer to European Centre for Higher Education, CEPES: http://www.cepes.ro/.
2 Thank you to Simone Leonhartsberger, Birgit Peterson, Irene Rauch and Pamela Wahl.

References

AcWriMo (2011) *What is AcWriMo?* Available online: http://www.phd2published.com/acwri-2/acbowrimo/about (accessed 6 December 2012).

Baty, C. (2004) *No Plot? No Problem? A Low-stress, High-velocity Guide to Writing a Novel in 30 Days*, San Francisco, CA: Chronicle Books.

Bolker, J. (1997) 'A room of one's own is not enough', in J. Bolker (ed.) *The Writer's Home Companion*, New York: Henry Holt.

—— (1998) *Writing a Dissertation in 15 Minutes a Day: A Guide to Starting, Revising, and Finishing Your Doctoral Thesis*, New York: Henry Holt.

Girgensohn, K. (2007) *Neue Wege Zur Schlüsselqualifikation: Autonome Schreibgruppen An Der Hochschule*, Wiesbaden: Deutscher Universitäts-Verlag.

Gray, P. (2012) *Free to Learn: Why Unleashing the Instinct to Play Will Make Our Children Happier, More Self-Reliant, and Better Students for Life*, New York: Basic Books. Available online: http://www.alternet.org/books/why-students-learn-better-playful-environment?page=0%2C0 (accessed 10 January 2014).

Lamott, A. (1995) *Bird by Bird: Some Instructions on Writing and Life*, New York: Anchor Books.

Chapter 13

The Studio Model
Developing community writing in creative, practice-led PhD design theses

Welby Ings

Introduction

In the corridor outside my office there is a sofa. It is bright red and, in the glancing afternoon light, it resembles something from an elegantly lit film set. In summer the sun slopes down in oblique rays and divides it into segments.

I have always thought it looked isolating; its plush upholstery and uniformity. Across many years, highly gifted design students have sat on it. With their laptops, dreams, and anxieties they wait here for a first meeting. When they come into my office, I make them a cup of tea and they glance anxiously at my bookcase, then somewhere early in the conversation they look down at the floor and tell me they are afraid of writing.

For most designers, writing in a professional context is an integrated part of thinking. They arrange ideas, draft information, and relate images to text as part of a seamless flow of ideation and refinement. But when they enter university in higher degree study, their confidence often falls apart. They encounter new voices and feel terrorised by them. In reaction to this they clumsily attempt to imitate what they don't understand, or stumble under mounting anxieties of inability and ineptitude. They wait on red sofas with crumbling faith in their potential, having come to believe in an inability that doesn't exist.

This situation isn't helped by the fact that many universities seek to address writing anxieties through a process of separation and divorce. Aitchison and Lee (2006) note that writing at PhD level is often institutionally isolated from the experience of research; it is often divided off and allocated to 'specialist bodies ... positioned largely outside mainstream doctoral studies programs' (266). This institutional method of addressing what is perceived as a deficit unfortunately reinforces a false belief that written thinking can be disconnected and outsourced.

However, if we perceive writing as an integrated part of how we organize and express thought, we understand it as *knowledge-creating* rather than a skill used in post-research write up (Kamler & Thomson 2006). Because we are social animals, expressions of the self (including writing) are socially constructed and socially situated (Aitchison & Lee 2006; Kamler & Thomson 2006; Maher *et al.* 2013). If we think about this idea, we are able to consider alternative approaches to writing pedagogies and rethink environments for PhD students undertaking practice-led PhD design theses. In so doing we might draw upon useful cultures of practice from the studios in which their professional thinking normally develops. This is particularly important because a PhD thesis in practice-led design research is often a combination of a project and a written exegesis. It is the purpose of the exegesis to contextualize the work produced by discussing methodology and method(s), critical ideas and knowledge relating to the inquiry. As such, what is written must speak authentically and perceptively to the designer's practice.

Writing as design

I work part time in such a studio. At any time of day or night there are five or six people scattered around the suite. From the back of our computers small luminous apples appear to demarcate this world into separate entities. But this is an illusion. Although at any time we might be working on different parts of a project or on different projects, our worlds are not discrete. The results of what we create occur through synergies of connection, co-creation and critique. Design is a collective activity.

The design writer John Wood (2012) says: 'The kind of academic research that is needed in the twenty-first century is a *collective* activity that requires imagination, self-reflexivity, empathetic awareness, ingenuity, resourcefulness, adaptability, clarity, insight, rationality, passion, scepticism and perceptiveness' (13–14). He acknowledges in this statement that designers are collaborative constructors. By orchestrating multiple levels of spatial, visual and word-led thinking, designers employ collaborative, discursive, open-ended processes. Through these they are able to move beyond the problematized mind-set towards what Lawson (2006: 43) calls 'solution focused' thinking.

Professionally, the most valued skill designers have is their ability to communicate with an identified audience in an empathetically focused and articulate manner. The uniqueness of their 'voice' is a quality that Wood (2004, 2012) sees as integral to both their creative and social integrity. When this voice is confidently developed, it negates the tendency towards plagiarism. When designers talk about their work, nuances of an authentic self in written form can become the basis of communicable integrity. Their voice can bring into concord research practice and *how* it is discussed. However, more importantly, this voice, whether spoken, visual or written, also operates as a vehicle for thought.

In one room of the studio where I work is a wall that can be wiped clean with a rag. It is positioned at the end of a table where we gather to collectively wrestle with potential. Across its surface ideas are clustered, catalysed, re-ordered and discussed. Here, key words, fragments of sentences and quick sketches are drawn into relationships. We work as a group to find solutions.

I suggest a similar approach might be applied to academic writing. Lockheart and Raein (2012) argue that there is a need 'for design writing (for and by designers) to reflect the thinking styles of the designer's processes and methods'

(281–2). In the world of professional design, solutions occur as a consequence of strategic, group-oriented thinking. The Studio Model for developing community writing draws its pedagogical inspiration from this practice.

At the university there are five kinds of tea in packets on my windowsill. Although I drink the common variety with milk and two sugars, the PhD candidates with whom I work have more refined tastes. Drinking tea and eating together has become an expression of an intimacy that I believe underpins all learning (especially that associated with addressing anxiety). In an environment where policy-driven pressure is often applied to 'get students through' their PhDs (Aitchison & Lee 2006; Marginson 2004), such intimacy and the time it takes to develop may seem antithetical. But it is a sound investment. If, as McCormick and Paechter (1999) note, 'learning is the *social* construction of knowledge' (xi), then we are presented with alternative horizons for growing researchers whose development transcends the production of their theses.

This said, writers' groups are not merely self-indulgent experiences. They are used to activate and develop skills in an environment where time has become money, and where there are high pressures to achieve quality and effectiveness (Aitchison & Lee 2006; Curtis & Matthewman 2005; Marginson 2004; Robertson 2007). Evidence suggests that collective approaches to writing at PhD level improve both quality and writing output (Aitchison 2010; McGrail *et al.* 2006; Maher *et al.* 2013). Strategically aligned with the realities of limited time and the desire for authentic, quality communication, community writing initiatives can be both progressive and transformative.

The Studio Model

The Studio Model approaches writing as a design activity. In this regard it embraces content, style and structure, as well as layout, typographical concerns, and the negotiations between image and text that are fundamental to how designers shape information. It enables gifted practitioners who may be less familiar with formal approaches to academic writing (either because their past research has been largely professionally based, or their first language is other than English) to use recognizable communicative tools and processes. Incrementally, as they work socially, they are able to develop increasingly confident, scholarly, reader-focused writing inside a familiar and supportive environment.

The model takes two forms but with similar tenets. The first is a collective that operates as a facilitated critique and writing group. The second group is an independent online development that has surfaced as a consequence of the first.

The facilitated critique and writing collective

This social collective normally meets fortnightly. Because it is voluntary, the group's size fluctuates slightly but generally there are between three and four people. We bring food to share and, wherever we are, we work in front of a large whiteboard. The aim of the collective is to support the development of any nominated body of writing relating to the thesis, whether it is chapter drafts, information design, or updated commentary on practice. Any work proposed for discussion is dropped into a shared online folder at least three days in advance. This enables everybody to read and make notes on material to be considered. Generally, people who post work are asked to provide a question or problem so the group is able to use this part of the session purposefully. These statements often say things like 'I can't get this to flow properly and it's wandering. How can I tighten it up?', or 'I'm not sure what aspect of my practice to talk about first. How can I break this down?', or 'My introduction feels repetitive. How do I stop it sounding like my abstract?'. Any statement or question is positioned as a preface to a posted piece of writing. This is so other participants can understand the nature of the perceived problem. This way of working has its origins in the culture of undergraduate reading groups. Here texts and focus questions are made available in advance and people come together to engage in informed discussion and analysis.

Normally sessions are divided into three parts. In the first session (which runs for 60–90 minutes) we work through each writer's focus question. We try to divide time evenly between the participants. Normally the writer leads the discussion and the facilitator will pull things back on task if the discussion begins to

Figure 13.1 Working through each writer's focus question. As in design studios, whiteboards are used to make thinking explicit. They may be used when someone doesn't know how to begin writing, or freezes in mid-process. A facilitator will ask the writer to simply talk about their ideas. The facilitator writes these onto the board as bullet points so they can be overviewed collectively. Advanced listening skills and astute questioning enable the thinking to be diagrammatically shaped into a structure that can later be turned into sentences or paragraphed sequences.

drift. Although as the candidate's supervisor I initially adopt the role of facilitator, as skills in productive questioning, recording and reflection develop, this position is increasingly assumed by members of the collective. The role of the facilitator is to question astutely, *not* to offer advice. This shifts the dynamic towards collective problem solving and away from a traditional tutorial. It also empowers people in the group to become active problem solvers for colleagues, and through this develop a more socially supportive, scholarly practice. It also removes me from the role of galvanizing agent. Although I endeavour to prioritize these collective meetings, if I am away at a conference or on research leave, the collective continues to function productively because it has become self-actuating. This is important because I am aware that other candidates might view an initiative like this as a form of supervisory favouritism. Because a number of students choose not to use this form of writing support, the decentring of my commitment (in terms of facilitation) is gradually seen in the context of a range of other, equally available, supervisory initiatives.

The second part of the session is devoted to each person writing a new draft of their posted material based on discussions and feedback. Often students photograph the board to keep as a reference, and some audio-record discussions about their work. Writing time in this phase is normally silent and generally participants withdraw to other rooms or quiet spaces. Before they go, each writer says what they will work on, even though this will normally only be an initial draft or reshaping of material. Normally one to two hours is devoted to this activity. The idea behind the withdrawal space is that it should be discrete and uninterruptible (all cell phones are contractually turned off). Some writers take music with them; some work in silence.

The last phase is normally preceded by a tea break and sharing food. Talking, laughing and eating is interspersed with a requirement that each writer reads their revised draft or presents the redesign of the structural issue they have attempted to address. At the end of each feedback session the writer nominates what they will have completed before the next meeting, and everybody notes this down. This contractual arrangement places emphasis on realizable progress. It also lets everybody know what is being undertaken by their colleagues; for those with poor organizational or time management skills, this demonstrates in a subtle but pervasive way how their colleagues create effective strategies for pacing work.

This process on average takes between three to four hours. Because of this, we have found that future collective meetings are best planned at the end of each session so participants can book arrangements at least two weeks in advance.

The independent online writing group

The second initiative may be described as an independent online writing group. This unit grew out of the writing collective. Using Facebook and its privacy settings, members control who sees and comments on their work. The only information shared is material relevant to agreed participants. It is up to the members to invite each other to become friends. Although many universities set up more formally based forums for students (for example, Google Drive's sharing option, and Moodle sites constructed to involve a specified group), the students in this collective prefer the discrete social environment of their familiar, 'friend nominated' sites.

Discussions within the group are not only about writing, but also about where to find relevant information, including upcoming social and academic events. People can also ask questions and talk about the nature of the program or the supervision of their thesis without worrying that what they say might impact in a negative way on how they are perceived by faculty. Significantly, the online writing group does not include supervisors or facilitators. Writers post work and agree on contracted progress. For instance, a writer might say 'I will work on this section this afternoon and post it up before midday tomorrow'. They can upload work they produce as either docx, jpeg or pdf files. This means written text *and* its relationship to images and layout can also be discussed and critiqued.

The online writing group attracts a significant number of international students. Some feel more comfortable in this environment because it removes the issue of people looking at them, waiting for an answer that has to cross language barriers. Writers can post comments in their own time. They can also select discrete postings so they can check written work with close friends before they share it with members of the wider group. This is important to certain cultures where loss of face is a significant impediment to progress while studying. Being able to rephrase sentences or, more importantly, seek cultural validation for ideas before sharing them means that higher levels of cultural authenticity gradually begin to permeate the writing. One online writer described it this way:

> Sometimes I wish to write about a certain Chinese philosophical or aesthetic idea, but I don't know how to translate the concept into English. This is not about translating words, but about communicating complex ideas (like Yi Jing) that have no Western equivalents. I will initially e-mail my writing to mentors in Shanghai for feedback, or I will talk to other Chinese students in the university who I know have a deep understanding of the concept. Not only do they provide me with helpful ways of wording the idea but they also put me in touch with recent writing that has not yet been translated into English. Once I am certain of the clarity of the concept, I share my writing with the wider group. That way I know it is *my writing* and not the idea that might be unclear. I do not feel embarrassed. In a room with everybody sitting around, I can't do this. If somebody questions a draft of what I am writing I do not have time to consider my response so I normally say nothing.

For both local and international students in design, the electronic posting of work in progress is not an unfamiliar process. Online sharing and critique has an established history in disciplines like photography and illustration where candidates post work on international sites like Flickr, Tumblr and Instagram. Other sites like

CONCEPTART.org, deviantART (dA), CGhub.com, Pixi, and art community groups on Facebook can be used to elicit critique from more advanced professional practitioners. These communities enable levels of networking and exposure that reach beyond published material. Researchers are kept abreast of developments as they emerge. The contextual knowledge they provide extends beyond the limitations of published material, and the delays that can accompany such processes. Moreover, these communities often become support networks that offer useful critique because the subscribers themselves are advanced practitioners.

Increasingly, design practitioners are becoming more active online, gathering followers and supporters of their work, while simultaneously contributing by posting critique, seeking advice and engaging in forum discussions. This offers important international exposure to the industry and enhances the potential for post-doctoral employment.

A recent development in this regard is the use of live-streamed screencasting (broadcasting one's computer screen to viewers in real time). Because chat rooms can be attached to the stream, in digital art communities, researchers can share their processes and watch other community members and leading creative researchers engaged in practice-led problem solving. An increasing number of prominent professionals now use live-streaming with voice-overs to explain their work processes, answer questions from the chat, and update community members about research developments. The potential for this form of social critique to fold out into thesis writing is considerable. One of my current thesis students says:

> I recently streamed some of my own work—after sharing a link to my livestream.com channel on a couple of sites ... I immediately had a dozen people join the stream and begin discussing my work ... *live*. This approach is currently quite popular in the US. I haven't seen anything similar with regards to thesis writing yet, although I have heard that there are a few published writers of fiction who live streamed their work as they roughed out a chapter in Microsoft Word.
>
> (Hanna 2013)

The independent online writing group is an extension of the facilitated writing collective. It operates effectively on a very simple platform where members of a voluntary community assist each other in the development of contracted writing through sharing, critique and social support. Although some writers prefer the intimacy of shared time and direct engagement, the online community offers a number of alternative advantages. When PhD candidates travel or are engaged in research activities overseas, they can remain active in this community. Similarly, some writers who work part time or have family commitments use the online community as a means of supporting contracted regimes. In addition, unlike the facilitated writing collective, participants in the online group are able to tailor the constitution of their community and meet at diverse times. This offers them a higher level of control over who engages with their work.

Teaching initiatives in the studio model

The two writing collectives are not mutually exclusive, but they do meet different needs for different people. Being social collectives, they are always in a state of making. In this regard it is useful to consider some of the teaching initiatives that have developed as a consequence. These initiatives are predicated on the principles of community learning. They all relate to approaches taken to student enablement, and respond to the specific requirements of practice-led thesis writing in art and design.

Critique as debate

Aitchison and Lee (2006) note that, in writing groups, 'the opportunity to practise the language of analysis and critique [is] a key element of pleasure and success' (271). Often the analysis of another person's work enables us to gain useful insights into our own practice. Building on this idea, once a year the facilitated writing group meets to critique three completed practice-led theses. These are downloaded from online repositories. For each thesis, participants write an examiner's report and an assessment. Critique is shaped as a debate where individuals argue the merits or otherwise of the work they have examined.

While the initiative generally leads to a lively exchange, its true value lies in demonstrating a variation of approaches to thesis construction. The analysis underscores the importance of writing about one's practice intelligently and authentically. Because participants are given an examiner's briefing pack from which to work, they also become familiar with expectations pertaining to their own theses. In reviewing diverse journeys across related academic terrain, differences are brought into very sharp focus, enabling developing writers to talk through effective or problematic approaches in relation to their own exegeses. In considering these completed theses, participants discuss diverse stylistic relationships between methodology, context and individual practice. Collective analysis helps to build a rich, discursive environment where discrete scholarly voices can be analysed and appreciated in terms of their communicative effectiveness. The environment also allows for anxieties to be voiced, new approaches to be considered, and deeper appreciations of clarity and authenticity to be developed.

Writing the self

Often practice-led theses become derailed when they are not *led* by the practice. If the wider university structures are not cognizant of the unique nature of such inquiries, the research can be impaired by generic emphases on prescribed methodologies, definitive literature reviews and fixed research questions. By their nature, practice-led PhD theses are protean. Scrivener describes them as spiraling 'through stages of appreciation, action and re-appreciation, whereby the unique and uncertain situation comes to be understood through the attempt to change it, and changed through the attempt to understand it' (Scrivener 2000: 8). In such research, reviews of contextual knowledge change as the inquiry shifts, and research design must be flexible enough to accommodate emerging needs in the inquiry. In a significant number of these theses, designers 'turn the analytic lens on themselves ... writing, interpreting, and performing their own narratives about culturally significant experiences' (Chase 2005: 60). Even if the researcher avoids this, their thesis remains fundamentally subjective. This is because, as Griffiths (2010) notes, 'the self is inescapable, because the person creating, responding to, working on, developing or evaluating performances, artifacts and practices is central to those activities' (185).

Because writing can be a mode of thinking, writing collectives *accompany* research; they do not lead it. Finding one's voice as a writer is integral to being able to think through one's thesis, so an early activity I introduce in the facilitated writing group is the drafting of a personal statement. This text positions the researcher, explains why he or she is doing the project, and contextualizes the thesis in relation to past work.

This personal writing also helps to set the tone for a thesis. It greets the reader in the opening pages and may be seen as a kind of threshold across which a relationship with the reader is established. Such writing, because it frames itself as personal, can be written without many of the anxieties that initially accompany crafting a 'scholarly voice'.

Normally, new writers enjoy writing material like this. Being short, the personal statement is often a confidence builder that is later refined and developed outside of the facilitated group. This confidence building is important because, as Ahern and Manathunga (2004) note, doctoral students can encounter cognitive as well as social and emotional blocks. While cognitive issues may be comparatively easy to identify and tackle, social and emotional blocks are often not obvious until they become disabling. Low self-confidence may be partly addressed by alleviating the isolation that unsupported thesis writing can engender. By working in a collective and using familiar modes of address early in the doctoral experience, one can often kick-start a sense of ownership and engagement inside an appreciative environment.

Writers are encouraged to craft this text as a letter aimed at an intelligent reader whom they have never met. They assume, however, that the reader is interested in their project and their relationship to it. The text is normally quite short (less than a thousand words) and can be used to develop skills in concise, personal writing that clarifies intention. Different modes of writing, including lyrical, personal and documentary forms, are encouraged and shared.

The following, from the opening of Gabriella Trussardi's (2012) PhD thesis, 'Patterns of corporeality: Text/ile evidence of the body', provides an example of how such writing may be used to introduce and position a thesis:

> I always knew that textiles spoke. My mother's quilts shared stories of the garments she'd worn before I was born, and those of my childhood. The untouched painted linen and wool threads in the cardboard box illustrated with a dainty lady

in 18th century dress, told me of my grandmother's wish for relief from the realities of post-WWII rural Kaingaroa.

The hand-stitched table linens kept in the china cabinet, and saved for 'best', whispered the importance of managing appearance. My 1990 needle worked teenage Ninja Turtles pillows shouted a wish to marry pop culture with domestic craft in a pre-internet world.

Throughout my life I learned every textile skill I could find … crochet, embroidery, quilting, appliqué, screen printing, needlepoint, cross stitch, dyeing, shibori, and garment construction: enlarging the vocabulary with which I spoke.

Once I joined the fashion industry I learned the dialects with which clothing talked to the world on our behalf, and the quiet desperation people felt when they couldn't find the right words. Working in costume for theatre and film let me fine-tune my understanding of the language of textiles; how colour, texture, pattern, size, and shape might speak worlds into being.

My Master of Art and Design thesis spoke about a childhood spent being both between, and at the edge of cultures and places. I lined garments made from upholstery fabric with textiles printed with childhood snapshots, and featured large buttons with resin-encapsulated images.

In this PhD thesis a range of textiles; digitally printed, embroidered, and with handpainted devoré, speak about a contemporary lived life framed as a grotesque subject.

My daughter's birth sampler in my hallway

… and the quilt that now lies on my bed, but once covered my grandfather's sparse cooling frame in a hospital have taught me in very intimate ways

… that fabrics speak.

(Trussardi 2012: 21)

The use of diagrams

Graphic designers are information architects. Professionally, they orchestrate often quite complex information to make it comprehensible. Although in doctoral theses conventional approaches to writing assume that this is done via sentences, paragraphs and tables, designers often communicate using elegant, mutually dependent relationships between image and written text. Where in conventional thesis writing diagrams are normally used to present accumulated data, designers often employ them as a mode of thinking. By this I mean they clarify and arrange thought visually. Not only does this approach enable them to process ideas multidimensionally, it can also, at a glance, enable others to understand relationships between complex bodies of thought.

Although diagrammatic thinking has a long history, it is most commonly identified as the radial tree associated with Buzan's (1974) process of mindmapping. This technique grew out of his assertion that readers do not scan information from left to right and top to bottom, but instead consider entire areas in a non-linear manner.

When doctoral students in design have trouble writing, I often find it useful to ask them to *draw* out their idea. By talking through visual connections they are able to overview relationships using a very familiar process. By utilizing insightful questioning and suggestions from their writing collective, they can quickly check what lacks coherence and what will need elucidating in explanatory text. This approach to developing writing from visual mapping can help in two ways. First it can be used as a process for creating paragraph headings when sequencing ideas, and second (at a more complex level), it can be used to present multidimensional information in the thesis that may be expanded upon using keys or written commentaries. Talita Tolutau's information graphic (Figure 13.2) offers a useful example.

The pedagogical use of emergent diagramming is very helpful in exegesis design. The architecture and written clarity of this document can be usefully processed in a group. This approach is very familiar to designers. Participants critique what is being arranged on the board in front of them. They suggest alternative approaches and ask for elaboration where something isn't clear. This collaborative approach to structural analysis and comprehension means that clarity can be simultaneously

Figure 13.2 Talita Tolutau's information graphic. A diagram of phases and relationships in the indigenous methodology Kakala employed in the explication of her PhD thesis (in development 2013). The information graphic sets out the core principles in the research methodology, then positions methods in relation to phases in which they operate. The subsequent writing in her chapter is used to unpack each of these in turn, and apply them to specific actions undertaken during the research.

constructed and critiqued. In this process, writing and reading become part of a socially supported, integrated dynamic of instantaneous trial, feedback and collaborative remodelling. Here hearing and integrating the views of others becomes part of a familiar process of design, re-design and evaluation.

The architecture of the exegesis

Lockheart and Raein (2012) note that design thinking has increasingly moved from monologue models to more conversational approaches. So too have its approaches to academic writing. The essentially modernist construct of the authoritative, singular voice has been challenged by the potential for conversations to be embedded inside theses (Scrivener & Ings 2009). As a consequence, designer/writers continue to seek effective ways to build articulate relationships between image and text, and to develop systems of narration that facilitate effective links between ideas and their expression in scholarly texts.

This means that in certain PhD exegeses, traditional constructs of writing as linear and cumulative have been renegotiated. When artists and designers talk about the content and thinking in their work, they often oscillate between the written self and the context of ideas inside which the self resides. Accordingly, they may rethink traditional scholarly writing devices (Figure 13.3) or design exegetic texts that contain more than one voice (see Sinfield 2009; Nepia 2012; Ings 2006).

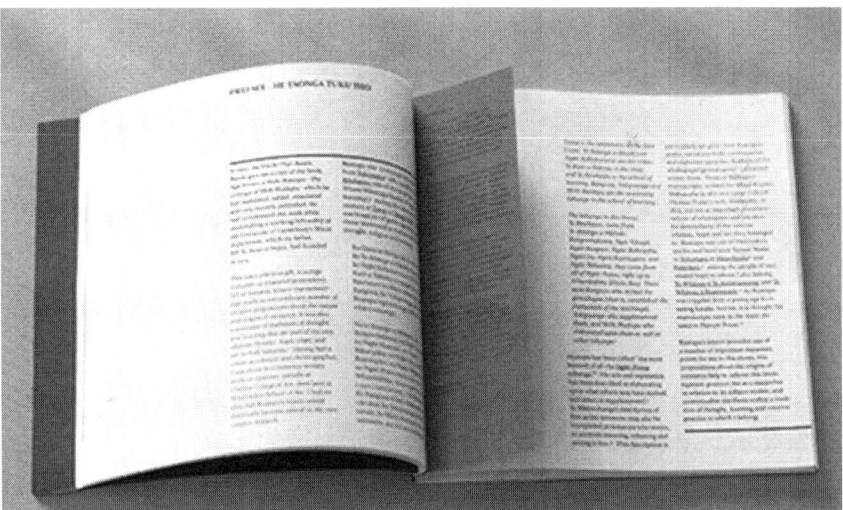

Figure 13.3 Volume two from Moana Nepia's PhD thesis 'Te Kore: Exploring the Maori concept of the void' (Nepia 2012, pictured in soft focus). Here footnotes are designed as extended bodies of clarification or elaboration. While interfacing with the main text, they are bound on separate pages; thus, one voice discusses critical concepts while another adds embellishment.

In conclusion

The Studio Model, with its critique and writing collective, the independent online writing group and the pedagogical initiatives discussed above have one thing in common. They are predicated on accepting that writing is a social practice of social beings. We communicate with others and, in so doing, the self becomes part of a social phenomenon. In the initiatives outlined, supervision moves from instruction to a more subtle process where growth is conceptualized as a learner-enabled process. In the quietness of my office I think about this.

As I do, I notice that outside it has begun to rain. Water runs down the window in small rivulets. Each drop flows in a similar direction and each makes a unique journey across the same piece of glass. In a few minutes a small cluster of writers will flow in through the door. They will bring steaming dishes for the microwave and packets of exotic tea. Most of all they will bring hope. Some will have writing they contracted to complete; some will have issues with new material. Some will have processed drafts through online environments and one or two will have compositions of image and text they need to discuss.

The worlds they inhabit have moved beyond the traditions of the solitary scholar. They gather in communities, be they physical or online, so that their writings are instantiations of social practice. While the PhD might be considered an offering of new knowledge, on a more profound level it can draw new identities into being (Johnson *et al.* 2000). These identities are both personal and social; they populate the academy and the profession … and in time I hope they may make the need for red sofas redundant.

References

Ahern, K. and Manathunga, C. (2004) 'Clutch-starting stalled thesis students', *Innovative Higher Education*, 28(4): 237–54.
Aitchison, C. (2010) 'Learning together to publish', in C. Aitchison, B. Kamler, and A. Lee (eds) *Publishing Pedagogies for the Doctorate and Beyond*, London: Routledge.
Aitchison, C. and Lee, A. (2006) 'Research writing: problems and pedagogies', *Teaching in Higher Education*, 11(3): 265–78.
Buzan, T. (1974) *Use Your Head*, London: BBC Books.
Chase, S. (2005) 'Narrative inquiry: multiple lenses, approaches and voices', in N. K. Denzin and Y. Lincoln (eds) *The Sage Handbook of Qualitative Research*, Thousand Oaks, CA: Sage, pp. 651–95.
Curtis, B. and Matthewman, S. (2005) 'The managed university: the PBRF, its impacts and staff attitudes', *New Zealand Journal of Employment Relations*, 30(2): 1–17.
Griffiths, M. (2010) 'Research and the self', in M. Biggs and H. Karlsson (eds) *The Routledge Companion to Research in the Arts*, London: Routledge.
Hanna, J. (2013) 'Online sharing'. E-mail (22 April 2013).
Ings, W. (2006) 'Talking pictures: a creative utilisation of structural and aesthetic profiles from narrative music videos and television commercials in a non-spoken film text', unpublished PhD thesis, Auckland University of Technology.

Johnson, L., Lee, A. and Green, B. (2000) 'The PhD and the autonomous self: gender, rationality and postgraduate pedagogy', *Studies in Higher Education*, 25(2): 135–47.

Kamler, B. and Thomson, P. (2006) *Helping Doctoral Students to Write*, New York: Routledge.

Lawson, B. (2006) *How Designers Think: The Design Process Demystified*, Oxford: Architectural Press.

Lockheart, J. and Raein, M. (2012) 'No one expects the design inquisition: searching for a metaphorical solution for thinking, researching and writing through design', *Journal of Writing in Creative Practice*, 5(2): 275–89.

McCormick, R. and Paechter, C. (1999) *Learning and Knowledge*, London: Paul Chapman and Open University Press.

McGrail, M., Rickard, C. and Jones, R. (2006) 'Publish or perish: a systematic review of interventions to increase academic publication rates', *Higher Education Research and Development*, 25(1): 19–35.

Maher, M., Fallucca, A. and Mulhern Halasz, H. (2013) 'Write On! Through to the PhD: using writing groups to facilitate doctoral degree progress', *Studies in Continuing Education*, 35(1): 193–208.

Marginson, S. (2004) 'National and global competition in higher education', *The Australian Educational Researcher*, 31(2): 1–28.

Nepia, M. (2012) 'Te Kore: exploring the Maori concept of the void', unpublished thesis, Auckland University of Technology.

Robertson, J. (2007) 'Beyond the "research/teaching nexus": exploring the complexity of academic experience', *Studies in Higher Education*, 32(5): 541–56.

Scrivener, S. (2000) 'Reflection in and on action and practice in creative-production doctoral projects in art and design', *Working Papers in Art and Design*, Available online: http://sitem.herts.ac.uk/artdes_research/papers/wpades/vol1/scrivener2.html (accessed 23 April 2013).

Scrivener, S. and Ings, W. (2009) 'Framing the typography extract from the exegesis of the thesis Talking Pictures', *Studies in Material Thinking*. Available online: http://www.materialthinking.org/sites/default/files/papers/ss_wi.pdf (accessed 19 March 2013).

Sinfield, D. (2009) 'Under the surface: reflections on workers' narratives from below the minimum wage', unpublished thesis, Auckland University of Technology.

Trussardi, G. (2012) 'Patterns of corporeality: text/ile evidence of the body', unpublished thesis, Auckland University of Technology.

Wood, J. (2004) 'The culture of academic rigour: does design research really need it?', *The Design Journal*, 3 (1): 44–57.

—— (2012) 'In the cultivation of research excellence—is rigour a no-brainer?', *Journal of Writing in Creative Practice*, 5 (1): 11–26.

Chapter 14

An intimate circle

Reflections on writing as women in higher education

Agnes Bosanquet, Jayde Cahir, Elaine Huber, Christa Jacenyik-Trawöger and Margot McNeill

Introduction

An extensive body of literature on writing circles or groups in higher education for doctoral students, and increasingly early career researchers, focuses on supporting emerging scholars to develop research capability. This literature has explored the history of writing groups for student learning, pedagogies of writing groups and principles for effective operation—including identification as writers, peer review, community building and establishing the business of writing as everyday practice. Only in passing, however, does this body of work address the gendered membership of writing circles. Where the gender of participants is indicated, the groups discussed in the literature consist predominantly of women members. Lee and Boud (2003), for example, do not identify participants but note in the acknowledgements that one of the writing groups published a paper in the proceedings of a conference focusing on women and university culture. Five of the six members in Lassig *et al.* (2009) are women. Aitchison and Lee (2006) are more explicit, stating: 'All group members were women in the midstages of their career' (272) and noting the shared points of identification this offers. More commonly, however, the heterogeneity of the group is emphasized, despite the predominance of women: 'we are birds of very different feathers [with] varying backgrounds, motivations and research interests' (Pasternak *et al.* 2009: 361). Although there are published examples of women writing together (Galligan *et al.* 2003; Dwyer *et al.* 2012), there is little discussion of experiences as women writers in these contexts.

There are some notable exceptions exploring subjectivities as women writers and the specific challenges of academic life for women, including 'hidden' workloads or academic 'housework', under-representation at senior levels, competing responsibilities, career interruption and differential research outcomes (Aronson & Swanson 1991; Grant & Knowles 2000; Grant 2006; Faulconer *et al.* 2010). The literature demonstrates that mothers in particular struggle to maintain research activity and publishing output (Acker & Armenti 2004; Ward & Wolf-Wendel 2004; Probert 2005). Writing circles for women offer a pleasurable and productive social space that can ameliorate some of these challenges.

The authors of this chapter are a group of women who have been members of a writing circle together for almost three years. This chapter builds on our previous reflective evaluations on learning in a writing group context (Bosanquet *et al.* 2012) to examine our practice as women writers in higher education. What does it mean to write as women and among women? How do writing circles support women to develop academic writerly identities? The discussion brings together feminist theory and pedagogy on writing as women and scholarship on intimacy and affect. Our reflections reveal the multitude of roles and myriad of identities that we perform as writers and women; enabling these observations is the protected space of our intimate writing circle.

Context

Our writing circle was established as part of a wider program of initiatives to raise the research profile of a centralized learning and teaching development unit at a research-intensive metropolitan Australian university. The process of establishing the group has been previously described (Bosanquet *et al.* 2012). Unlike other writing groups that are maintained by an expert facilitator, our writing group is made up exclusively of early career researchers in a collaborative network. The current membership consists of two academic developers, two research project officers and an educational developer; that is, both academic and professional staff who are active researchers in the field of higher education teaching and learning. Diverse disciplinary backgrounds are represented, including cultural studies, education, engineering, music and communication technologies. All members have postgraduate qualifications, with three members having completed PhDs (two since the establishment of the group) and two members currently undertaking PhDs. All five members are women, although this constitution of the group was unintentional. In response to an open call for participation, the initial membership was seven women and one man. Subsequently, three members withdrew from the writing group as a result of workload issues, a change in role or leaving the university. The establishment of the writing group was not underpinned by a feminist pedagogy like those reported by Grant and Knowles (2000) and Grant (2006); nevertheless, the gendering of the group has impacted its practice, and the writing retreat reflections reported in this chapter were preceded and informed by a discussion of feminist scholarship on writing as women.

Writing as women

Since the 1970s, French feminist scholars including Cixous, Kristeva, and Irigaray have developed an influential and wide-ranging theoretical field defining and analysing *écriture féminine* or women's writing. Literary critic Moi notes the challenge of translating *écriture féminine* into English: 'Does [it] mean "female" or "feminine" writing? How can we know whether this or any other such expressions refer to [biological] sex or to [socially constructed] gender?' (Moi 2002: 95). Cixous coined the phrase *écriture féminine* in her essay 'The Laugh of the Medusa': 'Woman must write herself: must write about women and bring women to writing ... Woman must put herself into the text' (Cixous 1981: 246). Irigaray uses the similar term *parler-femme* (speaking as woman): 'I am a woman. I write with who I am' (Irigaray 1993: 53). In her canonical book *This Sex Which is Not One* (1985), Irigaray writes 'a collection of questions' that cannot readily be answered, including: How can we speak (as) women? She suggests a possible way: 'By going back through the dominant discourse. By interrogating men's "mastery". By speaking to women. And among women' (Irigaray 1985: 119).

Irigaray's complex and challenging writing not only explicates *parler-femme*; she performs it: sentences are frequently left incomplete; grammar and syntax do not follow the rigid guidelines one has come to expect: ideas are fragmentary, elliptical, playful; her styles are various, multiple, and changeable mid-sentence. To exemplify this, in *This Sex Which is Not One* she writes:

> Hers are contradictory words, somewhat mad from the standpoint of reason, inaudible for whoever listens to them with ready-made grids, with a fully elaborated code in hand ... One would have to listen with another ear, as if hearing an 'other meaning' always in the process of weaving itself, of embracing itself with words, but also of getting rid of words in order not to become fixed, congealed in them.
>
> (Irigaray 1985: 29)

Hers are contradictory words. As feminist theorist Grosz says, 'the moment one feels relatively confident about what she means in one context, one loses grasp of other related passages which seemed comprehensible when they were read' (Grosz 1989: 101). Irigaray invites contradictory readings: 'no two readings, even by the same reader, are identical' (Grosz 1989: 102). This is a deliberate technique which offers an active rethinking of woman's relationship to text, language and theory. In *Speculum of the Other Woman*, Irigaray omits punctuation and referencing because 'in relation to the working of theory, the/a woman ... does not have to conform to the codes theory has set up for itself' (Irigaray 1985: 365).

Irigaray's writing articulates the plurality of feminine subjectivity in order to challenge the 'sameness' of men's and women's voices in scholarly and literary writing:

> We have so much space to share. Our horizon will never stop expanding; we are always open. Stretching out, never ceasing to unfold ourselves, we have so many voices to invent in order to express all of us everywhere, even in our gaps, that all the time there is will not be enough ... If we don't invent a language, if we don't find our body's language, it will have too few gestures to accompany our story.
>
> (Irigaray 1985: 213–14)

This project of *parler-femme* or *écriture féminine* is an attempt to break up phallocentric discourse or 'jam the machinery' of patriarchal language (which is understood to dominate scholarly work) by creating a new type of writing that could correspond to a model of 'being two' (Irigaray 1985: 78). In *Philosophy in the Feminine*, a critical reading of Irigaray's work, Whitford (1994) describes this process by articulating two possible reading and writing positions—the masculine and feminine. To write as a man, she suggests, 'is to assert mastery, to be in control of meaning, to claim truth, objectivity, knowledge'. On the contrary, to write as a woman is 'to refuse mastery, to allow meaning to be elusive or shifting, not to be in control, or in possession of truth or knowledge' (Whitford 1994: 50). Similarly, using the term 'anecdotal theory', American feminist Gallop (2002) distinguishes between traditional critical theory and a playful or erotic approach, characterizing the former as masterful, abstract and powerful. Anecdotal theory, on the other hand, is performed as a 'struggle for mastery' and an attempt to think through 'situations which tend to disable thought' (Gallop 2002: 15). Disrupting this binary logic, Whitford (1994) proposes a third reading and writing strategy—'a double reading, hovering between the two possibilities' (25) in which the male and female would operate together in 'a kind of creative and fertile partnership' (25).

Australian feminist scholar Bartlett pictures 'jamming the machinery' in a more literal sense:

> The machine I imagine being jammed is a printing press, a massive machine that generates words, texts, theory. It's a dirty black metal giant. The jam is strawberry: pink and glassy with bits of pieces held in suspension amid the transparent spread ... In the end, the quotidian rules; everyday domesticity overwhelms modernist industrialization ... The machinery Irigaray refers to ... is the upstanding and unbending patriarchal academy ... Writing as a woman, rather than through the narrative machinery of patriarchy, is a style: a disruption to conventional reading and representational practices that resists the steely authority of linearity and logic, arguing instead from subjective and historical specificity. It's the jam of theory, having to locate yourself in your writing.
>
> (Bartlett 2006: np)

For most women writing in academia, there is a gap between the exhortations of feminist literature to write the self, and the rigid criteria and norms of writing in research contexts. What can be taken from feminist theory is a focus on the pleasures of text and attention to the affective aspects and intimacies of writing. Describing an affective exchange between authors, readers, translators and their writings, Still uses Irigaray's (2002) evocative phrase 'poetic nuptials': 'Poetic nuptials are an alternative to ways of reading such as critique which demand a particular distance between what become subject and object' (7). She describes 'poetic nuptials' through her experiences translating the words of Irigaray's

Passions élémentaires into English. She and fellow translator Collie sit at the kitchen table, surrounded by the detritus of wine, dips and pitta bread, half-hidden beneath papers and French and English versions of Irigaray's books. At any given time, they might be rereading the 'sacred' text, shouting suggestions at one another, arguing for or against a particular translation, scrambling through dictionaries, or trailing hummus over work already completed, ready to be dismantled later. They pause to sip red wine, or to mop up a spillage, laughing hysterically, offering unusual word choices, sometimes shouting 'yes' and punching the air, then sheepishly taking another sip of wine and scooping up some more dip. Still calls this:

> An intellectual collaboration, an exchange of gifts, an emotional experience and a labour of love: rolling words around your tongue, letting them fall from your lips to have them reverberate in another's labyrinthine inner ear echoes your hopes for further passionate encounters between the text and other readers.
>
> (Still 2002: 20–1)

Several writers note the gap between affect and writing in higher education. As an academic developer, Manathunga (2007) mourns the absence of theory in educational literature. Similarly, Peseta (2007) identifies a disconnection between the pleasures of textuality and the work of academics, noting that the 'wonderful laughter and energy of our practice; occasionally its sadness, longing, regret, and desire, the confusion of difficult decision making; and at other times, the joy and celebration of collaborative successes' (17) is missing from scholarly narratives. Feminist writers offer pleasure in abundance. The writing woman described by Cixous (1981) finds herself overflowing: 'Time and again I, too, have felt so full of luminous torrents that I could burst' (246). Feminist writer bell hooks (the lowercase rendering of her surname is itself a way of jamming the machinery) similarly writes of the rapture, sacredness, grace and ecstasy of words and writing: 'I write to live' (hooks 1999: 45). This is juxtaposed against the challenges of academia: 'I was constantly walking a tightrope, trying to fulfil the requirements that would lead to tenure while searching for the space to write' (hooks 1999: 133).

Writing groups have been advocated as one method of overcoming the challenge of providing space to write, offering a community of practice, particularly to support early career researchers (Lee & Boud 2003) in developing their research profile in an increasingly casualized, cash-strapped and time-poor environment (Bazeley 2003). Issues faced by women establishing careers in academia are elegantly analyzed by Maher *et al.* (2006) when reflecting on experiences of working collaboratively during study leave. These female academics use the term 'peer mentoring' to describe the process of rotating their research presentations and reviewing writing and promotion applications. This was essentially a writing group, although the members did not describe it this way; it was a group of women who understood the challenges of career progression and mentored one another towards career development and advancement.

Dwyer *et al.* (2012) focus on early career academics (ECAs) breaking through or transitioning to the role of academics. The authors, all women, argue that writing groups can provide a chance for ECAs to write, review and debate ideas, and analysed this through the discourse of pleasure. Writing in and writing for a cohesive group enables ECAs to experience 'being' or 'becoming' competent academic writers taking pleasure in 'doing' writing (Dwyer *et al.* 2012). Written with the 'publish or perish' doctrine in mind, Galligan *et al.* (2003) describe the evolution of their all-women writing group over a three-year period. They focus on the benefits of increased productivity, collegiality and leadership, with the language used to describe the group tending towards the transactional—invest time and gain (publishing) rewards. In contrast, Aitchison (2010) describes writing group pedagogies (peer review, writing to know and knowing how to write, working together to write for others) which resonate with the collegiality and curiosity thematic in feminist theories about women as writers. The reflections of our writing group, written in the context of a retreat and discussed in the following section, articulate both the transactional and pleasurable aspects of writing together.

Reflections

Previous evaluations of our writing group found that making time for scholarly writing and incorporating writing into workloads is increasingly a challenge for members (Bosanquet *et al.* 2012). In 2012, the group organized a writing retreat to enable intensive writing, feedback, planning and workshop sessions. The retreat offered an ideal opportunity to explore the gap between the restrained realm of scholarly writing and the poetics of writing as a group of female friends, and provided time away from work to become immersed in academic writing interspersed with the sharing of food and conversation akin to the emotional and intellectual collaboration described by Still (2002). The retreat also gave writing group members an opportunity to explore creative possibilities, such as anecdotal theory and poetic nuptials, and to engage in critically reflective practice on writing as women in higher education.

There are multiple theoretical and practical approaches to critical reflection in different contexts, and reflections can be documented in various forms, structured to a greater or lesser extent, including through action research, collaboration, storytelling and journals. A critically reflective stance can lead to inclusive and collaborative ways of working, as researchers strive to incorporate perceptions determined via different lenses, in this case those of colleagues or peers (Brookfield 1995). This information can be used to reframe, evaluate and negotiate practice. Commonly, the focus of a reflective evaluation would be on whether an experience of reflection has been transformative or emancipatory, with the outcome a change in practice, belief or identity. In this case, our writing group took an approach to critical reflection similar to autoethnography, a qualitative research method that investigates the voice of the researcher through self-writing (Ellis & Bochner 2000) and prioritizes affect, embodiment and the construction of identity. As Peseta (2007) describes it, autoethnography supports a creative writing space and enables researchers to reimagine ideas, practices and strategies. This kind of reflection was possible because of the intimacy allowed by the size and longevity of the writing circle. By participating in a writing retreat together, we were responding to the call of feminist theorists to make space for speaking and writing to and among women.

The guiding questions that our writing group used for reflection during the retreat included: How would you describe your academic writing identity? To what extent and in what ways does being a woman impact on your writing and research? In what ways does being 'women only' impact our writing group? How effectively does the writing group address the challenges you face as a woman writer in higher education?

Two dominant themes emerged from the reflections as evidenced in the extracts which follow. The first concerned the multiple responsibilities and identities of writing group members as women writing in higher education: PhD students, casual employees, professional staff members, academics and/or mothers. Attempting to develop and maintain a writerly identity while juggling fragmented roles provoked anxiety for members. Identifying as writers and researchers was a contested process contingent on finding the time and space to write regularly. This is but one aspect of 'the upstanding and unbending patriarchal academy' to which Bartlett refers above (2006: np).

> I would describe my academic writing identity as emerging ... I am comfortable talking about 'my writing' but not 'my research'. In my position, I do not own the research I conduct—I execute and project-manage somebody else's ... My current professional space does not allow enough time, resources or 'street cred' to initiate my own research from which writing could flow. A PhD will change that ... to a degree. It will have to happen on top of serving and contributing, and, therefore, at the expense of personal time and family commitments.

For this writing group member, being categorized as professional staff means not having the opportunity to lead a research project. This results in a lack of ownership and agency around research, and a disconnection from an identity as writer and researcher. For professional staff, academic writing is not necessarily recognised as a part of workload and is therefore relegated to unpaid or 'hobby' time (Murray, 2013). Other members reinforced the challenges of family commitments:

> I feel that my time to write is not all mine and needs to be shared with my family. This is hard to negotiate. There is also my position to consider. As a

professional staff member I do not have workload associated with research and writing ... Therefore any writing I do is always in my own time which ... belongs to my family and now of course also to my PhD ...

Another participant wrote:

> We all juggle being employed/staying employed with family commitments, with the demands on early career researchers/writers/academics. Somehow our male colleagues do not seem to have quite so many balls in the air. We recognize ourselves in each other. Support and understanding, even intimacy flows from this.

Evident in these reflections is the complex interplay between roles in the workforce and roles at home, with attempts to dedicate after-hours and weekends to family and friends. Academic writing for women is not an activity separate from everyday responsibilities. Frequently, writing is interrupted, and identifying as a writer occurs in opposition to work roles and family time. Murray (2013) demonstrates that academics need to disengage from other tasks in order to write: 'writing ... may be absent from academic workplaces and workloads, just as if it were, indeed, a hobby' (80). An already tenuous identity as an academic writer is further fractured by insecure employment. One member of the writing group found that reflecting on her identity as a writer prompted anxiety:

> The sheer panic that there may not be an available job that will allow me to develop my potential as an academic writer and researcher outweighs the unfortunate realities that many women face when mothering or caring for elderly parents ... I am still at the starting line unable to begin because of the over casualisation of the academic workforce.

Identifying as a writer is compromised by the reality of job insecurity. An idealized vision of the academic writer—owning research, having sufficient time to write and secure employment—is not realized for many. This all too common situation is described as the 'ivory basement'—a spatial and symbolic locale where academics work in casual lower-level university positions, haunted by the possibility of unemployment (Eveline & Booth 2004). To some extent, participation in the writing group does legitimize writing and reading during work hours for all members, with reflections referring to task-focused, structured writing and placing an emphasis on outputs, strategies, impacts and deadlines. However, the constraints of casualization remain and the language used in the reflection above is in stark contrast to the affective aspects of writing practice described by participants in permanent or ongoing employment: 'Writing is a core part of my identity; it is one of my passions'. The literature describing the experiences of women academic writers (such as hooks 1999, above) frequently emphasizes the pleasures associated with writing with other women in a social context: playing with words, sharing food and wine, talking by the fire, walking and swimming (Grant & Knowles 2000). Writing is personal. Reading and writing are undoubtedly affective practices; the experience encompasses pleasure, joy and love on the one hand and, on the other, frustration, anxiety, doubt and fear. Putting your words on a page can be like laying yourself bare; this level of exposure requires trust and closed spaces. Writing groups can provide this space for disclosure, an inner circle, which is built upon shared experience and framed by equality.

Our reflections referred to the affective aspects of writing within the context of a group, both positive and negative—curiosity, inquisitiveness, empathy, lack of confidence, love, passion, insecurity, uncertainty and power.

> Being women only has enabled the development of much more intimacy than I imagine would be otherwise possible. For example, we have enjoyed the opportunity to get to know each other and share our stories about motherhood and family etc that may have been different with a mixed gender group. We have shared meals, conversation and laughter in a relaxed atmosphere, sometimes over breakfast in our PJs [pyjamas] ... I have benefitted from the different perspectives and areas of expertise the diverse group brings to our discussions and feel supported [by] my friends as well as colleagues.

The second major theme to emerge from the reflections concerned intimacy. In describing intimacy in research contexts, Fraser and Puwar (2008) refer to the affective and sensory aspects of scholarship—'rhythm, smell, sense, tension and pleasure' (2)—that are usually edited out in academic writing. The term 'intimacy' evokes a cluster of images and notions: personal, private, loving, belonging and sharing to name a few. It consists of a variety of feelings—closeness, warmth, tenderness—and is connected to a range of human relationships (Pratt & Rosner 2012). In our writing group, participants used phrases such as 'shared realities' and 'protected space' to describe the intimacy of our writing circle:

> I know that I would not have said some of the things that I have said if it was a male dominated group. We have shared stories and we have supported one another. The group is very empathetic considering that we have experienced shared realities. We also know that we can trust one another with privileged information. Over time I have also found that I have told the group things that I would only tell my friends.

> I feel more comfortable in a 'women only' group. I enjoy the intimacy of the group, and the way in which we blend conversations about writing, work and our personal lives. I talk about things that I wouldn't in a mixed group. I feel comfortable sharing work in progress ... I feel like we have carved out a special and protected space.

Intimacy is both affective and performative. These two dimensions of intimacy were key elements to emerge when we analyzed the specific characteristics of our writing circle and our retreat. Contributing to its ongoing success was the connection we developed as a group of women with a common focus on writing as one part of our work, sometimes compressed between competing influences in our lives. Sharing stories and laughter enabled friendships to develop, and reflecting and writing together about our experiences as a writing circle strengthened the bonds between us. As Berlant (1998) puts it, 'Intimacy involves an aspiration for a narrative about something shared, a story about oneself and others ... set within the zones of familiarity and comfort' (281). This affective component of intimacy was played out in actions that made the group stronger and more successful. One example is our increasing tolerance of the time pressures we all experienced at different phases, ranging from work project or study priorities, to family illnesses, scheduled holidays and pregnancy. Intimacy led to a generosity where we all stepped in to fill the gaps and help as required. The writing retreat made manifest the performance of intimacy. Five women with family, work, social and study commitments chose to put aside all these demands and spend time together. In an unfamiliar context that exceeded the usual boundaries of work, we exposed aspects of ourselves we would not otherwise have shared—in our pyjamas, preparing, eating and cleaning up meals, spending downtime together discussing our lives. Our writing similarly overflowed from the usual conventions of writing group meetings; at the retreat we critiqued each other's writing but also had an opportunity to observe how others approach the practice of writing.

Associated with intimacy is the sense of trust that flourishes when we reveal the things that we keep hidden or disclose to a select few. Intimacy engenders these protected spaces that can either contract or expand depending on the situation. Busier *et al.* (1997) note the 'revelation of, and respect for, personal vulnerabilities' (165) in intimate research contexts; this is evident in our reflections, especially in relation to job insecurity. The scope of intimacy in feminist scholarship encompasses feelings and affect; attachments to friends, families and lovers; and the personal (Pratt & Rosner 2012). One aspect of the latter is the theoretical and practical work of writing ourselves as described in this chapter. Feminist theory opens up the diverse ways in which the discourse of intimacy can be connected to women's writing groups.

To confirm our findings on roles and responsibilities, intimacy and affect, we entered the text of our reflections into NVivo and produced a word cloud of the top 50 words. The relative size of a word demonstrates its frequency and acts as a proxy for its importance as a concept. There is a rich representation of roles and responsibilities impacting on practice in the words 'time', 'challenges', 'issues', 'identity', 'career', 'position' and 'family'. The word cloud also represents the priorities of generating and thinking differently about intimacy. Words associated with creating and maintaining intimacy include 'support', 'friends', 'share', 'comfortable' and 'enjoy'. Central to these two themes are the practicalities of balancing academic life, writing, and research—the reasons for establishing our writing circle three years ago.

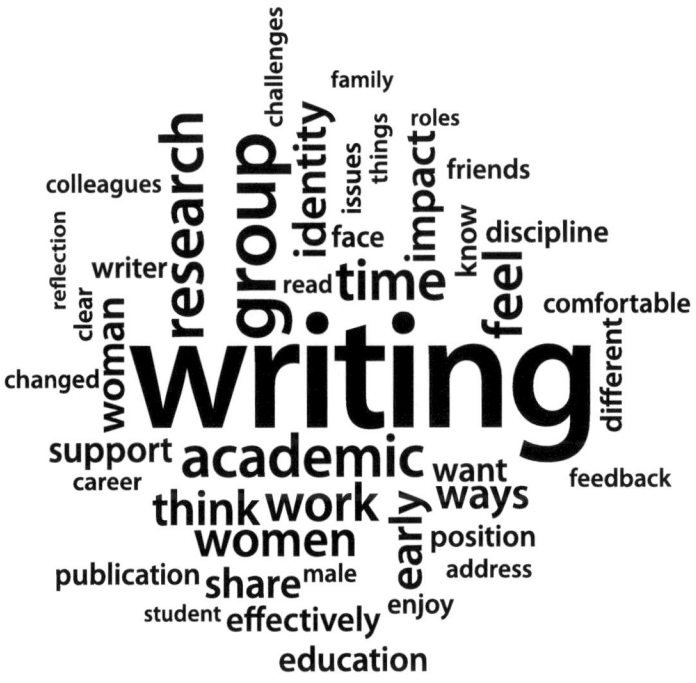

Figure 14.1 Word cloud of writing retreat reflections.

Lying dormant beneath the everyday practice of research writing are systemic issues of policy and pedagogy as our reflections have revealed. Writing groups can help members navigate some of these complex issues because of their reliance upon pedagogical principles of peer review, communities of practice and the view that writing is synonymous with research (Aitchison & Lee 2006). Writing groups with all women membership, however, can confront these challenges and more, as such groups can provide a subversive response to the dominant highly competitive and individualistic writing culture within academia (Grant & Knowles 2000). They offer an opportunity to 'jam the machinery' of academia by making space for writing amidst the constant juggling of roles and responsibilities.

Conclusions

This chapter has discussed issues surrounding the membership of academic writing groups in higher education, examining them through the reflective lens of a writing circle for women. Feminist literature on the affective and intimate aspects of women's writing offers insight into the experiences of our group. Irigaray (1985) advocates rewriting dominant discourse by speaking and writing to and among women. This is not restricted to the words we choose but also encompasses the experience of writing and how it intersects with other aspects of our lives. Our starting point was to acknowledge the gendered constitution of writing circles in the scholarly literature. From there, we located our own group within the theory, *writing ourselves* as women writers in higher education through a process of critical reflection. Our reflections emphasize the conflicting demands of writing for pleasure and for work, and the challenges of establishing and negotiating our many roles and responsibilities as carers, academic or professional staff, students and, above all, writers. Writing is a personal process, which exposes us to criticism and, at times, insecurity and guilt. Managing critique in a sensitive and collegial manner cultivates a level of trust, and sharing our writing experiences and challenges creates intimacy within our group. Our reflections indicate that intimacy flourishes with the building of trust and disclosure of experiences and challenges that are particular to women writers.

The path through academia is better travelled in the company of others—call them our peers, our friends, our allies. Our group of early career researchers has been able to communally celebrate successes and commiserate over disappointments and so progress along the treacherous path of publishing. Our writing circle is now entering a new phase in the ebb and flow of change and transition, as one member takes up a promotion at a new institution and another takes maternity leave. Decisions are to be made about shifting membership and future group goals; however, due to the existing level of intimacy, these decisions are more easily debated and collaboratively decided. Working together in a women's writing group provides a successful approach to ensuring our disparate roles are acknowledged and supported. It allows us to bridge the gap between the alienating world of publishing and the intimacy of feminist theory and affective practice, lessons which may be of interest to others grappling with the myriad challenges of academia.

References

Acker, S. and Armenti, C. (2004) 'Sleepless in academia', *Gender and Education*, 16(1): 3–24.
Aitchison, C. (2010) 'Learning together to publish: writing group pedagogies for doctoral publishing', in C. Aitchison, B. Kamler and A. Lee (eds) *Publishing Pedagogies for the Doctorate and Beyond*, London: Routledge.
Aitchison, C. and Lee, A. (2006) 'Research writing: problems and pedagogies', *Teaching in Higher Education*, 11(3): 265–78.
Aronson, A. L. and Swanson, D. L. (1991) 'Graduate women on the brink: writing as "outsiders within"', *Women's Studies Quarterly*, 19(2/4): 156–73.
Bartlett, A. (2006) 'Irigaray makes jam', *M/C Journal*, 9(6). Available online: http://journal.media-culture.org.au/0612/07-bartlett.php (accessed July 21 2007).
Bazeley, P. (2003) 'Defining "early career" in research', *Higher Education*, 45: 257–79.
Berlant, L. (1998) 'Intimacy', *Critical Inquiry*, 24(2): 281–8.

Bosanquet, A., McNeill, M., Huber, E., Cahir, J. and Jacenyik-Trawöger, C. (2012) 'Reflection, speed dating and word clouds: evaluating a writing group for early career researchers', *Compendium* 2(5): 9–18. Available online: http://etc.dal.ca/ojs211/index.php?journal=C2 (accessed 17 May 2012).

Brookfield, S. (1995) *Becoming a Critically Reflective Teacher*, San Francisco, CA: Jossey-Bass.

Busier, H.-L., Clark, K., Sech, R., Glesne, C., Pigeon, Y. and Tarule, J. (1997) 'Intimacy in research', *International Journal of Qualitative Studies in Education*, 10(2): 165–70.

Cixous, H. (1981) 'The laugh of the Medusa' (trans. K. Cohen and P. Cohen), in E. Marks and I. de Courtivron (eds) *New French Feminisms: An Anthology*, New York: Pantheon Books.

Dwyer, A., Lewis, B., McDonald, F. and Burns, M. (2012) 'It's always a pleasure: exploring productivity and pleasure in writing group for early career academics', *Studies in Continuing Education*, 32(4): 129–44.

Ellis, C. and Bochner, A. (2000) 'Autoethnography, personal narrative, reflexivity: researcher as subject', in N. Denzin and Y. Lincoln (eds) *The Handbook of Qualitative Research* (2nd edn), Thousand Oaks, CA: Sage.

Eveline, J. and Booth, M. (2004) 'Don't write about it: writing "the other" for the ivory basement', *Journal of Organisational Change Management*, 17(3): 243–55.

Faulconer, J., Atkinson, T., Griffith, R., Matusevich, M. and Swaggerty, E. (2010) 'The power of living the writerly life: a group model for women writers', *NASPA Journal About Women in Higher Education*, 3(1): 207–35.

Fraser, M. and Puwar, N. (2008) 'Introduction: intimacy in research', *History of the Human Sciences*, 21: 1–16.

Galligan, L., Cretchley, P., George, L., McDonald, K. M., McDonald, J. and Rankin, J. (2003) 'Evolution and emerging trends of university writing groups', *Queensland Journal of Educational Research*, 19(1): 28–41. Available online: http://education.curtin.edu.au/iier/qjer/qjer19/galligan.html (accessed 17 May 2012).

Gallop, J. (2002) *Anecdotal Theory*, Durham, NC: Duke University Press.

Grant, B. (2006) 'Writing in the company of other women: exceeding the boundaries', *Studies in Higher Education*, 31(4): 483–95.

Grant, B. and Knowles, S. (2000) 'Flights of imagination: academic women be(com)ing writers', *International Journal for Academic Development*, 5(1): 6–19.

Grosz, E. (1989) *Sexual Subversions: Three French Feminists*, Sydney: Allen & Unwin.

hooks, b. (1999) *Remembered Rapture: The Writer at Work*, New York: Henry Holt.

Irigaray, L. (1985) *This Sex Which is Not One* (trans. C. Martin), Ithaca, NY: Cornell University Press.

—— (1993) *Sexes and Genealogies* (trans. G. C. Gill), New York: Columbia University Press.

Lassig, C. J., Lincoln, M. E., Dillon, L. H., Diezmann, C. M., Fox, J. L. and Neofa, Z. (2009) 'Writing together, learning together: the value and effectiveness of a research writing group for doctoral students', in *Proceedings of Australian Association for Research in Education 2009 International Education Research Conference*, Canberra, November–December, Melbourne: AARE.

Lee, A. and Boud, D. (2003) 'Writing groups, change and academic identity: research development as local practice', *Studies in Higher Education*, 28(2): 187–200.

Maher, J., Lindsay, J., Peel, V. and Twomey, C. (2006) 'Peer mentoring as an academic resource: or "My friend says…"', *Australian Universities Review*, 48(2): 26–9.

Manathunga, C. (2007) '"Unhomely" academic developer identities: more postcolonial explorations', *International Journal for Academic Development*, 11(1): 19–29.

Moi, T. (2002) *Sexual/Textual Politics: Feminist Literary Theory*, London: Routledge.

Murray, R. (2013) '"It's not a hobby": reconceptualizing the place of writing in academic work', *Higher Education*, 66(1): 79–91.

Pasternak, D., Longwell-Grice, H., Shea, K., and Hanson, K. (2009) 'Alien environments or supportive writing communities?: Pursuing writing groups in academe', *Arts and Humanities in Higher Education*, 8: 355–67.

Peseta, T. (2007) 'Troubling our desires for research and writing within the academic development project', *International Journal for Academic Development*, 12(1): 15–23.

Pratt, G. and Rosner, V. (2012) *The Global and the Intimate: Feminism in Our Time*, New York: Columbia University Press.

Probert, B. (2005) '"I just couldn't fit it in": gender and unequal outcomes in academic careers', *Gender, Work and Organization*, 12(1): 50–72.

Still, J. (2002) 'Poetic nuptials', *Paragraph*, 25(3): 7–21.

Ward, K. and Wolf-Wendel, L. (2004) 'Academic motherhood: managing complex roles in research universities', *The Review of Higher Education*, 27(2): 233–57.

Whitford, M. (1994) 'Reading Irigaray in the Nineties', in C. Burke, N. Schor and M. Whitford (eds) *Engaging with Irigaray: Feminist Philosophy and Modern European Thought*, New York: Columbia University Press.

Chapter 15

Shut up & Write!
Some surprising uses of cafés and crowds in doctoral writing

Inger Mewburn, Lindy Osborne and Glenda Caldwell

Introduction

Providing research degree candidates with writing help during their degree is difficult. Candidates come into their studies with widely varying needs and levels of experience. Providing writing assistance within a less structured, voluntary workshop format has been trialed with promising results (Boud *et al.* 2001; Catterall *et al.* 2011; Devenish *et al.* 2009). While semi-structured approaches, such as writing circles and peer-to-peer support groups, have been developed and studied in some detail, little attention has been paid to the potential for creating informal learning opportunities to support doctoral writing.

In this chapter we explore a 'writing movement' that has been taken up at various locations in Australia and around the world through the auspices of social media (so called 'Web 2.0' sites such as Twitter and Facebook). 'Shut up & Write!' is a concept first used, as far as we can determine, in the café scene in San Francisco Bay area in 2007, publicized via a 'Meetup' website (http://www.meetup.com/). A meetup is similar to 'birds of a feather' sessions, a common feature of the academic conference scene. The format of the meetings is simple, as the SF Bay area website states:

> Making the time to write one hour per week is an empowering and ultimately rewarding experience but it needs to serve as the foundation of your daily discipline. If you RSVP that you are coming, then please arrive 10–15 minutes before the start of the Meetup. The facilitator will lead introductions and then the group will write for an hour. There will then be 15–30 minutes of social time to get to know each other and possibly discuss personal writing successes such as getting published or overcoming writing resistance in some small way. No critiquing, exercises, lectures, ego, competition or feeling guilty.
>
> (http://www.meetup.com/shutupandwriteSFO/)

This paper reflects on the process and outcomes of setting up Shut up & Write! groups in two Australian locations: at Royal Melbourne Institute of Technology

(RMIT) University in Melbourne, and Queensland University of Technology (QUT) in Brisbane. Although both groups took a slightly different approach to implementing the Shut up & Write! concept, both preserved the basic features in the description from the San Francisco group. A group of writers used social media (Facebook and Twitter) to arrange a weekly meeting in a café on campus. Some time would be set aside to drink coffee and share news of the week, then all would write together in silence for a period of time. At the end of the session the writers would spend some time socializing over coffee, where writing practice may or may not be discussed. Unlike other writing groups described in this book, Shut up & Write! has very little in the way of structure; it is really a way to create a community of practice around the process of academic writing, rather than its products.

This 'community of practice' approach (Wenger 1999) temporarily transforms writing from a solitary practice into a social one. In this chapter we compare the experience of facilitating Shut up & Write! sessions over a period of approximately a year at RMIT University and QUT using a narrative inquiry approach. We argue that this kind of informal learning practice can be exploited to assist research students to orientate themselves to the university environment, share vital technical skills and create inter- and intra-peer group bonds. We tease out the differences between this kind of informal learning practice and more structured approaches to doctoral education and explore the role of social media in both the spread of the movement and the facilitation of the groups. Finally, we reflect on the value that this approach offers to doctoral students and other professional writers who inhabit university spaces.

In our view there is much untapped potential in the Shut up & Write! model to promote sustainable, flexible and productive writing practices within the research degree experience. Moreover, these kind of spontaneous, opportunistic writing practices can be carried on into and through the early career researcher period and beyond, enriching scholarly practices beyond the PhD.

Shut up & Write!

Conventionally, academic writing skills are acquired through immersion as an undergraduate in a disciplinary community that has shared writing practices. The assumption underpinning the traditional apprenticeship model of PhD pedagogy is that the candidate has enjoyed this kind of uninterrupted immersion and therefore 'knows' how writing is done, even if they are not yet an expert writer themselves. The job of the supervisor in this arrangement is to help the candidate refine their skills.

However, as various scholars have pointed out, the landscape of doctoral education is rapidly changing and undergoing 'massification' (Boud & Lee 2006; Pearson 1999). Supervisors are more likely now to encounter students who are changing disciplines or have had a significant break before taking up further studies, not to mention students with diverse cultural and linguistic backgrounds.

The apprenticeship model is under pressure at the same time that the regulatory frameworks surrounding doctoral education are becoming more rigid. The introduction of the Australian Qualification Framework will force Australian institutions to provide evidence that candidates are attaining a common set of learning outcomes. In response to these pressures the temptation is to call for more formal coursework to ensure equity—but is this the only way?

Doctoral education has never really been about the classroom and herein lie many of the problems that plague those who are dedicated to supporting doctoral students. Gathering students together to provide support may be preferable in terms of economies of scale, but is not always easy in practice because 'appointment learning' is not a consistent part of the doctoral experience. Coursework may seem like an ideal way to provide parity of experience, but we should not be too quick to assume that coursework will cure what ails us. Research education does, after all, aim to produce the independent researcher who is largely self-teaching, not one who is dependent on organized teaching and learning activities to acquire knowledge and skills. How to achieve this most effectively is a question best answered by turning to the nature of the work itself.

While writing is an intellectual activity, it is also a set of practices that are learned through, and by, doing (Schön 1999). The nature of this doing—where and how it happens—forms the background to the learning. When we set out to write this chapter we performed a search on Amazon.com using 'academic writing' as key words and turned up 17,240 results—an extraordinary number of resources which reflects, perhaps, the level of anxiety that people can experience when faced with writing for their academic peers. Doctoral candidates usually write in private and present their writing to their supervisor, who is meant to provide feedback and critique on the text. The text can be thought of as the primary site for 'doing supervisor' (Petersen 2007). Candidates, for the most part, do not do their writing in the presence of their supervisor, so the process of learning through doing writing occurs mostly in isolation. Anxiety coupled with isolation forms the background to many doctoral students' experience of learning to write a thesis.

There has long been awareness of these issues, so research educators have been exploring ways to surface and share writing practice by turning writing into a social, transparent activity, rather than a private, opaque one. Academic support within a social setting can combat what Lovitts (2001) calls 'pluralistic ignorance' (candidates assuming that the problems they are experiencing are unique to them and therefore a sign that they are not cut out for doctoral study).

Writing circles, journal clubs and other semi-structured learning environments provide opportunities for doctoral candidates to learn how to learn writing from instructors, and also from their peers (see Boud *et al.* 2001; Stracke 2010; Devenish *et al.* 2009; Lee & Aitchison 2009). Peer-to-peer learning can be empowering, creating the space for students to experience a greater sense of agency—which is important in doctoral education where the aim is to develop an independent researcher. Importantly, peer-to-peer learning can allow students to take on different roles, albeit temporarily, particularly as instructor or 'knower'. Through critiquing the work of others, students can extend their own knowledge base.

While writing circles and peer-to-peer groups could be called semi-structured learning environments, Shut up & Write! is best described as a 'movement'. The concept—to join others for a period of silent writing in public—is both simple and portable, but creates the opportunity for complexity to develop. Shut up & Write! is 'performed', not 'delivered'. There are no pre-determined learning outcomes and no teacher, therefore it is best described as a set of practices and, as such, resists easy categorization or description. The Shut up & Write! concept enables both teaching and learning but does not rely on a centre—the figure of a 'teacher'—to come into existence. As a performance, Shut up & Write! does need actors and, importantly, not all of them are human.

Method

Informal learning can be a tricky beast to study. By its very nature, informal learning is unpredictable, emerging in the cracks and margins where a researcher armed with a plain language statement may be viewed as an unwelcome intruder. For this reason we decided to explore the Shut up & Write! movement via the narrative enquiry method. Narrative enquiry, as described by Conle (2000), involves the gathering of 'experiential stories that combine the social and the personal' on the assumption that such stories give voice to 'tacitly held personal knowledge ... without abandoning the particular, the contextual and the complex'. We approach narrative research bearing in mind Frank's (2005) caution that qualitative research is only ever 'one person's representation of another' and that we can never arrive at a final and complete picture of another's experience.

Narrative accounts can help us to understand the particularities of Shut up & Write! as it is performed in different environments and experienced by its various members. To this end, in this chapter we offer three different accounts of experiencing the Shut up & Write! movement. These accounts, each using a distinctive 'voice', describe the way the Shut up & Write! concept has been taken up and used within two different institutional settings in Australia. The first, from Inger Mewburn, explains how the concept was imported from the United States and spread through social media. Lindy Osborne's story discusses the origin and facilitation of the QUT group from the point of view of a practicing academic who is also a part-time doctoral student, while Glenda Caldwell, also from the QUT group, highlights the learning experience for a PhD student and academic who is a regular participant in Shut up & Write! meetups.

Collectively our stories highlight 'ways of getting on' with learning, and doing, writing outside of conventional structured approaches, but they also trouble the idea that writing needs to happen in solitude, or that the fruits of writing need to be shared in order for writers to learn new writing techniques and approaches. These accounts also offer designers of learning environments food for thought about the kind of infrastructure that is needed to facilitate such learning experiences, and suggests that effective teaching and learning environments can be more lightweight than previously imagined.

We explore the composition of Shut Up & Write!, specifically its success factors, using concepts drawn from Actor Network Theory (ANT). ANT is a body of work originating in studies of science and technology that is not a theory *per se*, but a way of collecting and examining data in order to attend to practices and how they make (and make durable) what we might otherwise think of as objects. For example, a university can be seen not as a thing, but a collection of practices that assemble resources (academics, computer hardware, libraries, parking lots and so on) to produce effects, such as 'research', 'teaching' and 'learning'. Often called 'the performative turn', ANT—and 'Post ANT'—draws on the work of scholars such as Bruno Latour, John Law and Annemarie Mol. The overall project of ANT is to break down categories such as nature/culture—or learning/teaching—and instead pay attention to practices: to how the work is done to produce 'culture' or 'learning'. Subjected to this kind of close examination, we can see that inanimate actors (tables, chairs, cafés, coffee) all become important to the story we have to tell about Shut up & Write!—valuable information in any attempt to replicate its effects (that is, a community of writers) across time and space.

We hope these stories serve as vehicles for describing the various practices that have been employed to start the 'movement', give it momentum and sustain it over time. After these accounts we reflect on the common elements and differences. We hope these stories will inspire other practitioners, writers and candidates to take up and adapt the practices to their specific circumstances.

Inger's story

I am a researcher, educator and blogger specializing in research education. My position includes very few regular teaching commitments, which enables me to trial new teaching and learning approaches for helping doctoral candidates hone their so called 'generic skills'. I heard about the concept of 'Shut up & Write!' in which a group of creative fiction writers in San Francisco had regular 'meetups' to write together in local cafés. The San Francisco Shut up & Write! group had set up a web page to advertise the location and the general format of the sessions. Intrigued, I trialled the concept with another member of RMIT staff, Jonathon O'Donnell, in a café on campus. I used this initial session to write a meta-reflection on the activity of writing in the company of another person:

> It's a curious thing, but Jonathan's relentless key tapping reminds me that I should be writing, so my fingers keep moving. All the hubbub in the café doesn't bother me—in fact it feels comforting … this mode of writing is a bit like doing an aerobics class at the gym. Although my fingers are feeling a little bit tired already, and this bench I am sitting at is ever so slightly too

high for comfortable typing, I keep going. I don't want to look like the fat, unfit person up the back of the class who isn't keeping up. This is peer pressure of the best kind!

(http://thesiswhisperer.com/2011/06/14/shut-up-and-write/)

I then suggested a regular meetup time be established at a popular café on campus. From this initial experiment has grown a collaboration with Dr Tseen Khoo and Jonathon O'Donnell of 'The Research Whisperer' blog. Through our social media contacts (primarily Twitter, blogs and email) we encouraged students and our peers to join in. The RMIT Shut up & Write! group has met every Friday morning at a local café ever since. The group varies from six to sixteen and the meetings usually last around an hour and a half.

Through social media, it was brought to my attention that there was a Shut up & Write! group active in Brisbane, which used Facebook as a way to organize themselves. Lindy Osborne, the facilitator of the group, and I became friends via social media and began to exchange ideas and information. The two groups have kept in contact via Twitter, eventually translating into face-to-face meetings and collaborations, such as this book chapter. The movement gained considerable momentum after coverage in a newspaper article which featured the Thesis Whisperer blog and Lindy's Shut up & Write! group.[1]

The sessions at RMIT are held in a commercial leasehold café on campus and therefore open to the public. This enables members of other universities to attend, so RMIT Shut up & Write! attracts a diverse crowd of research students, early career academics and professional staff, all of whom have a common interest in producing large amounts of writing. Some of the participants are deadline driven, with a thesis to write, while others use the group as a way of setting aside productive writing time during a busy week.

Social media has been the key to facilitating and sustaining Shut up & Write! Melbourne. Jonathan O'Donnell and his collaborator Dr Tseen Khoo took up the idea to support early career researchers and wrote a post which outlines the structured approach to the sessions.[2] The pair started a companion Google map for Shut up & Write! locations, which provides a series of contact points for potential participants who might be travelling and want to drop in and meet new people.[3] A 'recipe' for others who might be interested in starting their own group can be found at http://thesiswhisperer.com/shut-up-and-write/.

It is essential to have one or more people who are guaranteed to show up at the appointed time; Jonathan, Tseen and I play this role at RMIT and use a Twitter account @tweeting_tomato to muster the events. Although all of us are university staff members, none of us take on an explicit 'teacher' role. The composition of the group changes over time and grows through existing social networks. Students from undergraduate to PhD level attend; all participants are united by the common problems of being professional writers, not by our identity as either 'staff member' or 'student'. This is an entirely different kind of space from a classroom. We have found that it doesn't appeal to everyone; often people will only attend one meetup and never return, or attend irregularly.

Our group endures, we believe, because the fun, social aspects of the meetup concept are emphasized over the learning and productivity aims. Some participants decide to read, do data analysis or filing instead of writing during the silent 25-minute writing sprints. There is no expectation that participants will show the products of their writing to each other or offer critique. The conversation between sprints is the key 'informal learning space' as it allows the exchange of ideas and thoughts about workplace practice, that is, 'shop talk'. Shop talk is a powerful way to learn technical skills for writing, for instance, to enhance computer skills by looking at how others organize their digital workspaces and use short-cuts, or to seek advice on software. We also share the way we feel about our work, seeking support and sometimes consolation from each other about difficulties in writing, deadlines, problems in collaboration and managing family life with academic work. Sometimes the talk touches on 'real-world' issues in the working life of an academic/writer, such as rejections from peer review journals, committee meetings, dealing with cantankerous colleagues and other 'mundane' aspects of the lived experience of academia.

Lindy's story

I am a full-time lecturer and part-time PhD student at Queensland University of Technology (QUT). I have difficulty differentiating between my academic research, teaching and service, as they are intertwined. As a member of the Design Learning Collective at QUT, my research focus is on architectural education and learning environments. My 'real-world' teaching approach draws extensively on my professional architectural practice experience, and my service activities revolve mainly around the orchestration of my school's social media portfolio and serving on the Australian Institute of Architect's Education Committee. Because of the interrelated nature of all aspects of my academic life, I find it difficult to isolate my 'PhD research' and set aside the time to work on it, alone, without continuous interruptions and distractions. As a full-time lecturer, I supervise and support other postgraduate students in their research, so much of the time I feel somewhat disengaged from my PhD student body, a situation which is not helped by the fact that I am located in a different area from them, physically. In addition to this, my PhD supervisors are my work colleagues and my friends too. My life as a PhD student feels like a complex inter-tangled web.

After reading Inger's blog post about the Shut up & Write! idea, I was instantly sold on it. Could this really be the Mecca that I had been so desperately searching for? I immediately sent out a tweet to gauge whether there was sufficient interest to start a regular Brisbane meetup. The result was a resounding 'yes', and Shut up & Write! Brisbane was born. I did not have to apply for grant funding, put in a request for a room booking through timetabling, develop a web site, get an ethics approval nor submit a risk assessment. It was organized instantly—all in under the 140 character limitations of Twitter. All I needed was a few interested people, a coffee shop in a convenient and accessible location, and the determination to make this format work. To date the sole expenditure of our group has been a $1.99 giant red plastic tomato, which takes pride of place in the centre of our meetup table, and acts as a symbol for newcomers. We disseminate information at no cost through social media (mainly Facebook and Twitter) and occasionally bring home-made baked goods along to our meetups to fuel the writing process.

When Shut up & Write! Brisbane was first established we met for one and a half hours, once a week, at a centralized coffee shop on our main campus. The coffee shop was selected primarily because it provides long tables that enable large groups of people to meet and collaborate. The environment is busy and noisy, and during the summer it is very hot, but it is the best physical environment on campus for our meetings. Our current format is to start with 15 minutes of introductions and discussions about what we are currently researching and/or writing about, and then we get started with the writing. We use a digital timer using the Pomodoro app to count down 25 minutes of writing time. After the Pomodoro app relieves us of our duties, we chat informally for five or ten minutes before a second 25-minute writing block. We finish off the meetup with a short discussion about our achievements, before heading off to face the rest of the day. Sometimes people stay and continue to chat or work, and we have been know to add in a 'bonus' third Pomodoro session. The length of the sessions is dependent on what time of year it is. During the teaching semester, we tend to run the standard one and a half hours; however, over the summer break three hour meetups become more common.

Our group has grown from strength to strength after receiving media coverage in a newspaper[4] and a radio interview.[5] The frequency of Shut Up & Write! Brisbane meetups varies. We started with one meeting a week at the Gardens Point Campus and then quickly grew to four weekly meetups—three at Gardens Point and one at Kelvin Grove Campus. This was difficult to sustain, so we have now pulled back to one at each campus per week. This growth has allowed more participants to work Shut up & Write! around their busy schedules and has accommodated us meeting across two campuses. Meetups can vary from only three people to a 'full house' of about 10–12 people, with the ideal size being five or six people (which comfortably allows for one or two conversations in the break). One of the ways that we have grown our group is through using social media, primarily Twitter. We have participants that have moved to Brisbane from interstate or overseas, and who had made contact with us prior to moving to Brisbane. We are all Facebook and Twitter users, and primarily use these social media to stay in contact with each other. Recently we have had virtual participants who have joined in the discussions by phone or via Twitter. Weather can impact on personal comfort and has sometimes lead to cancellation or early termination of our outdoors orientated meetups. We continue to experiment with alternative formats to encourage a supportive and inclusive environment.

While the 'core' group stems from the School of Design, we also attract new participants from different schools and faculties, which results in interesting discussions about divergent research areas and exciting research collaboration opportunities. Attendees consist mainly of PhD students, but post-doc researchers, academics, Masters students and, occasionally, people who are considering enrolling in higher degree research, also join us. This mixture of participants developing different stages of their research degrees has lead to much valuable mentoring and information sharing within the group. Mentoring is informal and a wonderful by-product of the Shut up and Write! meetups. Roles are flexible, and in any one meetup participants can find themselves being both a mentor and a mentee. All participants have differing levels of experience and areas of knowledge or expertise, so everyone has something to offer. The participants who attend the most regularly tend to enact the role of mentors more frequently, but this is not always the case. Mentor/mentee relationships tend to extend beyond the confines of the weekly meetings, so our meetups seem to be the catalyst for building positive collegial relationships.

I love Shut up & Write! because it allows me to be a PhD student instead of a lecturer with all the answers. I can be vulnerable or feel exposed, and I have the opportunity to learn from those who are more advanced in their research careers than I am. It's safe. Shut up & Write! allows me to ask questions and receive mentoring from colleagues who have been through the process, but are not my supervisors. In turn, it allows me to mentor and encourage other Masters and PhD students; I learn more about my own practice through sharing and reflecting with others. I have learnt many techniques to assist me with my writing and productivity, which I continue to utilize outside of the Shut up & Write! meetups. Probably the most important lesson has been the Pomodoro technique of writing to time.[6] Other lessons might also be more practical, for example, how to insert/link Endnote citations into a Scrivener file, or the free data analysis tool Dedoose. There is no hierarchy in our group; we all have something different to contribute and to learn.

The Monday meetups act as a catalyst to trigger research activities for the rest of the week, while the Friday meetups help me to consolidate and reflect on what I have achieved during the week and plan out a strategy for the following week. I treat my Shut up & Write! time as sacred; it is booked into my diary weeks in advance and nothing is more important or takes precedence over it. It is protected 'me time', where my research writing comes first. Often it is the only 50 minutes of writing time that I achieve the whole day. Shut up & Write! is fun and social, and my productivity has increased immeasurably since forming the group. (Much of this book chapter, for example, was written during meetups, and using techniques and software learnt from peers in our group.)

Glenda's story

I have been attending the Shut up & Write! meetups at QUT since they commenced in 2011. I have blocked out the meetup times in my diary so that I can attend as often as possible. I am committed to Shut up & Write! for both professional and social reasons. My experience with this group has been positive in many ways and has helped me as a newly enrolled PhD student and as an academic.

Shut up & Write! is informal and voluntary; both aspects are critical to its success. The composition of our community has changed weekly, depending in part on the time of year, and our individual academic schedules. The experience of Shut up & Write! is different for each person, as everyone is in a different stage in their academic or professional careers. This diversity is the beauty of our group.

I have learned something from each of the different Shut up & Write! participants: the established research fellow, the progressing PhD students and the Masters students (who have joined to catch a glimpse of what is expected if they commence a PhD). The group is not exclusive to PhD writing. There are times when I have simply written a 'to-do' list and used the time to organize my life. Most of the time I have used the time to map out or write papers for publication, plan research projects, or draft grant applications.

For me, Shut up & Write! is not the time to check my email or phone messages, nor to think about my family and friends; it is my time to write, my time to listen to the inspiring keys clapping away next to me while sipping coffee. It is my time to relish my academic headspace and feed off the motivating presence of my colleagues.

My favourite times during the Shut up & Write! meetups are the discussions revolving around our goals for the day, and at the end when we share what we have achieved. Never is judgement passed, only pure encouragement. It is often difficult to stop the conversation and begin what we are all there to do—write—because it is wonderful to hear what everyone is doing. It is both stimulating and encouraging to listen to what others are going through, what they have done and where they are headed. We are all on different trajectories and, in spite of this, we still learn from each other. Shut up & Write! provides me with the time and place to be productive and to learn, at the same time. It is a place where I am exposed to the unexpected; ranging from learning about new apps that help to edit pdfs, learning how to best organize my Twitter feed, finding out which conferences are coming up, being mentored on starting a grant proposal, to what school would be best for my son. The best part is learning and knowing that I am not alone.

I often try to encourage others to join our meetups, because I want them to discover the benefits that this social and academic time offers. Through our Shut up & Write! group, I have met people that I would not normally have the opportunity to talk to. Our lives are busy, leaving little time for meeting and greeting. Our group is usually small in number, indicating that it does not always appeal to all people. Shut up & Write! motivates me, and it has helped me to accomplish some major goals.

Often people will say they are too busy to come to our weekly meetups. I too am too busy and that is why I attend Shut up & Write! almost religiously. Because I have committed to this group, I feel obliged to attend. When I was younger, I was dedicated to team sports. I don't enjoy exercising on my own but I do well in a team or class environment; writing is the same. In eight months I have written four papers, two grant proposals, and my PhD research proposal. Before Shut up & Write! I had completed only two papers in two years.

Discussion

In our narratives a range of common elements emerged as 'outcomes' of the Shut up & Write! movement:

- sharing productivity techniques and technical 'tricks';
- sharing and talking about the affective dimensions of writing and academia; and
- sharing 'mundane' dimensions of academic practice (conferences, committees, peer reviewing, dealing with cantankerous colleagues, etc.).

Three aspects of the narrative accounts call for closer attention: (1) the part location—or more precisely *materiality* (both physical and digital)—plays in the success (or not) of the groups; (2) the types of learning which are described in the accounts; and (3) the 'meta' commentary on identity and identity work which pervades all of the texts.

The setting in which learning takes place and the materiality which is implicated in those spaces affects the kinds of learnings, identities and work which can be performed. Seen ANT-wise, traditional classroom learning and teaching is performed by time and space as well as more invisible actors, such as policy and regulation. Teachers and students enact curriculum within sometimes tightly constrained boundaries. We could call this formal learning in contrast to informal learning—that learning which is not planned as an intentional outcome but takes place in the margins where instruction is intermingled with social interaction in the hall outside lecture theatres, or between students sitting up the back of a classroom. Informal learnings can involve teachers, but often they don't. Sometimes the informal learnings are not what the teacher intended (or wanted); therefore processes exist in classrooms to stifle it ('Eyes to the front!', 'No talking up the back!'). Informal learning happens most frequently in places like Facebook where students congregate after (and during) class time. Shut up & Write! is an attempt to mobilize informal learning processes, to create a space for them.

Scholars of informal learning practices have noted that places or spaces, both physical and virtual can provide opportunities for alternative learning experiences (Mathison *et al.* 2007). Some have claimed that explorations of linkages between space and pedagogy are a critical factor in the design of successful learning landscapes (Fisher 2007; Neary *et al.* 2010). Others have discussed the importance of campus design in facilitating rich learning experiences. For example, Neary *et al.* (2010) argue that the most effective spaces are flexible, technologically rich, open 24/7 and with a sufficient occupation capacity to allow different disciplines to connect.

Our stories add to these understandings of how physical and digital spaces collaborate in creating a learning environment. Repurposing of public cafés into work and study areas is not always smooth, and some participants find the noise and bustle of these spaces off-putting. While Shut up & Write! Melbourne takes place in a sheltered café, Shut up & Write! Brisbane is more exposed to the elements and sometimes weather gets in the way of the performance. It is not just the physical spaces, but also digital ones that are part of this performance. It has been noted that communities of practice and informal learning are enabled by mobile devices and the ability to connect virtually outside of the physical classroom (Skiba 2011). Online spaces figure in our accounts as alternative methods of structuring engagement between potential and actual participants. In all our accounts, social media enabled both inter- and intra-group bonding to occur in between and during sessions. Like Cain and Policastri (2011), we have found that the choice and extent of social media use must be left to the participants.

However, while learning and teaching should be the key drivers behind learning landscape design, there appears to be a disconnect between these two in practice (Barnett & Temple 2006). Neary *et al.* (2010) have shown that space planners and managers tend to become preoccupied with the availability and serviceability of furniture, finishes and technology selections, to the detriment of spontaneity, comfort and pedagogy. Our accounts complicate the notion that facilitating spontaneous and technologically enriched learning always requires an investment in physical infrastructure—or, at least, classroom infrastructure. The wide-scale adoption of wireless technology and development of cloud technology and social media enables the 'classroom' to be a practice which is enacted anywhere that bodies can be seated to write.

Shut up & Write! is one way of providing the kind of cohort experience that is possible in the classroom without the need for 'content' or a facilitator to provide direction, and without 'critiquing, exercises, lectures, ego, competition or feeling guilty'. As we noted in the introduction, 'Shut up & Write!' is not a learning and teaching experience which is delivered, but an emergent phenomenon performed into being by physical spaces, tools and the presence of peers. This could be called a 'community of practice' (Wenger 1999)—but Shut up & Write! also resists this definition. 'Community' and 'learning' emerges from this performance and is not defined or predictable, but fluidly re-created (de Carteret 2008) by the diverse people and places that are drawn into this performance.

Finally, what can we learn about research student 'identity work' from these accounts of Shut up & Write!? No longer is there a teacher or even a student, but a loose collection of colleagues united by common problems. One does not have to be an officially sanctioned member of the university community to participate. The porous nature of contemporary university campuses—the fact that cafés are now semi-privatized spaces, open to members of the public—means that institutional boundaries start to melt away. Larcombe *et al.* (2007) suggest that writing circles help doctoral students solidify their identity by working with an identified group of peers; by contrast Shut up & Write! productively de-stabilizes this identity. Since each participant takes responsibility for their own work, the most salient 'role' which this kind of performance makes possible is 'writer'. However, other identities are possible too: colleague, student, friend, etc. One way these identities are enabled is through the talk, which is strategically allowed in between periods of intense work. Often the sessions are characterized by what Mewburn has referred to before as 'Troubles Talk'. She cautions that:

> When PhD students tell stories about the self, especially of the self in some kind of trouble, we should be alert to the need to listen closely: students may not always, or only, be looking for sympathy and help.
>
> (Mewburn 2011)

Mewburn draws on the work of Jefferson (1984) to show troubles talk tends to follow a pattern or repertoire which can perform a knowledge and sense-making role as well as a way to 'blow off steam' and bond with others. Shut up & Write! provides further evidence for the 'learning' function of such talk. Troubles talk is not structured into Shut up & Write! sessions: it happens spontaneously. Some, like Glenda, are both active partakers in this talk and 'legitimate peripheral participants' (Lave & Wenger 1991): consuming the talk in order to vicariously experience other aspects of the professional life of a working academic.

Conclusion

The experiences we have reported on in this chapter suggest there is untapped potential within activities like Shut up & Write! to promote informal learning and peer-to-peer bonding within the research degree experience. These robust informal learning practices, once instigated and promoted, can be a sustainable way of providing an alternative support network for some candidates. As our stories noted, Shut up & Write! activities are not for everyone. Some who come to a meetup never return because they do not find the environment conducive to productive work. It is impossible, without further research, to find out why it works for some and not others, or what attracts people initially, but we do know that social media habits were strongly correlated with attendance. Those with stronger social ties within the group seem to persist longer and these social ties were actively maintained with contact between sessions through Twitter or Facebook. These social ties may pre-exist participation in the group, but often they don't; social media therefore provided a way for strangers to more rapidly become intimates and, perhaps, feel more comfortable and motivated to continue. A further development of this work is underway in both institutions as we trial the key feature—working quietly together in focused bursts—within more traditional classroom environments.

Acknowledgements

Inger would like to acknowledge the hard work and dedication of Dr Tseen Khoo and Jonathan O'Donnell to the success of the RMIT University group. She would also like to acknowledge that it was her sister, Anitra Nottingham, who first told her about the Shut up & Write! concept.

Lindy and Glenda would like to acknowledge the commitment and extremely valuable presence of Dr Ben Kraal at the Shut Up Write! sessions at QUT. The group would not be the same without his mentoring and knowledge sharing.

Notes

1 'Lonely PhD student? Just log in' (http://www.theage.com.au/national/education/lonely-phd-student-just-log-in-20110808-1iixu.htmlgroup).
2 http://theresearchwhisperer.wordpress.com/2011/08/16/shut-up-and-write/.
3 http://maps.google.com/maps/ms?msa=0&msid=205250474487578475457.0004b4049c6a7b892ce16.
4 'Cafe culture helps with the thesis' (http://www.theaustralian.com.au/higher-education/cafe-culture-helps-with-the-thesis/story-e6frgcjx-1226486848950).
5 http://blogs.abc.net.au/queensland/2012/11/shut-up-and-write.html?site=brisbane&program=612_morning.
6 The 'pomodoro technique', invented by Francesco Cirillo, is a way of 'time boxing' or focusing on a single task for a specified time. Cirillo used a tomato-shaped timer in his initial experiments, hence the name 'pomodoro' which means 'tomato'.

References

Barnett, R. and Temple, P. (2006) *Impact on Space of Future Changes in Higher Education*, Higher Education Funding Council for England.
Boud, D. and Lee, A. (2006) 'What counts as practice in doctoral education?', paper presented at *Knowledge Creation in Testing Times: Proceedings of the Quality in Postgraduate Research Conference*, Adelaide, April.
Boud, D., Cohen, R. and Sampson, J. (2001) *Peer Learning in Higher Education: Learning From and With Each Other*, London: Routledge.
Cain, J. and Policastri, A. (2011) 'Using Facebook as an informal learning environment', *American Journal of Pharmaceutical Education*, 75: 10.
Catterall, J., Ross, P., Aitchison, C. and Burgin, S. (2011) 'Pedagogical approaches that facilitate writing in postgraduate research candidature in science and technology', *Journal of University Teaching and Learning Practice*, 8(2): 7.
Conle, C. (2000) 'Narrative inquiry: research tool and medium for professional development', *European Journal of Teacher Education*, 23(1): 49–63.
de Carteret, P. (2008) 'Diverse pleasures: informal learning in community', *Australian Journal of Adult Learning*, 48(3): 502–21.
Devenish, R., Dyer, S., Jefferson, T., Lord, L., van Leeuwen, S. and Fazakerley, V. (2009) 'Peer to peer support: the disappearing work in the doctoral student experience', *Higher Education Research and Development*, 28(1): 59–70.
Fisher, K. (2007) 'Pedagogy and architecture', *Architecture Australia*, 96(5): 55–57.

Frank, A. W. (2005) 'What is dialogical research, and why should we do it?', *Qualitative Health Research*, 15(7): 964–74.
Jefferson, G. (1984) 'On the organization of laughter in talk about troubles', in J. M. Atkinson and J. C. Heritage (eds) *Structures of Social Action: Studies in Conversation Analysis*, Cambridge: Cambridge University Press.
Larcombe, W., McCosker, A. and O'Loughlin, K. (2007) 'Supporting education PhD and DEd students to become confident academic writers: an evaluation of thesis writers' circles', *Journal of University Teaching and Learning Practice*, 4(1): 55–63.
Lave, J. and Wenger, E. (1991) *Situated Learning: Legitimate Peripheral Participation*, Cambridge: Cambridge University Press.
Lee, A. and Aitchison, C. (2009) 'Writing for the doctorate and beyond', *Changing Practices of Doctoral Education*, London: Routledge.
Lovitts, B. E. (2001) *Leaving the Ivory Tower: The Causes and Consequences of Departure from Doctoral Study*, New York: Rowman & Littlefield.
Mathison, C., Wachowiak, S. and Feldman, L. (2007) 'School in the park', *Childhood Education*, 83(4): 206–10.
Mewburn, I. (2011) 'Troubling talk: assembling the PhD candidate', *Studies in Continuing Education*, 33(3): 321–2.
Neary, M., Harrison, A., Crellin, G., Parekh, N., Saunders, G., Duggan, F., Williams, S. and Austin, S. (2010) *Learning Landscapes in Higher Education*, Lincoln: University of Lincoln.
Pearson, M. (1999) 'The changing environment for doctoral education in Australia: implications for quality management, improvement and innovation', *Higher Education Research and Development*, 18(3): 269–87.
Petersen, E. B. (2007) 'Negotiating academicity: postgraduate research supervision as category boundary work', *Studies in Higher Education*, 32(4): 475–87.
Schön, D. (1999) *The Reflective Practitioner*, New York: Basic Books.
Skiba, D. J. (2011) 'On the horizon mobile devices: are they a distraction or another learning tool?', *Nursing Education Perspectives*, 32(3): 195–7.
Stracke, E. (2010) 'Undertaking the journey together: peer learning for a successful and enjoyable PhD experience', *Journal of University Teaching and Learning Practice*, 7(1): 8.
Wenger, E. (1999) *Communities of Practice: Learning, Meaning, and Identity*, Cambridge: Cambridge University Press.

Index

Abbott, R.D.: and Gere, A.R. 131
abstracts: writing abstracts 26
academic culture 155
academic development 205; academic developers 79, 129, 138
academic integrity 156
academic life 3–4, 71, 99, 102, 111, 130–2, 204, 211; normalized conventions 65
academic literacies 9
academic writing 155–7; development of 219, 145–6
Actor Network Theory 222
Adcroft, A. 53, 54
affect 211, 213–15
agency 61–2, 94, 171, 220, 221; in feedback 57, 62, 194–5; in writing 210
Aitchison, C.: 6, 8, 10, 11, 12, 14, 25, 30, 34, 35, 36, 54, 55, 61, 69, 79, 85, 91, 94, 106, 133, 146, 150, 153, 154, 190, 197, 204, 209, 214; and Haas, S. 30; and Lee, A. 4, 7, 30, 35, 38, 55, 65, 69, 84, 106, 119, 158; and Paré, A. 4, 35; and Mowbray, S. 4, 171
Amundsen, C.: and McAlpine, L. 86
Antal, B.: and Richebé, N. 130, 132, 134
anxiety 220
applause 12, 177–89
apprenticeship: cognitive apprenticeship 86–90, 91; model of doctoral education 219–20
Asghar, A.: and McAlpine, L. 6, 133
authorship: co-authorship 23, 85; joint 23; as legitimate 52
Austin, E.A. 86; and McDaniels, M. 86
Austria 182

Badley, G. 30, 35, 37, 38, 52
Bakhtin, M.M. 12, 20–2, 25, 167, 172–3
Barnett, B.G.: and Caffarella, R.S. 6, 30, 54, 102, 133, 153, 154
Bartholomae, D. 24, 25
Barwarshi, A.S.: and Reiff, M.J. 66
Baty, C. 179, 185, 187
Bazerman, C. 66; and Prior, P. 67
Becher, T.: and Trowler, P. 85
Belanoff, P.: and Elbow, P. 30
Belcher, W.L. 84
belonging: and connection 12, 128, 128; 136, 168, 212–14 and identity 12, 26
Beltechi, A.: and Gabrys, B.J. 86
Berger, P.: and Luckmann, T. 20
Bitchener, J.: and Basturkmen, H. 145
Bizzell, P. 22
Bolker J. 12, 177–81, 185
Boote, D.N. 83
Bosanquet, A. 11, 12, 13, 14, 205, 209
Boud, D. 131, 218; and Lee, A. 5, 6, 8, 10, 30, 35, 55, 65, 69, 90, 94, 131, 163, 208, 219
Bourdieu, P. 3
Brehony, K.J.: and Deem, R. 145
Bruffee, K.A. 22, 131
Butler, J. 51

Cadman, K.: 145, 168; and Cargill, M. 54
Caffarella, R.S.: and Barnett, B.G. 6, 30, 54, 102, 133, 153, 154
Caldwell, G. 10, 12, 13, 14
Cahir, J. 14
Can, G.: and Walker, A. 54, 55
Canagarajah, A.S. 8

candidature: progress of 4, 178
Cargill, M.: and Cadman, K. 54
Carter, S. 149
Catterall, J. 4, 218
citation practices: cultural differences 156
Cixous, H. 205, 208
Clark, W.M. 30, 34
Clegg, S.: and Rowland, S. 111
Clughen, L.: and Hardy, C. 108
coaching 88–9
cognitive apprenticeship 82, 84–90
coherence: behavioural 94, 100–2; cognitive 94, 102–3; social 94, 103–7
collaboration: collaborative settings 7, 111, 114, 128; collaborative learning 18, 19, 22; collaborative writing 9, 18, 22, 23; collaborative revision of drafts 148–9
collective: writing as 23–6, 85
collegiality 12, 61, 117, 118, 121, 123–6
communication: with technology 12, 164, 218
community: building 9, 72–3, 79, 114–5, 122, 128, 130, 134, 139; lack of 73–8; of practice 85, 99–100, 128, 219; disciplinary community 26, 132; discourse communities 22, 24, 150; interpretive communities 21; speech communities 21; and voice 24, 26
composition: and rhetoric 18
compulsory participation in writing group 35, 74
conference: attendance 26
confidence 186, 190; building 9, 30, 57, 102, 125, 128, 132, 139, 198; lack of 4, 145; ESL writers 150–2, 154, 158
connection: and belonging 12, 10, 145, 177
conversation: about writing 72, 85, 89, 99, 106, 117, 157; in writing groups 58, 89, 105, 135–6; with disciplinary community 24–7
Cotterall, S. 145, 171
creative practice-led and creative practice-based doctorates 191–203
critical: thinking 72
critique 128, 132, 154; as debate 197, 215; online 194–6

culture: cultural psychology 20; and cognition 20; diversity in writing 155–8
Cumming, J. 85
Cunningham, E.: and Murray, R. 96, 103
Curry, M.J.: and Lillis, T.M. 3, 8, 9
Cuthbert, D.: 34, 163; and Spark, C. 6, 30, 36

Danby, S.: and Lee, A. 5, 10, 11
Deem, R.: and Brehony, K.J. 145
demystify writing 87, 91, 118
Devos, A.: and Manathunga, C. 5
diagrammatic thinking 200
dialogism 21, 52
disciplinary differences 67, 150
discipline-specific writing 67, 84, 88
diversity: in doctoral education 219, linguistic 8, 146; student 146, 157–8; in writing spaces 94
doctoral education 3–6, 25, 65, 84
doctoral writing pedagogy 11

early career researcher 4, 122, 205, 208–9, 215, 220, 223–4
Ede, L.S.: and Lunsford, A.A. 22, 23
editing 116
Elbow, P. 34, 35, 37, 38, 39, 163; and Belanoff, P. 30, 38
emotion 102–3, 120–1, 125, 150–1, 165–176, 188, 215; fear 179; laughter 162–176, 79; negative 12, 84, 91; nurturing 12, 13; pleasure in writing 117
Engeström, Y. 20
English: culturally and linguistically diverse (CALD) 8; English as an additional language (EAL) 8; English as a second language (ESL) 8, 138, 145, 159; hegemony of 8; native English speaker 8; non-native English speaker 137–9; non-English-speaking background (NESB) 8; terminology 8
exegesis 201
expert peer review 53

Faigley, L. 21, 22; and Miller, T.P. 23
Faulconer, J. 30, 35, 36, 204
feedback 25, 30, 53–4, 76–7, 115, 123, 215; and affect 54; and agency 57; and authority 57, 137; and ESL writers 137–9 150–3; dissatisfaction

with 53–4, 124; multiple sources of 14, 56–60; oral 58; from peers 20, 38, 88, 14, 131–3, 135, 153–5, 158–9, 193; soliciting feedback 193; from supervisors 59–60, 89–90, 134–6; feedback vs. review 52–5; rejection of 56–7, 137–9; uptake of 56–60, 153–5; written 58
feminist: theories of writing 13, 205–9
Ferguson, T. 6, 30, 34, 128, 139
Fingar, J. 35, 38
Fish, S. 20, 21
food 37, 184, 192, 194, 209, 225; creating atmosphere 13, 83, 114; and social bonds 13, 114, 133–4
fear of writing 179, 185, 189, 190
freewriting 37, 101

Gabrys, B.J.: Beltechi, A. 86
Galligan, L. 30, 34, 35
Game, A.: and Metcalfe, A. 130
gift exchange: as theory 12, 129–31; as practice 13; feedback as gift 124; negative gift 136–7; rejected gift 137–9
global: setting for doctoral education 5
gender 121, 179; and race 71–3; and writing 11, 12, 204–217; at writing retreats 97, 111, 181, 205
generative writing 37
Gere, A.R. 6, 18, 38; and Abbott, R.D. 131
Girgensohn, K. 35, 36, 40
goals for writing 38, 117, 121, 179–83
Golde, C.M.: 91; and Walker, G.E. 5
Grant, B.M. 5, 30, 111, 113, 120, 204, 205; and Knowles, S.S. 10, 12, 13, 14, 110, 111, 117, 204, 205, 212, 214
Green, B. 4, 6, 25, 70, 135; and Lee, A. 4
Green, I.: and Guerin, C. 135
Grosz, E. 51, 206–7
group dynamics 183; group writing 191
Guerin, C. 4, 6, 8, 10, 12, 13, 14, 35, 69, 77, 128, 139; and Green, I. 135

Haas, S. 6, 9, 10, 13, 35, 37
habits: of writing 84, 95–103, 116, 123–5; *see also* routines
Halliday, K. 51
Hardy, C.: and Clughen, L. 108
Hatcher, T.G.: and Rocco, T.S. 5, 6

Hemmings, B.: and Kay, R. 4
Herman, C. 168, 171
hierarchy: in writing groups 7, 8, 13, 35, 137; in universities 134
hooks, b. 208
Hunter, D.E.: and Kuh, G.D. 84
Hutchins, E. 20
Hyland, K. 150

identity: scholarly identity formation 6, 9, 26, 91, 122–3, 129, 131–2, 136; multiple identities 117; in writing 25, 61, 68, 73, 110, 113, 114–5, 117, 120–1, 209, 211, 224, 228–230
individualism: in writing 23, 133; opposed to collective 25, 111; relationship between individual and group 123
informal learning 118–19, 219, 221–31
Ings, W. 8, 10, 12, 14
institution: institutional setting 3, 65–9, 83; institutional support, lack of 3, 4, 99, 100, 104; non-institutional support for writing 4, 99, 105–6, 177–89
international students 137–9, 145, 157–9, 195–7
intertextuality 21, 52
intimacy 192, 204–17
isolation 30, 71, 74–5, 85, 89, 118, 119, 133, 145, 177, 188, 202, 220; *see also* solitude

Jacenyik-Trawöger, C. 14
James, B. 51
Johnson, W.B.: and Mullen, C.A. 83

Kamler, B. 85: and Thomson, P. 4, 5, 6, 65, 67, 83, 91, 106, 170, 190
Kaplan, R.B. 156
Kay, R.: and Hemmings, B. 4
Kemmis, S. 9
Kiley, M. 83
kindness 110, 111, 124
knowledge: knowledge construction 9, 67, 78, 91; disciplinary approaches 67, 196; as social 20–4; as gendered 207, 215
Knowles, S.S. 54, 55, 124, 153: and Grant, B.M. 10, 12, 13, 14, 110, 117
Kristeva, J. 20, 21, 205
Kuh, G.D.: and Hunter, D.E. 84
Kumar, V.: and Stracke, E. 54

labour: writing labourers 4
labyrinth 10, 13, 110, 112–3, 120, 125–6
language: expressive language 19; as heuristic 19; risk-taking in language 150–3; terminology 8, 159; writing in foreign language 4, 145, 150–3, 155–8; *see also* English
Larcombe, W. 6, 229
laughter 14, 133, 139, 162–76, 179
Lave, J.: and Wenger, E. 20, 85, 131
learning: environment 145, 220, 228–30
Lee, A.; and Aitchison, C. 4, 7, 30, 35, 38, 55, 65, 69, 84, 106, 119, 220; and Boud, D. 5, 6, 8, 10, 30, 35, 55, 65, 69, 90, 94, 131, 171; and Danby, S. 5, 10, 11
legitimacy as an author 52; to write 103
Li, L.Y. 8, 9, 12, 14, 37; and Vandermensbrugghe, J. 6, 137, 154
Li, S.: and Seale, C. 55
Li, Y.L.: and Wang, T. 137, 145, 153, 155
Lillis, T.M.: and Curry, M.J. 3, 8, 9
liminality 112, 113, 121–2, 125
literature: writing the literature review 89
Lonka, K. 30, 37
Lovitts, B.E. 5, 220
Luckmann, T.: and Berger, P. 20
Lunsford, A.A.: and Ede, L.S. 22, 23

McAlpine, L.: and Asghar, A. 6, 133; and Amundsen, C. 86
McClafferty, K.A.: and Rose, M. 106
McDaniels, M.: and Austin, E.A. 86
MacFarlane-Dick, D.: and Nicol, D. 53
McGrail, M. 5
MacKay, G. and Murray, R. 30, 35, 36, 37
McKenna, C.: and Creme, P. 119
McLeod, 30, 94, 95, 96, 103
McWilliam, E. 162, 169
Maher, D. 6, 128, 139,
Maher, M. 10, 12, 13, 14, 84, 85, 190, 192, 208
Manathunga, C. 90; and Devos, A. 5; and Ahern, K. 198, 208
marathon 11, 13, 177–89
materiality of writing 228–30
Mauss, M. 128, 129–30, 133–4

mentoring 87–8; in writing groups 82, 85, 90, 226, 227; cascading mentoring 90–91
metaphor: labyrinth 13, 112–13; marathon 13, 177–89; seed to fruit 121–2; sprint 13
Mewburn, I. 10, 12, 13, 14, 230
metalanguage: for discussing writing 76–8, 157–8
micro-group 10, 94, 96–9
Miller, C.M.: and Nerad, M. 85
Miller, T.P.: and Faigley, L. 23
modeling 10, 86, 87–8, 121
Moore, S. 94; and Murray, R. 95
motivation 30, 104, 178–9
multi-disciplinary writing groups 34, 60, 76–7, 146, 162, 226; feedback from multi-disciplinary readers 124
multilingual writers 8, 145, 157–8, 159, 195
Mullen, C.A. 6, 128, 139; and Johnson, W.B. 83
Murray, R. 4, 5, 6. 10, 12, 14, 35, 37, 38, 94, 95, 100, 111, 117, 150, 210, 211; and Cunningham, E. 96, 103; and MacKay, G. 30, 35, 36, 37; and Moore, S. 6, 95; and Newton, M. 30, 36, 37, 38, 95, 96, 99

NaNoWriMo 179–81
narrative: methodology 221
Nerad, M.: and Miller, C.M. 85
Newton, M. and Murray, R. 30, 36, 38, 95, 96, 99
Nicol, D. 54: and MacFarlane-Dick, D. 53

observation of writing 87
online: writing groups 35, 194–7, 218–231; online writing programs 179–181; online tools 193, 195–6; online critique 195–6
Osborne, L. 10, 12, 13, 14

Paltridge, B.: 145; and Starfield, S. 147, 150
Paré, A. 4, 12, 13, 24, 51, 54, 55, 70, 85; and Aitchison, C. 4, 35; and Starke-Meyerring, D. 67
Parker, R. 6, 163
Parry, S. 5, 85
pedagogy: definition 11; doctoral education 163; writing pedagogies:

8, 191, 214; the Studio Model 192–203
peer: expert peer review 53; peer learning 6, 22, 131–2, 151–3, 163, 220, 230; peer editing 20, 22; peer review and feedback 24, 25, 56, 77, 88–9, 118–19, 150–5, 158–9, 164–5, 221; peer review vs. feedback 52–5; peer pressure as constructive 105; peer support 180, 181
performativity 11, 51, 111
personal writing: writing for self 169
Pick-n-Mix: metaphor 9, 39–40
plagiarism 21, 191
pleasure 117–18, 209
pomodoro 13, 22
power 54, 62, 87, 90–1, 137, 163, 167, 172–3
practice: practice turn 11; practice theory 9; writing as practice 220
practice-based doctorates 5, 190–203
pre-writing 20
Prior, P.: and Bazerman, C. 66
process and product of writing: process writing 9, 19, 44, 145, 147, 219
professional: doctorate 5
publication: politics 3; learning for 55; institutional reward for 3; institutional support for 69–7; pressure to 106, 108–9

qualitative research: and writing 209–210, 221
quotation: overuse 156

race 71–2
reading: reading audience 156; reader-response criticism 21
reciprocity 113, 128, 129–33, 136
records: of writing group meetings 40
redrafting 194
reflection: reflective journals 39–41; on institutional environment for writing 65; in cognitive apprenticeship 86; on writing 90, 158
reflexivity: in research 209–10; and writing 209–14
Reiff, M.J.: and Barwarshi, A.S. 66
relationships: intimate 209–14; student–supervisor 90–1, 135; teaching/learning 10; of trust 19; in writing groups 130, 133, 137, 139, 147

research: research culture 67, 73, 76–7
research education 3–6, 79, 219–20
retreat: writing retreat 10, 39–43, 209; communal vs. solitary 119; continuing beyond 94–108; discipline of 123–5; internet and email access during 115–16; residential 114–15; structure of writing retreat 95, 110–11
rewarding writing 184
rhetorical: arhetorical institutional culture 66–9; and composition 18, 155; contrastive 156–8; and invention 19; rhetorical genre theory 9, 145, 147
Richebé, N.: and Antal, B. 130, 132, 34
risk 12, 25, 26, 68, 104, 136–7, 150–3, 162–76, 187
Robinson-Pant, A. 145, 158
Rocco, T.S.; and Hatcher, T.G. 5, 6
roles: supervisor roles 68–78, 83–5, 128, 131, 135, 145, 150, 169, 170, 192–4, 197–201, 220, 225, 230; work and domestic 210–12
Rorty, R. 20
Rose, M.: and McClafferty, K.A. 106
Rosenblatt, L. 20–1
Rosenthal, L. 35
routines: for writing 9, 10, 84, 120; *see also* habits
Rowland, S.: and Clegg, S. 111
rules for writing groups 7, 114

scaffolding: writing 88–9
Schatzi, T.R. 9
Schön, D. 220
Scrivener, S. 197
scholarly publishing: value of 211; *see also* publishing
scribbling and scribing 37
Seale, C.: and Li, S. 55
second language speakers *see* English
secrecy about writing 30, 87, 91, 99; *see also* demystify
self-help writing support 4, 195–7, 204–17, 224–6
sharing 88, 104, 114, 118, 130, 228
situated: learning 20; writing 23, 202
skills: writing as skill and practice 4, 13
Skype: for writing group contact 36, 195–6; for writing group facilitation 223

social constructivism 22
social contexts of writing 103–7
social media 218–19; for bonding 230
social practice: writing as 8, 18, 51–2
social sciences 74, 76
sociality 74–8, 79, 113
South Africa 162–76
space: institutional space 65–9; writing space 3, 94–108, 118; personal writing space; physical 12, 114; psychological and emotional 12; supportive 71, 113–15, 158; virtual 12; writing group spaces 36, 88
Spark, C.: and Cuthbert, D. 6, 30, 36
sprint: as metaphor 13
Starfield, S.: and Paltridge, B. 147, 150
Starke-Meyerring, D. 10, 12, 14, 53, 66, 68; and Paré, A. 67
Stracke, E. 6, 139: and Kumar, V. 54
structure: cultural difference 155–8
subversion: writing as 12
supervision: and writing 70, 192–4, 219; and meetings 192–4
supervisor: fear of 150; and feedback 55, 59–60, 89–90,134–6; relationship with student 5, 121, 122, 165; roles and responsibilities 25, 219; as writing teacher 4, 70, 84, 86, 219
sustainability of writing groups 39–43; of retreats 111, 120
Swales, J.M. 22
symbol: food and celebration 13; pomodoro 225
Systemic Functional Linguistics 51

tacit knowledge 53
Tardy, C.M. 147, 150
technology: for communication 12; for writing 224; for writing groups 194–7
terminology: alternatives for writing groups 7
textual ideologies 8
theory: academic literacies 9; Actor Network Theory 222; feminist theories of writing 13; gift exchange 129–30; practice theory 9; process approach 147; rhetorical genre theory 145, 147; sociocultural theories 20–2; theory of cognitive apprenticeship 82; of writing development 78

Thesen, L. 7, 10, 11, 12, 14; and Cooper, L. 8
Thomson, P. 53: and Kamler, B. 4, 5, 6, 65, 67, 83, 91, 106; and Walker, M. 5
time: to write 111–12, 210–11, 218, 226, 227; protecting writing time 95, 114–16, 226, 227; timing writing 96–101, 224, 218
timely completion 5, 27, 178
transferability: in doctoral education 5; in writing space 105
transition: from undergraduate to doctoral writing 24, 219; from early career researcher to academic 209
transparency: in doctoral processes 5; in writing 86–90, 220
Trowler, P.: and Becher, T. 85
trust 114, 128, 135, 138, 213
typing pool: writing group model 12, 31, 38, 40, 95
typologies of writing groups 14; see also Haas 30–47
Twitter 223, 225

undergraduate writing: shift from 24
United Kingdom 5, 97, 170
United States 83, 222

Vandermensbrugghe, J.: and Li, L.Y. 6, 137, 154
verbal language 21
voice in writing 26, 90; authoritative 21, 26, 58–61; multivoiced 52, 58–61
voluntary participation in writing group 35, 82, 146, 164, 188, 194–7, 224–8
vulnerability 211
Vygotsky, L. 20

Walker, A.: and Can, G. 54, 55
Walker, G.E.: 82, 86; and Golde, C.M. 5
Walker, M.: and Thomson, P. 5, 6
Wang, T.: and Li, Y.L. 137, 145, 153, 155
Washburn, A. 30, 36
wellbeing 100, 103, 108
Wellington, J. 150
Wenger, E.: 20, 219, 229; and Lave, J. 20, 85, 131
Wisker, G. 83
Wolfsberger, J. 11, 12, 13, 14,

women: as writers and scholars 11, 178–9, 181; all-women writing group 13, 204–17
work–life balance 107, 111
Write On! 83, 87
Writer Development Course 39–43
writer's block 103, 117, 125, 165, 185
writing: as conversation 24; habits 10, 116, 123–5; as fun 181–9, 224; as design 191–2; as knowledge making 7, 8, 67, 68, 78, 190; as marginalized 65–6; as practice 191; as social practice 9, 21–5, 67, 106, 119, 133, 190, 203–24; as skill 77, 219; as research 67; as women 204–17; emotion 68–9, 84–5, 103, 125, 150–1, 166, 171–4; in a foreign language 4, 145, 192; observing 87–8; personal writing 198; practice 108, 116–17, 220; process 87, 147, 219; structural differences 155–8; targets 179, 181; theory 13, 145, 18–23, 205–9; and materiality 167; and thinking 26, 198; and talking 26, 76, 123–5, 193, 230; and identity 68, 204–17; websites and blogs 5
Writing Development in Higher Education (WDHE) 30

writing development: formal programs 39–43; informal 204–17; institutional support 69–71; lack of support for 71, 107; revision of drafts 147–50; websites and blogs 5
writing collectives 190–203, 204–17
writing groups: and cultural diversity 155–8; as multidisciplinary 76–7; as social 58; as supportive 69–71, 103–7, 150–3, 158; as sustainable 39–43, 73–8, 219; activities 88, 98–9, 122, 146, 147, 183–4, 192–7; alternative terms 7; environment 113–14; facilitation 145–62, 164, 194; failure of 73–8; history 18–27; formation 34, 40, 55, 71–3, 82–3, 129, 146; ground rules of 91, 104; longevity 36, 73–8; membership 55, 145, 164, 204–7, 223; and play 177–89; practices 56, 83, 98–9, 148–54, 192–7, 164; relationships between members 130, 133, 137, 139; size 34, 83, 146; theory 18–25
writing productivity 36, 39, 82–4, 102, 104, 117, 177, 209, 224, 226; pressure for 4, 5, 11,
writing skills: of doctoral candidates 68

Zuber-Skerritt, O.: and Ryan, J. 145